STUDYING TV DRAMA

STUDYING TV DRAMA
BY
MICHAEL MASSEY

auteur

First published in 2010 by
Auteur
The Old Surgery, 9 Pulford Road, Leighton Buzzard LU7 1AB
www.auteur.co.uk

Copyright © Auteur Publishing 2010

Designed and set by Nikki Hamlett at AMP Ltd, Dunstable, Bedfordshire

Printed and bound in Poland by Polskabook www.polskabook.com

Cover: *Life on Mars* © BBC Television

British Library Cataloguing-in-Publication Data
A catalogue record for this book is available from the British Library

ISBN 978-1-906733-04-9 (Paperback)
ISBN 978-1-906733-05-6 (Hardback)

CONTENTS

AUTHOR'S NOTE

In each of the following chapters, specific scenes are discussed from episodes of the dramas to illustrate generic conventions and specific issues relating to *mise-en-scène*, etc. In most cases these descriptions have been lightly illustrated with frames from the scene, but this has not been possible in every case. However, readers might like to know that at the time of writing, many of these scenes, including those from *Casualty* and *Holby City*, not illustrated herein, were available for viewing on YouTube.

PREVIOUSLY ON.....

Books about television drama are not legion, especially at the level at which this one is aimed. The ephemeral nature of television makes it a difficult subject to write about. Students are not likely to have seen much, if any, drama from last year, let alone from the last six decades. Even the continuing dramas, such as *Casualty* or *Coronation Street*, will have changed considerably over time, especially with regard to the central characters.

Obviously DVD boxed sets have preserved some of the drama of previous years, but availability is subject to marketing choices on the part of the producers and the survival of the material itself. Most of the early dramas no longer exist except in the memories of the creators and viewers, if they are still alive. Sometimes scripts have made it through, but they are no substitute for the actual production.

I was conscious at every stage of the writing of this book that the dramas I have selected were already 'out-of-date' as their details hit the page, notwithstanding the time-lapse before publication. Constant revision allowed me to add references to later editions or series. So *Life On Mars* is joined by *Ashes To Ashes*, *Bleak House* by *Little Dorrit*, and an earlier episode of *Casualty* is balanced by a more recent one from *Holby City*, so that at least some of the characters may be recognisable to the contemporary audience.

The purpose of this book is to provide students with the analytical resources to take a piece of television drama apart, find out what makes it tick and put it back together again in the shape of an informed discussion of its content and the processes which have combined to create it. The dramas I have chosen are merely examples of what different forms of television drama might look like and sound like. I am very well aware that there are glaring omissions, and I apologise for that. I make no apologies for the dramas I have selected, believing them to be significant and interesting examples of the genre which provide students with a range of opportunities for examination and discussion.

I am grateful to Colin Dear for his willingness to be a sounding board for my ideas, and I have found his suggestions and advice very helpful. I am grateful, too, to my publisher, John Atkinson, for his constant encouragement and belief that this project could actually work. I am more than grateful to the myriad writers, producers and actors who have made the process of watching television drama such a delightful, informative and often life-enhancing way to spend my time.

Special thanks must go to Jon and David Massey, who spent much of their hard-earned cash on providing me with boxed sets to watch, and to Emily, Rob and Dawn Stowe, for allowing me to raid their own DVD collections.

Finally, I could not have written this book without the constant support, help, guidance and cups of tea so generously provided by my wife, June, to whom it is dedicated with much gratitude and love.

ANALYSING TELEVISION DRAMA

This book is about how television drama works. It is not a comprehensive history, nor can it possibly hope to cover the whole range or variety of dramatic productions created by the TV companies during the last sixty years – serials, series, single plays, two-parters, soap operas, drama-documentaries, crime dramas, medical dramas, period dramas, costume dramas, literary adaptations, classic theatre plays – the list seems endless. What this book aims to do is to use some landmark productions from the last six decades as a way into the exploration of the techniques, technologies, aesthetics and values of television drama, and how these have developed during that time.

Most of the emphasis will be on UK drama, but this introduction will also look briefly at the development of drama on US television, and one of the detailed case studies will review the contemporary US medical drama, *House*.

The following introduction is designed to provide you with an overview of the varying types of TV drama and their technical and stylistic development over the last sixty years.

INTRODUCTION TO TELEVISION DRAMA

'Television is the most important medium of communication. You view TV with all defences down in a relaxed social setting (like an audience at an Elizabethan theatre).' Dennis Potter (1977)

'…(the single TV play is) the most important new indigenous art form of the 20th century…' David Hare (in The Guardian, 8 June 2002)

'Telling stories is one of the most valuable means we have of finding out about the world…' Dennis Potter (1983)

We now take television drama for granted. A quick glance at the main terrestrial and freeview channels alone, for any one week, reveals about 200 hours of all kinds of drama – one-off plays, drama serials, soap operas, adaptations, drama-documentaries, new and repeats. It is very likely that you will be a regular viewer of at least one soap opera, or keep up with a weekly visit to a hospital or police station. And even if you are not a great fan of television dramas, you will be aware of the amount of 'TV chat' they generate.

The purposes of television drama are many and varied. Some dramas are heavily issue-based, attempting to raise public awareness of current social controversies. Others provide interesting historical perspectives. Still others provide deliberate escapist fantasies. In television drama we can see the three primary aims of public service broadcasting – to educate, to inform, to entertain.

However, television drama does not operate in a vacuum. It is one strand in the larger scheme of televisual output, and cannot be entirely detached from it. It is part of what the media critic Raymond Williams called (1974) 'televisual flow'; or, as John Ellis (1982) put it, just one of the 'segments' of televisual output.

Williams would have us believe that we must regard a piece of drama as one element in his notion of 'televisual flow'. He maintains that television presents us not with discrete artefacts, such as a film in the cinema, or a play in the theatre, but with a continuous flow of images whose juxtapositions and associations construct meanings which 'are not made explicitly in the text, but are devolved to the viewer, where their associative nature will allow them to be made subconsciously'. 'Flow' also suggests that the output of television is, or should be, endless. The advent of 24-hour broadcasting, largely unknown to Williams, has made this comment uncannily perceptive.

The notion of 'flow' would seem, at first glance, to militate against the concept of a single dramatic presentation, a 'TV drama slot', a 'one-off production'. Dennis Potter himself speaks enthusiastically of the opportunities afforded by this cultural oasis:

'There, in the middle of the news bulletins, the ads, the sports, entertainments and party politicals, there, in virtually every home in the land, seen with the social guard down and the texture of the modern world all around it, is a precious space for drama; the great playwrights of the past would surely have sought to use this medium to address their fellow-citizens.'

On the other hand, Ellis turns our attention to the notion of 'segmentation', arguing that television outputs its texts in 'small, sequential units of images and sounds, whose maximum duration seems to be about five minutes'. News stories, commercials, music videos, title sequences and scenes from narrative drama are examples of such segments, and Ellis maintains that flow occurs as the segments follow one another without apparent connection. Even within a genre like soap opera or a regular crime series, the segments switch swiftly from one narrative strand to another, often without logical narrative cause. It could even be argued that the process of segmentation works in opposition to the linear narrative progression of television drama.

1950S

It wasn't always like this. When BBC television began to take over from radio as the mass broadcasting medium in the UK in the early 1950s, nearly all programming was live. Only the occasional item, shot on 16mm cinefilm, provided relief from the relentless output of live, 'as-it-happens' broadcasting. Live television meant that a play, lasting anything from sixty to ninety minutes, was transmitted as it was acted from beginning to end, with no breaks. The actors had to learn their entire parts, just as they did for a theatre production. Every camera move, every lighting change, every scene change had to be planned down to the last detail — there was no room for error. If anything did go wrong, everyone had to carry on as though nothing had happened until the end.

Such plays were broadcast from one of the TV studios at Alexandra Palace, with sets built indoors and the bulky electronic cameras had to move between them according to a carefully pre-arranged plan. If a short outdoor scene had been shot on cinefilm, it had to be slotted into the studio transmission at precisely the right moment in order to avoid awkward interruptions in the flow of sequences. Such points were indicated in the director's script as 'telecine', and getting them to fit seamlessly into the whole live production was a skilled job.

All of this meant that early TV drama was often a slow and cumbersome affair. A single shot from one camera might last anything up to twenty seconds before a cut to a second shot. The size of the cameras made them difficult to move smoothly from one position to another, resulting in a need to make many of the shots static and of similar style. Zoom lenses had not been invented, so calling for close-ups and long shots usually meant that a cameraman had to change lenses between shots (most studio cameras had a rotating turret of four lenses) for different types of shot. Such restrictions seriously affected the pace of productions, and the 'studio-based' nature of sets contributed to a very basic and somewhat 'amateur' look to early drama, compared with the quality of today's electronic digital output.

The only transitions available to the first vision mixers were dissolves, cuts, wipes and fades. Titles and captions had to be written or printed in white on a black background and superimposed on a live picture by a simple dissolve. Rolling credits were wound by hand on rollers in the same way. Any other visual 'special effects' (very limited in scope and number) could be provided on cinefilm (cinema had made greater progress in this direction), but such luxuries were expensive to design and shoot, and so were used very sparingly. There were, of course, no CGI or digital effects available.

Other aspects of early *mise-en-scène* included a monochrome picture shot in a 4:3 ratio on low-resolution cameras (405 scanning lines), seen by viewers on small domestic receivers with nine or, at best, twelve-inch screens. The small size of the viewing screen quickly determined one of television's most enduring shooting styles – the emphasis on big close-ups of talking heads – still much in evidence in today's soap opera conversations and confrontations. Even though the screens get bigger, the 'in-their-face' intimacy of such shots remains a vital ingredient of most TV drama.

Despite the technological limitations of the medium in this period, playwrights, producers and directors collaborated on some remarkably creative productions. Unfortunately the lack of any systematic recording procedures means that virtually all of those early TV programmes have not survived, except in the memories of those involved, in the scripts of those plays not consigned to the dustbin, and in occasional photographs taken on set.

The recordings of one or two productions have been preserved for posterity by a process known as 'telerecording'. A cinefilm camera was set up in front of a good quality television monitor, and this filmed the TV programme as it was being broadcast live. This was something of a technical challenge, not least because of the different 'frame' rates of film and television – film runs at 24 frames per second; television is scanned at 25 frames per second. Such telerecordings were often used only as a means of repeating a transmission of the programme at a later date, and not with a view to maintaining any kind of archive of broadcast work. Consequently such 'films' of TV programmes were destroyed as the economics of storage became an issue, or simply because even those involved with its production did not regard television as a medium worth preserving. Actors also objected to telerecordings, preferring to repeat a performance live and receive a second fee, which, at that time, they did not get when telerecordings were broadcast.

Many early television dramas were adaptations of theatre plays or taken from novels. There was some original writing, but almost all of this early material has not survived. The BBC's head of television drama from 1950–2, Val Gielgud, is on record as regarding TV drama as essentially radio plays with pictures. It isn't surprising, therefore, that early TV drama continued to be heavily influenced by the conflicting aesthetics of film, theatre and radio.

In 1952, Michael Barry became head of television drama and brought with him his belief in the 'power of the televisual image'. Convinced that television drama writers and producers needed to find new ways of presenting their productions, he was instrumental in promoting such innovation by commissioning two productions which are said to have stood out from other contemporary work for their groundbreaking use of the medium as a means of engaging the television audience with what was, indisputably, television drama: *The Quatermass Experiment* (1953) and *Nineteen Eighty-Four* (1954).

It is fitting, perhaps, that the first two episodes of *The Quatermass Experiment* are the earliest surviving examples of television drama. This science-fiction narrative, an original script by Nigel Kneale, traced the story of a manned space flight which goes horribly wrong, leaving the sole survivor to mutate into a giant piece of vegetation, which meets its destruction in Westminster Abbey. It was broadcast as a six-part serial. Kneale died in 2006, the year after the BBC decided to broadcast an up-dated version of his drama as a one-off live production, now something of a risky rare event, with Jason Flemyng and David Tennant (later to be The Doctor in the new *Doctor Who* series) in the lead roles.

Later commentators have regarded the original production as an example of the contemporary preoccupation with 'Cold War' fears of military attack from the Soviet Union and predictions of atomic mutation following a nuclear war. Many sci-fi films from the late 1940s and early 1950s had used this theme to great effect, but *The Quatermass Experiment* was television's first serious venture in this direction, and an original script as well. Obviously the televisual style was very static and slow-paced by today's standards, much constrained by the technical limitations described above. There were 'outdoor' filmed inserts, but much of the live action was staged in the studio. The surviving

The Quatermass Experiment

sequences may seem awkward to us now, but the fact that the programme was broadcast live meant that all involved were very aware of their own tensions and excitements, which some have seen as an important factor in generating such responses in the viewing audience.

With so much early TV drama not surviving, it is impossible now to state definitively that *Quatermass* was a revolutionary televisual event. It was not the first serial drama – Francis Durbridge had written several thriller serials before it – nor was it the first exploration of a fictional future; it does, however, seem to have been one of the first dramas to take television as a serious medium of dramatic entertainment which could be quite different from cinema, radio or the theatre. The fact that someone decided it was worth telerecording may also suggest that it had been recognised as something out of the ordinary. We shall never know for certain.

Two of its characteristics – an original script and the serial drama form – foreshadow some of the defining features of much later television drama, from *Doctor Who* in 1963 to *Holby City* in 2009; from the work of seminal TV playwrights and directors such as Dennis Potter and Ken Loach in the 1960s and 70s to more contemporary works by Lynda La Plante (*Prime Suspect*) and Tony Jordan (*Life On Mars*); from *Coronation Street* in 1960 to *Doctor Who* in 2008.

Barry's second commission, also adapted and written by Nigel Kneale, was, in some ways quite different: a dramatisation of George Orwell's novel, *Nineteen Eighty-Four*. It was an adaptation of a work of literature, and it was a complete play. The two-hour production was transmitted live on Sunday, 12 December 1954, and repeated on Thursday, 16 December, also live, when a complete telerecording was made. This bleak and powerful version of Orwell's vision of the future did even more to influence the development of TV drama – intimate close-ups of 'talking heads', address to camera, claustrophobic studio sets, extensive use of filmed inserts (fourteen sequences) to open out the production into a wider world, voice-overs to reveal inner thoughts, the treatment of serious and controversial social and political themes. For those who had not read the book, it also helped to widen the viewing public's familiarity with some of Orwell's most famous concepts: 'Big Brother', 'Room 101', 'New-Speak', 'Double-Think'.*

In the same year that *Nineteen Eighty-Four* was transmitted, the BBC had begun screening its first police drama series called *Fabian of Scotland Yard*. Each 30-minute episode was a

*The opening sequence of *The Quatermass Experiment* and the whole of *Nineteen Eighty-Four* may be available for viewing on YouTube.

complete story, and the character of Detective Inspector Fabian was based on a real-life Scotland Yard detective of the same name. The significant feature of the series was that it was shot on film, like the American cop shows of the period, which meant it was easier to edit, more flexible to schedule and more marketable to other countries of the English-speaking world than studio-based live productions. This third advantage was important because of the greater costs involved in making the programmes – film was (and still is) more expensive to produce than live television or (later) videorecordings – which could be recouped through international sales. The shooting style, with shorter shot-lengths than studio television and bigger close-ups, increased the pace of an episode and made it more intimate. Although not as action-packed as current police-themed drama, *Fabian of Scotland Yard* managed to reflect some of the gritty realism we tend to associate with cop programmes today.

The emphasis on realism which we now take for granted seems to have become an established feature of much television drama in the early 1960s, at a time when UK films, inspired by the early work of 'realist' film-makers in Europe, were taking both their themes and their images from the lives and experiences of ordinary people in familiar environments.

1960S

It is no accident that a low-key serial drama on the lives of a northern working-class community was first broadcast in 1960, just as UK cinema was beginning to feature films on precisely the same themes – personal, often troubled relationships; economic hardship; the bonds of family and community. In the cinema audiences watched films such as *Saturday Night and Sunday Morning* (1960), *Room At the Top* (1958), *A Taste of Honey* (1961) – all using the harsh industrial landscapes of northern Britain as their backdrops, and then came home to watch *Coronation Street*, that low-key serial drama which set the pattern for all soap opera-serial drama that followed it (see Chapter 2).

Coronation Street was not the first TV soap opera. The BBC had produced a family-based serial for children in the mid-50s called *The Appleyards*, and the idea was later developed into a twice-weekly serial drama for adults, called *The Grove Family*. This was hugely popular (even with royalty) and ran for three years. The central characters, Mr and Mrs Grove, their two grown-up children, two school-age children and irascible grandmother, were cleverly designed to appeal to a wide age range. The storylines were very 'worthy', often including helpful advice about home security or domestic projects (Mr Grove was a builder), and reflected the BBC's commitment to education as well as entertainment. However, the Groves were more of an ideal rather than a real family, which is why *Coronation Street*, produced by Granada Television for the relatively new ITV channel, was something of a shock and a surprise to the TV audience of December 1960.

From the very first episode a gallery of contrasting characters and a catalogue of serious themes set the tone for much subsequent drama: a working-class family with a university-educated son who finds his parents' small-minded attitudes hard to deal with; a flirty divorcee's arguments with her ex-convict son and a daughter who has run away to marry a 'foreigner'; the down-to-earth street-corner pub landlord and his snobby wife with pretensions above her social position; the nosy, gossipy elderly woman who looks after the church mission hall and manages to offend almost everyone in the street; the grumpy old soldier; the single father struggling to cope with the wayward behaviour of his lively teenage daughter. Over the last forty-seven years that list has become almost endless, and the storylines have broadened out to include ever-more serious, harrowing and tragic themes and issues. But, at the core, the drama is still about a community, about families in conflict, about relationships, about loyalty and betrayal, all underscored by the comedy of human life.

If gritty realism was the keynote of northern TV serial drama from ITV, the BBC at the beginning of the 1960s seemed still firmly rooted in a more comfortable view of the world. Their leading police series was *Dixon of Dock Green*, about the experiences of an ordinary London copper on the beat and his fight against crime. Each episode was introduced by PC George Dixon talking directly to camera ('Evenin' all'), and ending with Dixon again pointing out some moral lesson drawn from the very conventional storyline (criminal commits crime, cop arrests him, criminal learns the error of his ways). Despite its very positive view of policing and its very predictable storylines, it remained very popular for over twenty years, even when much other TV drama had 'grown up' around it, and its 'star', Jack Warner, was in his seventies!

The BBC also experimented at this time with escapism in the form of a science fiction drama serial featuring the adventures of a rather bad-tempered old man and his intelligent and resourceful granddaughter who travelled through space and time in a curious ship whose exterior resembled something to be seen on many street corners at the time – a blue police box, used by both policemen on the beat and the public to communicate by phone with police control centres in cases of emergency. Its interior, however, was vast, but its central control system was faulty, making it impossible for its owner to determine its destination with any accuracy. The programme's creators were probably equally unable to determine with any accuracy the ultimate destination or the popularity of their creation, as The Doctor and his Assistant continue to travel the universe some forty-five years later. *Doctor Who* (the programme, never the name of its leading character – see Chapter 6) has also been responsible for introducing one of television's most enduring icons, the Daleks, an interesting early example of how a TV drama can produce characters and objects which have a 'life' outside of the show itself.

Just as ITV had embraced the new realism with its serial drama, *Coronation Street*, the BBC followed a similar path, except that it chose police drama as its preferred route. The cosy world of George Dixon's loveable London bobby was shattered in 1962 by the arrival of *Z-Cars*. Set in the realities of the urban Liverpool of the day, *Z-Cars* presented to its audience life as it was, not just for the villains, whose shady and corrupt existence was not always as clear-cut as earlier police drama would have us believe, but also for the police, whose concepts of 'right' and 'wrong' were distinctly 'grey', and whose personal lives were often as messy as those of the law-breakers they were pursuing. The visual settings for *Z-Cars* often featured the protagonists in their patrol cars, thus creating a *mise-en-scène* of claustrophobia and tightly-framed close-ups of the characters, exposing to the relentless gaze of the camera their attitudes and emotions. An extreme close-up of the troubled expression on a patrol officer's face became a familiar feature of the programme, paving the way for similar visual intimacy in much TV drama of the 1960s.

Alongside the fascination for 'life-as-it-happens' drama, audiences in 1967 also hugely enjoyed *The Forsyte Saga*, a serial costume drama, set in the late-Victorian/early-Edwardian period. It was adapted from the novels of John Galsworthy and traced the story of an upper-class English family, focusing on the troubled interactions between its leading members, played by some of the top actors of the day. Originally scheduled for transmission by the new BBC2 channel as a means of encouraging more of the population to switch to the higher resolution (625-lines) service, it achieved its highest audience rating of some eighteen million viewers when it was shown later on BBC1. The press at the time were full of stories of pubs emptying and churches changing their service times, as people rushed home each Sunday evening to catch the latest episode, in the absence of any kind of time-shift videorecording. The combination of an aristocratic, period-costume setting and 'soap opera' style storylines proved to be a winner – a combination that has been repeated many times in the last four decades (*Brideshead Revisited*, *The Jewel in the Crown*, *Pride and Prejudice* and *Bleak House* are just a few examples).

While popular audiences were attracted to the new developments in serial drama, there was still a substantial draw for the single play, and some later commentators have regarded the 1960s as the 'golden age' of television drama. Such a description owes much to the recognition that the playwrights and directors of the time (David Mercer, Dennis Potter, Alan Plater, Jack Rosenthal, Tony Garnett, Ken Loach, et.al.) had the freedom to experiment – with subject-matter, themes, issues, and, equally importantly, with the form and style of the productions – in ways that commercial and ideological pressures, and audience demand have made almost impossible in later decades.

One such play, *Up the Junction*, is a good example of how these experimental freedoms were synthesised in a single drama.

BACKGROUND

Although much television drama in the 1950s and early 1960s attempted to transport its audience to unfamiliar times and places, a definite strand was determined to bring it face to face with the realities of life in the here-and-now. The new wave of *British* films

Up The Junction

in the early 1960s, with its focus on working-class lives confronting the issues that faced many people at the time, had its effect on the television drama of the period, as we have seen with such serial drama as *Coronation Street*; but such drama can now be seen as essentially re-active, attempting to reflect the day-to-day experiences of ordinary people everywhere.

However some playwrights and directors were convinced that even television drama could and should be pro-active, taking an important issue, offering a critique of the reactionary forces which were not willing to bring about change, and using drama as a way to make those responsible for the status quo sit up and take notice of the problems. Cinema, with its tradition of mass entertainment, was not seen as a viable medium for such social commentary. Television, on the other hand, reaching into millions of homes, and with a remit to educate as well as entertain, could be the channel for social reform.

Two such early practitioners were Tony Garnett and Ken Loach. In 1965 they began to work on an adaptation of Nell Dunn's novel, called *Up The Junction*. The book was a series of impressionistic scenes of working-class life in and around the South London area of Clapham Junction. It did not have an obvious linear narrative, but one of its central themes was the terrible fate facing young girls having to undergo illegal, back-street abortions. Although the topic was something of a political hot-potato at the time, it was not the sort of subject whom a conservative, reserved and prudish audience expected to see dealt with on television. For precisely these reasons, Loach and Garnett thought it would make an ideal subject for a play which would challenge the comfortable complacency of the middle-England audience, and focus their attention on the plight of those working-class young women who had no social or financial alternative to seeking help in this appalling way.

CAMERA AND EDITING

Apart from its subject-matter, the book seemed to have other disadvantages as the basis for a television play. There was no obvious storyline, no conventional character parts of varying weights to suit a casting director, and much of the novel was set on the streets, which the TV technology of the time could not realistically reproduce in the confines of the studio, as *Coronation Street* had shown. Loach and Garnett were very keen to shoot the whole production on film, but costs were prohibitive. What they didn't want was to have to combine the slower, less fluent studio-bound sequences with filmed sequences, because at this time it was very easy to see the edits where the filmed shots were cued into a production which was recorded live in the studio. What they wanted was to edit the play like a film, to give it pace and immediacy. Video editing at the time was clumsy, expensive and often technically inaccurate. Costs often limited the number of such edits that were allowed for any one production. After much thought, discussion and quite a few disputes with BBC drama department officials, they compromised by filming the output of the live studio sequences on the lower quality telerecording equipment, and then editing that film together with the filmed sequences shot on location. The differing quality of the two methods is certainly detectable, but it did allow them considerable flexibility during the editing of the play. This meant that they could achieve a very high level of documentary realism, which was one of their goals.

Another goal was to achieve a shooting style which would liberate the play from the perception that it was just another piece of televised theatre. The result was a series of sequences which had few establishing shots and even fewer clues about the storyline or character identity. Instead viewers were brought, literally, face to face with different characters shot in big close-up, mid-way through conversations which were often not resolved. The only obvious linking motif was the choice of three girls as the central characters, and around whom much, but not all, of the action took place. One of them, Rube, was singled out to be the vehicle for Loach and Garnett's major goal – the back-street abortion storyline, with which they wanted to enter the current public debate about abortion-law reform, by making mainstream television drama an influential medium in that debate. Forty-plus years on it is clear that they very largely succeeded in all three goals – the law on abortion was changed just two years later, and much TV drama owes something to both their technical and stylistic pioneering ideas. (Ken Loach is still making politically-charged films about his social and historical passions.)

ANALYSIS

The play begins abruptly with a big close-up of a pub vocalist singing 'Bad Girl', a song specially composed for the play. This diegetic song then becomes the title music under shots of Clapham Junction – the railway station, steam trains, shops, people, traffic, Battersea power station chimneys in the background, and then the three leading characters out shopping; Rube, Eileen and Sylvie – with the titles of the play superimposed. In the following scenes we are presented with snatches of conversation in the pub between the same three girls and a group of young men. The cheeky, light-hearted banter is all about going out, having a good time, fancying blokes, trying it on with girls, being married, thrown together in a montage of talking, laughing heads. The dialogue is inconsequential, anecdotal, random, and serves only to set a scene and an atmosphere, while focusing on the preoccupations of the characters.

At some point in all of this confusion and noise someone suggests that the three girls and the blokes they have linked up with should go for a late-night dip in a local outdoor swimming pool. After being thrown out by a night watchman, they hang around some of the local demolition sites (the more derelict parts of London were being extensively redeveloped at this time), going off as individual couples to make out amid this unpromising landscape. The fragile and furtive nature of these casual relationships (one of the men openly admits he's married) is somehow reflected by the dark, crumbling shells of the dilapidated buildings. Although time is not referred to during these sequences, we are to understand that they take place at a weekend.

The mechanical processes of destruction in the previous scene give way to an assembly line in a chocolate factory where we discover the girls at work. It might be Monday morning. The women who work in the factory represent all ages from fifteen to retirement. Their endless chatter as they work seems to focus on their relationships, marriages and the desperate plight of their impoverished lives. They have little time for the men in their lives, whom they regard as unreliable and inadequate, but are resigned to the depressing nature of their inescapable circumstances. A tea break brings them some music, even some impromptu dancing, until they are sent back to work by an unsympathetic male supervisor. Despite their humorous banter, the older ones seem careworn, and the younger ones can only look and see themselves in twenty or thirty years time. During the course of the chat, one girl informs her workmates that she will be getting married as soon as she's sixteen.

The scene then shifts abruptly to a sequence concerning a tally-man, who is driving around his patch, visiting his customers. This door-step mode of selling, once very common in many working-class areas, involved paying a deposit for an item, often clothing, and then paying an agreed sum each week until the cost of the item, plus interest, was paid off. As might be imagined, the customers, often women, would be talked into ordering more than they could afford, and would then be caught in a spiral of debt and repayments from which they could not extract themselves, frequently borrowing more money to pay off the existing bills. The tally-man delivers his cynical, materialistic thoughts on the system and his customers direct to camera, as though he is the subject of a documentary. During his one-man performance he displays much of the prejudice current on the streets in 1950s and 60s Britain, openly criticising the stupidity of his female clients, or patronising the black members of his community. This sequence serves to show the self-seeking predatory nature of the entrepreneurial class, ready to capitalise (quite literally) on the weaknesses and economic hardship of the client base, but also hints at a more general ethos, where those with even the smallest amount of power over others are quick to benefit from their victims. This theme is developed in subsequent scenes, where men attempt to control their wives and girl-friends, often forcing their desires on their unwilling partners, and where women like Winnie, the back-street abortionist, seek to profit from their sordid trade to the detriment of their 'clients'.

Three girls

We return to the three girls visiting a local laundry and swapping more tales of their dealings with the men in their lives.

There are further scenes in the pub, where, once again, the conversations are fragmented and incidental. The exchanges between the girls reveal more of their contradictory thoughts about men, sex and relationships generally. Rube expresses the opinion that sex is the gift that she is prepared to give to a man she 'loves', because it is the 'best' thing that 'you can give to a bloke'. This somewhat 'naive' viewpoint is betrayed when we learn that it is Rube who becomes pregnant and is desperate to have an abortion.

As we watch the girls walking around Clapham Junction, voice-overs from a variety of women and from a doctor are heard, discussing the issues of sexual relationships, unwanted pregnancies and abortions. This use of the voice-over continues to reinforce the documentary nature of the play.

Winnie

Loach and Garnett treat the abortion sequence in a detached and dispassionate way, letting the full horror of their subject speak for itself. Rube visits Winnie, the middle-aged back-street abortionist, who demands five pounds for her services, but is quite willing to accept the four pounds that Rube offers. This is made to look like the grubby, commercial transaction that it is. Big close-ups of Winnie's expression reveal an ingratiating smile that looks friendly, but conceals a deep scorn for her troubled client. Winnie puts the money in her handbag, as if to suggest that the girl's traumatic condition is nothing more than the source of some spare cash for her.

After 'the treatment'

We see nothing of the 'treatment'. Our next shot of Rube is the central, graphic scene of this whole sequence. She is lying on her bed at home, screaming in agony, supported by Sylvie and Eileen. She is covered in sweat and the big close-ups of her anguished face reveal the pain and terror she is enduring. This was probably the first time that a mainstream television audience had been exposed to the visual 'realities' of such an ordeal concerning a 'taboo' subject of this kind.

Some sort of equilibrium is restored as the girls resume their evenings out at the pub, being chatted up by the men, and generally joining in with the continuing uninhibited lifestyle of the community. Surrounded by reminders of old age and death (there are scenes of the laundrywoman, Mrs Hardy, socialising with her elderly friends, which then shift to shots of her funeral, while her friends discuss the shortness and hardship of life), the girls are seen continuing their apparently carefree life, while Rube's abortion becomes just another small motif in the fabric of life 'Up the Junction'.

Although much of the play seems almost to celebrate the light-hearted mood of the 'Swinging Sixties', it, nevertheless, has at its heart the very real desperation and hardship of working-class life in South London, and especially the lives of young women like Rube. Loach and Garnett's method of letting the camera observe this world, and building from the mosaic of images that this produces, a carefully constructed montage of juxtaposed details and sequences, allows them to comment subtly yet powerfully on the social climate of the time. We watch and listen to the three brash, up-beat and flamboyant girls as they enter, like prey, the lion's den of predatory masculinity. Their brazen speech and ebullient confidence belie their unconfident youth (they are still in their teens). They seem very self-assured and in control, but subsequent events reveal the fragility of that self-assurance and the hollowness of that control.

REPRESENTATION

It is significant that the central female characters of *Up The Junction* are intended to be in their late teens. This enables them to sport the latest fashions (shorter skirts and dresses, beehive hair-dos, extravagant make-up), and behave in a loud and cheeky manner. Most of the men appear older. They wear suits and ties, with neat hairstyles and shaven complexions. The older women wear headscarves, aprons and a variety of cheap, unattractive clothes.

Every single character in this play (except the professional voice overs) is represented as working class. They all have South London working-class accents, brash and abrasive modes of speech, and the subjects of their conversation reveal a combination of street-wisdom, naivety and a general lack of education. Housing, places of entertainment and the commercial environment all suggest a lack of money and a lack of resources.

The younger females both support the stereotype (as described above), but also appear to challenge it in terms of some of their characteristics (confident behaviour generally, attitudes and behaviour towards men, for example). Although they do exhibit an upbeat independence form time to time, much of their conversation reveals conventional attitudes towards sex and marriage. Having a good time means having a good time with a boy.

Influence

Television dramas like *Up the Junction* and its successor, *Cathy Come Home*, which dealt with the tragic effects of poverty and homelessness on families and relationships, and was largely responsible for the establishment of the housing charity 'Shelter', and a shift in government policy, were also very influential on scripting and production styles, narrative content and the representation of realism, not just in single dramas but in a variety of subsequent dramatic genres.

One significant feature of this kind of realism was what might be termed an impressionistic approach to visual narrative. Instead of a logical progression of establishing shots followed by carefully arranged shots and reverse shots, audiences were presented by seemingly haphazard and unpredictable shots which *suggested* a setting or a theme, rather than made details clear and obvious. The audience were expected to engage with the narrative and work proactively to make meaning from it. In this way the audience learnt how to 'fill in the gaps' of the narrative for themselves. As a result television drama gradually became more elliptical, leaving the audience to provide an understanding of the intervening action for themselves.

As has been noted above, Loach and Garnett insisted on making the play as a tightly edited 'televisual film', rather than as a studio-bound piece of broadcast theatre. When budgets have allowed, more recent dramas have usually been shot on film and edited to preserve narrative sharpness and economy. Contemporary developments in high definition video-recording now produce a film-like quality to much dramatic material, and the latest editing technologies easily allow the kind of precision that Loach and Garnett were striving for but were able to achieve only by painstaking effort with the available technology.

1970S

While the 1960s was undoubtedly the 'experimental laboratory' of challenging TV drama, the 1970s saw its consolidation in a variety of genres. The single play was still a very popular medium for the exploration of a wide range of contemporary issues and themes, and a random list illustrates this very clearly: *Edna, The Inebriate Woman* (1971) – homelessness and alcoholism; *Nuts In May* (1976) and *Abigail's Party* (1977) – lower middle-class pretensions; *The Bar Mitzvah Boy* (1976) – adolescence, religion and culture; *The Spongers* (1978) – middle-class deference to upper-class culture and hostility to working-class benefit dependency.

Meanwhile royal serial costume drama was achieving considerable success with *The Six Wives of Henry VIII* (1970), *Elizabeth R* (1971) – about Elizabeth I, *Edward the Seventh* (1975), and *Edward and Mrs Simpson* (1978) – about the abdication of Edward VIII in 1937.

'You're nicked!' Regan (John Thaw, left) and Carter (Dennis Waterman) of the Flying Squad in The Sweeney

Although the more realistic police dramas, beginning with *Z-Cars* in the 1960s, and continuing into the 1970s, the influence of American 'cop' cinema, with films such as Clint Eastwood's *Dirty Harry*, is clearly seen in series such as *The Sweeney* (1975–8). This hugely successful series created a very popular double-act, DI Regan and his assistant, DS Carter. Regan was the 'rogue' copper, like Dirty Harry, who played policing by his own unorthodox rules, and sometimes faced the disapproval of his colleague, Carter, for his brutal treatment of suspected offenders and his often underhand methods. Even its title – cockney rhyming slang: Sweeney Todd = Flying Squad – brought the audience face-to-face with down-to-earth coppers who behaved much like the villains they were chasing.

It might be argued that the first TV cop double act was Inspector Barlow and Sergeant Watt from *Z-Cars*, but Regan and Carter fore-grounded the special relationship of senior and junior copper, which has become a staple of TV policing ever since. One of its most recent incarnations, DI Hunt and DS Tyler from *Life On Mars* (see Chapter 8), obviously owes much to *The Sweeney*, even its early 1970s setting. Among its innovations were: a considerable increase in location filming, fast-paced editing, exaggerated action sequences, fast cars and an unashamed homage to US cop series of the time.

In 1978 the TV audience was taken completely by surprise. In the opening minutes of what appeared to be a drama serial about the hopes and frustrations of Arthur Parker, a 1930s sheet-music salesman, the leading character, played by Bob Hoskins, awakes to another depressing day, is rebuffed by his cold wife, Joan, and moves towards the bedroom window to open the curtains. As he does so, the lighting changes so that he is bathed in a Hollywood-style golden glow, a 1930s dance band tune is heard on the soundtrack, and as he turns back to look at his wife he opens his mouth, but instead of hearing his voice, we hear the tremulous voice of the band's female singer, Elsie Carlisle, coming from his lips – 'Somewhere the sun is shining, so honey don't you cry, there'll be a silver lining, the clouds will soon roll by.' The six-part drama was *Pennies from Heaven*, its writer was Dennis Potter, and in those first four lines of the song he both encapsulated and cynically underlined the very essence of Arthur's tragic story, and changed some aspects of television drama forever.

Potter had used popular music in one or two of his earlier plays, but this was his first attempt at what might be termed a 'television musical'. His aim was to use the popular songs of the 1930s as an emotional counterpoint to the thoughts and feelings of his characters, but to have those characters mime the lyrics to the voices of their original performers. Dance sequences were also included, and the studio lighting was always changed to reflect the mood of the music and to emulate the staged production numbers of the golden age of the Hollywood Musicals. It was a style and a technique which he used twice-more, in *The Singing Detective* (1986), where he employed 1940s tracks, and *Lipstick on your Collar* (1988) which was based on pop music from the 1950s.

Pennies from Heaven was controversial at the time of its first transmission. Some of the BBC officials themselves were sceptical of its quality and its likely impact on the audience – one even questioned whether the characters were going to 'sing' in every episode. Some sectors of the audience were concerned about the sexual explicitness of some scenes – a 'concern' about his work which was to hound Potter throughout the rest of his career. The biggest reservations seemed to surround Potter's deliberate flouting of the 'rules' of naturalistic drama by his introduction of 'non-naturalistic' features which appeared to disrupt the narrative flow and challenge the expectations of his audience. Once a critical distance had been achieved and the work could be judged for the undoubted brilliance of its conception and execution, audiences then began to look forward to future works, most notably *The Singing Detective* (see Chapter 3), which most commentators regard as Dennis Potter's masterpiece.

The 1970s also saw another first for TV drama. Alan Bennett, one of the four original writers and performers of the 1960 groundbreaking comic revue, *Beyond The Fringe*, wrote his first television drama, *A Day Out*. This filmed play, broadcast in black and white in 1972, just as colour television was gaining ground, is a straightforward, almost documentary account of a men's cycling club on a Sunday ride from Halifax to Fountains Abbey in 1911. It attempts to capture the quiet simplicity of the northern English countryside shortly before the cataclysm of the First World War changed everything for ever. The men exchange gentle, good-natured banter, while observing a degree of reserved politeness, addressing the older members as 'Mr.', rather than using first names. Bennett had already written for the theatre, and has continued to do so ever since, but *A Day Out* brought to a wider public his unerring ear for the subtleties and nuances of the everyday conversations and language of ordinary people, particularly those living in Yorkshire and Lancashire.

Bennett, by his own admission, always felt as though he and his family never quite fitted in, and many of his television plays feature characters who strive to be accepted and aspire to better things – as his own mother had – but never quite succeed. He even felt out of his depth and something of an impostor in the company of his fellow-performers in *Beyond The Fringe* – Jonathan Miller, a fiercely intelligent and articulate medic; Peter Cook, an anarchic comic genius; and Dudley Moore, a highly talented jazz pianist and comedian.

This social disjuncture found its ultimate expression in Bennett's series of dramatic monologues, *Talking Heads*, broadcast by the BBC in 1988, with a second series in 1998. Each play features just one character, usually a lonely person, excluded from the cut-and-thrust of everyday life, whose behaviour or personality leads them into situations they cannot control, often into the darker corners of the human soul – repression, depression, infidelity, criminal acts. 'A Lady of Letters', for example, depicts a local busybody, always writing to the authorities about perceived problems, usually of a trivial nature. Her concerns about a young family living opposite, however, spiral out of control and result in her making written accusations of parental neglect and abuse. She receives visits from the police and an injunction on her activities and she is told that the child is, in fact, seriously ill in hospital and not in danger of abandonment by her parents. 'Playing Sandwiches' follows the observations of a park keeper on his behaviour, as we learn of his apparently innocent befriending of a young mother and her little girl. The befriending of the little girl left in his charge, however, leads to sexual abuse and his imprisonment.

Bennett's plays are not comedies *per se*, but they do use the devices of comic observation and comic expression to highlight the personal circumstances, often tragic, of ordinary people living ordinary lives.

1980S

The significant televisual event of this decade was the opening of Channel 4 in 1982. The major contribution of this channel to TV drama was to fund a number of films (*The Draughtsman's Contract* (1982), *My Beautiful Launderette* (1985), *The Ploughman's Lunch* (1983)), which were destined for the big screen, but were also shown on television. In practice this meant bringing the production values of cinema to small screen drama.

In terms of such values (high quality, well-financed filmed productions, shot in lavish locations with bankable stars) and televisual styles, the 1980s, then, was something of a high watermark for TV drama. This decade saw big-budget drama serials, now named 'heritage drama', such as *Brideshead Revisited* (1981) and *The Jewel in the Crown* (1984), as well as those with a sharp social and political standpoint, such as *Boys from the Blackstuff* (1982) and *Edge of Darkness* (1985).

Brideshead Revisited, adapted from the novel by Evelyn Waugh, views the decline and fall of the aristocratic Marchmain family through the eyes of an outsider, Charles Ryder, who is seduced by the members of the family into their family, their world-view and, ultimately, their religion. The eleven-part serial was a glorious opportunity to exploit big-name stars – Laurence Olivier, John Gielgud, Claire Bloom – and exotic and expensive locations – Castle Howard in Yorkshire, Venice, North Africa, New York, Oxford and Paris – to attract the ordinary audience to what might otherwise have been a production of minority appeal. It was shot entirely on film and assumed the proportions of an epic-scale movie. It also demonstrated that the BBC did not have the monopoly of quality dramatic productions – *Brideshead Revisited* was made by Granada Television, one of the regional ITV companies at the time.

Three years later they repeated the success with a full-scale, eleven-episode adaptation of Paul Scott's four novels, *The Raj Quartet*, to which Granada gave the title, *The Jewel in the Crown*, the title of Scott's first novel in the series. This was an epic story of the British in India, before, during and immediately after the Second World War, leading up to Partition in 1947 and British withdrawal in 1948. Its landscape was vast, but the story was told through the events surrounding a series of significant characters belonging to, or in some way connected with one family. Once again well-known actors (Eric Porter, Peggy Ashcroft, Judy Parfitt, Frederick Treves) were cast in major roles alongside up-and-coming actors (Charles Dance, Tim Pigott-Smith, Art Malik, Geraldine James), and extensive location filming was undertaken in India. Its two central characters, the ex-grammar school white captain of police, Ronald Merrick, and the ex-public school Indian, Hari Kumar are at the epicentre of the rape of a young white upper-class woman, Daphne Manners, by unknown Indian assailants. Because Kumar is friendly with Daphne, a friendship of which the bigoted, middle-class Merrick strongly disapproves, the captain of police arrests him, interrogates and tortures him, and finally imprisons him for the crime, even though he is innocent. For this grave injustice, Merrick is persistently persecuted and finally 'executed' by Indian extremists, fighting for the independence of India from the British Empire.

Boys from the Blackstuff, a gritty social drama dealing with the issue of unemployment in Margaret Thatcher's Britain, was set largely in Liverpool and featured individual stories about each of the members of an out-of-work gang of tarmac layers. The series pulled no punches in its depiction of working-class men pushed to the brink of reason as they sought to hang on to their families, their friends, even their very lives and sanity, in the face of financial hardship and the oppression of unemployment. Its political stance and its biting critique of government attitudes towards the unemployed have, arguably, not been more sharply drawn than in this collection of five characters struggling with a system which they cannot beat but has demonstrably beaten them.

Social and political issues of a different kind, namely nuclear power and the well-being of the Earth itself, found expression in the eco-nuclear/sci-fi political thriller, *Edge of Darkness*. A senior police officer, devastated when his daughter, a college student, is killed, apparently accidentally, by a gunman, finds evidence among her personal belongings that she was deeply involved in an anti-nuclear movement whose activities were threatening US/UK collaboration on nuclear development programmes. The officer pursues his own investigations into his daughter's death and becomes mixed up in a web of international espionage, secret dealings and a plot to undermine the security of the West. Apart from its gripping storyline and topical subject-matter, this serial introduced some interesting features into the genre, including theme music specially composed and played by guitar legend, Eric Clapton, the use of real politicians and TV presenters playing themselves, as well as references to real locations, thus confusing the boundaries between reality and fiction.

Not all TV drama in the 1980s was issue-based or inspired by 'heritage' literature. In fact, the most original of all drama serials in this, or possibly in any decade, was Dennis Potter's *The Singing Detective*. The multi-layered complexity of the narrative, or narratives, remains one of the most remarkable examples of the TV dramatist's art. It will be fully discussed in Chapter 3. Employing the popular music of the 1940s, much as he had done the 1930s songs in *Pennies from Heaven*, Potter nevertheless uses it to far more savage and ironic effect. The six-part serial has four parallel but interconnected narratives – two are from the 'real' world (the leading character as an adult, Philip Marlow, in the present, a writer of detective fiction; and his former self as a child in the 1940s), and two are 'fiction' (the leading character, Philip Marlow, as a fictional private detective in 1940s wartime London; and his present self fantasising about his wife's infidelity with a fictional film producer anxious to procure the rights to Marlow's latest book, *The Singing Detective*, which is about a 1940s wartime private eye…). Potter's time-mosaic within the drama, with its constant and confusing shifts between all four narratives, is also overlaid with another stylistic mosaic, that of an intricately woven web of cross-references and intertextual juxtapositions which revisits most of Potter's previous writings for television. It is as though the detective story of these narratives is not just about 'whodunnit?', but also an investigation into the content and style of the playwright's whole output of TV drama.

On-going serial drama also came to the fore in the 1980s with two quite different productions from the BBC. Firstly, in an attempt to compete with ITV's continuing success with *Coronation Street*, the BBC sent two people to the Canary Islands for two weeks with the brief to create a soap opera from scratch. The result was *EastEnders*, which first aired in 1985, and has maintained a very high position in the ratings ever since. Just as *Coronation Street* had located its characters in a very precise geographical location – Weatherfield, a fictional suburb of Manchester – and had concentrated its storylines on the personal interactions of some very believable families, so *EastEnders* located its very colourful characters in a fictional area of East London – Walford – and used Albert Square as the central point for its realistic take on East End life.

The second production was intended to cash in on the ever popular subject of fictional 'doctors-and-nurses'. *Casualty* (see Chapter 5), which began its uninterrupted run in 1986, focused on the work of an A & E department in a city hospital, fictionalised as Holby City, but set in Bristol. From the very first episode the series had the pressures of working in an under-staffed and under-funded NHS hospital as one of its central issues, one which continues to be at the forefront of storylines to this day.

1990S

Middlemarch

For many this was the decade of the big-budget costume drama adapted from established works of classic literature. While the idea of televising classic literature has been a staple of broadcasting since it began, the 1990s brought to the mainstream audience a 'more modern' take on the old formula. All of these large-scale productions were shot on film, guaranteeing a high quality of image, both technically and aesthetically, and their editing style and sharply crafted script adaptations were designed to appeal to audiences more familiar with contemporary soap operas and popular drama serials.

Andrew Davies, who adapted both George Eliot's *Middlemarch* (1994) and Jane Austen's *Pride and Prejudice* (1995), was determined to emphasise the modernity of the characters, enabling their emotions and behaviours to be more readily recognised by contemporary audiences. In this way, for example, Trevyn McDowell's portrayal of the beautiful and ambitious Rosamond Vincey (*Middlemarch*) and Julia Sawalha's playing of silly and flirtatious Lydia Bennett (*Pride and Prejudice*) would not have been out of place in an up-to-date soap opera. Davies also realised the appeal of the power of sexual attraction to a contemporary audience, and deliberately underlined this aspect of the central characters in the romantic elements of these novels, most famously in the exchanges between Colin Firth's Darcy and Jennifer Ehle's Elizabeth Bennett in *Pride and Prejudice*.

The 1990s also saw another kind of period drama with ITV's *Heartbeat*. This highly successful drama series covered several bases – it was a police series which occasionally tackled serious subjects, but was set in the 1960s and, therefore, pushed the heritage and nostalgia buttons by featuring much of the popular music of the time on the soundtrack and by being located in the idyllic setting of a village on the North Yorkshire Moors. By making two of the central characters a London copper and his wife who had moved north, the series did not run the risk of alienating the southern audience. Finally, many of the rural scenes concentrated on the wild beauty of the moorland and on the (preserved) steam railway that runs through it, thus doing much for tourism in the area. The drama was completely undemanding but clearly had a wide appeal for many sectors of the audience: younger viewers enjoyed the crime stories, mini-skirts and pop music, older viewers remembered the music from the first time around and enjoyed the countryside locations and older characters.

This was also the decade of some ground-breaking approaches to familiar genres. Where *Heartbeat*'s nostalgic take on policing would not have been out of place in Dixon's Dock Green of forty-odd years before, *Prime Suspect* (1991) brought the force right up to date by making the leading copper a woman, DCI Jane Tennison, and a personally troubled woman at that. Facing the prejudice of her male colleagues, Tennison had to work twice as hard to establish herself as a serious professional and as a police officer who could crack a complex and unsavoury murder.

Other serious contemporary drama was not forgotten. In 1997 Tony Marchant wrote a multi-narrative serial drama, *Holding On*, about a group of characters who lived in the London of the late 1990s. Their lives were not directly connected, but the actions of some impinged coincidentally on others. Serious social issues of care in the community, corruption, clashes of ethnic groups were covered, but not necessarily resolved. Living in London was portrayed as a 'white-knuckle ride', and Marchant was content to leave his audience with untidy loose ends and a messy complexity of incident and character.

2000 ONWARDS

Contemporary TV drama continues to travel diverse routes. The soap operas carry on as usual, although they increasingly feature storylines dealing with serious social issues, for which 'helpline' contact details are now provided after each relevant episode – an echo of television's original remit as a public-service broadcaster. Other on-going serial dramas, such as *Casualty, Holby City, Heartbeat* and *The Bill*, continue to reflect society's perceived anxieties about law and order, and the NHS, as well as pandering to the public's eternal fascination with criminality and medicine. Drama serials, two-parters and single dramas, such as *Silent Witness, Midsomer Murders, A Touch of Frost, Doc Martin, Kingdom, New Tricks, Hustle* and *The Chase*, all continue the trend of high production values, big-name actors, health, crime and largely predictable storylines.

Some productions have taken a different tack. The revived *Doctor Who* (2005–present) has broken exciting new ground, in terms of characterisation, exotic storylines and extravagant special effects, competing to great acclaim with the offerings of sci-fi cinema. Literary adaptations have included a fast-paced, episodic approach to Charles Dickens' *Bleak House* and *Little Dorrit*, employing very atmospheric *mise-en-scène* and the cliff-hanger style of soap operas to keep the audience on its toes, while parading a wide array of well-known actors and TV personalities in cameo as well as larger roles.

The drama coup of 2006-7, though, was undoubtedly *Life On Mars* (see Chapter 8). This enigmatic psychological cop thriller cleverly combined two contrasting periods of our recent history – 1973 and 2006 – with contrasting policing styles and social attitudes, and also the contrasting TV treatment of the 'cop' genre in the 1970s (*The Sweeney*) and the present-day police serials, by featuring the time-travelling experiences of DS Sam Tyler, who appeared to be functioning as a copper in 1970s Manchester while in a coma as the result of an accident in 2006. Very little about this serial was predictable, least of all the ambiguous resolution, and the strong storylines, powerful ensemble playing by the central characters and careful attention paid to the minutiae of the production design all combined to reassure the audience that TV drama was, unlike its unfortunate protagonist, very much alive and well and living in the twenty-first century.

US TELEVISION DRAMA

Drama has been a significant part of US television programming since the late 1940s. The 'Kraft Television Theater' (sponsored by the Kraft Food Company) series began on 7 May 1947. The 'Philco Television Playhouse' (sponsored by an electrical goods company) was a close second. The plays were produced live and, like their UK counterparts a decade later, generated a lot of on-set tension among actors and crew alike.

One of the key features of US television drama was its relationship with the US film industry. The major studios were, of course, very suspicious of the new medium, but many actors who began their careers in television went on to achieve considerable fame on the big screen. James Dean, Paul Newman, Jack Lemmon, Charlton Heston, Humphrey Bogart, Lauren Bacall, Henry Fonda, Frank Sinatra and Grace Kelly are just a few of the famous names who appeared in US television plays in the 1950s. Some plays were also made into films during this period, most notably multi-Oscar winner *Marty* in 1955.

By the late 1950s, most American homes had television, and the wider audience seemed happier to settle for schedules filled with game shows, variety shows and formulaic 'genre' dramas, such as westerns. This was also the period when sitcoms formed some of the most popular output of the US television companies.

Serious drama was clearly a minority interest. It was not until the early 1960s that another, more enduring form of television drama caught the audience's imagination – the medical drama. Present-day series like *House* (see Chapter 9), *Grey's Anatomy* (2005-) and *ER* (1994-2009) can all be traced back to the popularity of 1960s series such as *Dr Kildare* and *Ben Casey*.

Whereas UK drama tended to have its origins in live theatre, US drama was more closely related to radio and film. Some of the major film studios, such as MGM, were quick to realise that it would be more profitable to invest in the new medium instead of trying to fight it. The result was a tradition of television drama shot on film, rather than the studio-bound productions of its UK counterpart.

That tradition has continued through the latter part of the twentieth and into the twenty-first century. Several major genres have been well represented during those decades including: police dramas, such as *Hill Street Blues* (1981-7) and *NYPD Blue* (1993-2005); legal dramas, such as *LA Law* (1986-94); and forensic crime dramas, such as the *CSI* series (2000-).

Science fiction is also represented by such blockbusters as *The X-Files* (1993-2002) and *The New Adventures of Superman* (1993-7). Big budget 'soap opera' style series, starting with such family-centred dramas as *Dallas* (1978-91) and *Dynasty* (1981-9), are now well represented by the like of *Desperate Housewives* (2004-). Historical drama also found a place, with such ground-breaking series as *Roots*, about the influence of the slave-trade on the historical and political development of America.

A more ground-breaking approach to US TV drama in recent years has been the emergence of Home Box Office - HBO - as a dominant force in quality serial production. A cable channel run on customer subscriptions, it is not bound by the same advertising-led restrictions that the US networks must negotiate, and is thus able to 'push the boundaries' in its programming choices. This has resulted in major critical (and occasionally commercial) successes, especially in the last decade or so, such as *Sex and the City* (1998-2004), *Six Feet Under* (2001-2005) and, especially, *The Sopranos* (1999-2007), the compelling story of a New Jersey mobster family's trials (literally) and tribulations.

Subsequently, HBO's *The Wire* (2002-7) has for many viewers redefined the possibilities of what TV could do with that most traditional of drama formats, the police series. This hard-hitting show, set in Baltimore on America's East Coast, deals with the challenging struggle confronted by the city's police force against organised drug-dealing, gang violence, political corruption and the sheer hopelessness of the city's youth in the face of unemployment and social deprivation. Using a combination of film noir, documentary and cinéma-vérité techniques, *The Wire* charts the drug wars between rival gangs and the police department's attempts to break the stranglehold of violence exerted by the gang leaders. Lines between cops and criminals are not clear-cut and the highly complex narratives try to simulate the haphazard happenings and loose ends of real life.

HBO's impact is now being felt across the wider US TV landscape. AMC's *Mad Men* (2007-) depicts the lives and loves of Madison Avenue advertising executives in the 1950s and 60s with a meticulous attention to detail bordering on the fetishistic. Its lengthy story arcs and sometimes glacial pace are remarkable even by contemporary sophisticated drama standards. AMC was previously known by its full name American Movie Classics when it was, essentially, a cable film channel. But since the mid-noughties it has increasingly invested in sophisticated original programming of the sort pioneered by HBO, of which *Mad Men* is only the most conspicuously successful example.

RESEARCH IDEAS:

Interview some older members of your family for their memories of the TV drama they watched in earlier decades.

Research the Internet for examples of earlier TV drama in both the UK and the US (YouTube and Google would be good starting points).

Compare dramas in similar genres from different periods in terms of:

- Narrative.

- Use of characters and actors.

- Representation.

- Settings and locations.

- Production values.

CHAPTER TWO – CORONATION STREET

Mike Baldwin (Johnny Briggs, left) and Ken Barlow (William Roache) settle their differences in Coronation Street

The grey, overcast skyline reveals the rooftops of drab, two-up, two-down, terraced houses, crowded together, hardly a hair's breadth between them. On the soundtrack we hear the brass band strains of a tune that manages to be both jaunty and melancholy. A rather shaky superimposed white title appears in bold capitals.

We make our very first visit to the street which will determine how we react as an audience to the concept of a soap opera, or serial drama, as its production company, Granada Television, insists on calling it, for the next forty-nine years.

Creator Tony Warren's gallery of back-to-back, working-class suburban characters, obsessed with their small, everyday concerns, and always ready to jump down each other's throats, laid the foundations for a community which was immediately recognisable to its audience (Tony had based many of his original characters on people known to him and his family), and whose 'descendants' seem to have maintained many of those same characteristics almost untouched.

The first episode opens with a shot of some children playing a game outside a corner shop. A woman is looking up at the 'registered owner' plate above the door: Elsie Lappin. She moves inside as the children run off and begins to talk to another woman who is standing inside. The dialogue reveals immediately that the second woman is taking over the shop. Her name is Florrie Lindley. The previous owner, Elsie, takes the opportunity of this 'handing-over' conversation to tell the newcomer something about the local residents of Coronation Street. This neat dramatic device enables us to learn about the Tanners at number 7 – Elsie Tanner is something of a tough customer, with a grown-up time-waster of a son, Dennis. The Barlows at number 3 have two sons. One, Ken, is a university student, and the family are steady and reliable. The conversation is interrupted by the arrival of a customer, Linda, Elsie Tanner's daughter, who 'married a Pole'. And so the 'scene-setting' continues as we move to the Tanner's house, where Elsie is arguing with her son about the 'disappearance' of some money from her purse. This second dramatic device requires a response from Denis. He denies stealing it, and within seconds we learn that he has just been released from prison, and that his mother is always ready to distrust anything he says or does. This is a confrontational household, and Elsie wishes it were more peaceful, 'like the Barlows at number 3'. Elsie's wish is a distinct piece of dramatic irony, as we discover that not everything is quite so peaceful at number 3.

We cut to the Barlow's house, where a meal is set, and Ida, the wife and mother, is worrying about the late arrival of her younger son, David. Her husband, Frank, and older son, Ken, are sitting at the table. Despite Elsie's perceptions about the peaceful nature of this house, we see almost immediately that there is considerable tension between father and son. Frank is very critical of what he regards as Ken's snobbish attitudes, now that he is at the university, and perceives Ken's every look as a negative comment on his behaviour at the table. Even small details, such as Frank's insistence on bread and butter and tea with his meal, act as a device to point up the perceived class differences between himself and his older son. Ida attempts to keep the peace and David's arrival defuses the atmosphere somewhat.

Back at the Tanners, the arrival of Elsie's daughter, Linda, acts as a narrative disruption. She announces she has temporarily left her husband, Ivan, and this causes more friction between her, her mother and her brother. Meanwhile, Ena Sharples, the resident caretaker at the Glad Tidings Mission Hall across the road, has called in at Florrie Lindley's shop, ostensibly to make a couple of purchases, but really to find out more about the new owner. Ena is a middle-aged woman with very little good to say about anybody, and is ready to say it with a sharp tongue and considerable disapproval. She is a woman of old-fashioned virtues and fixed attitudes, and people in general seem very wary of her barbed comments and sanctimonious criticism. The speed of her gossipy dialogue takes her from comments on the religious preferences of her neighbours to a request for a packet of baking powder without a pause for breath and without missing a beat. This use of dialogue allows the audience to acquire a clear and detailed picture of a character. We learn more from what she says than from what others might say about her.

- Identify some current characters who exhibit similar features to those described above.

GENRE

Coronation Street belongs to a television genre popularly known as soap opera. Having its origins in US radio serials designed to attract a daytime, generally female audience by featuring the manufacturers of domestic products as its sponsors, soap opera was quickly identified with on-going domestic narratives dealing with relationships, family matters, and the general business of day-to-day living in ordinary communities. All subsequent television versions of soap opera have exemplified these features:

- Tightly-knit communities, with clearly identifiable social hubs (pub, square, street, market, work-places, shops, cafes).

- A strong emphasis on family groupings.

- The development of recognisable characters.

- The typical issues and problems of ordinary life.

Among the gallery of recognisable characters, we may expect to find the following:

- A number of strong women of different ages, who represent the moral (or immoral) 'compass' of the community, and who derive much of their strength of purpose from their need to deal with the far less morally and emotionally secure men in their lives (Peggy Mitchell, Deirdre Barlow, Emily Bishop, Pat Evans, Denise Fox, Tanya Branning).

- An older figure, male or female: acts as an advisor or mentor for other characters, whether related or not. Dot Cotton, from *EastEnders*, or Ken Barlow and Emily Bishop from *Coronation Street* are good examples.

- Independent younger males: can be mischievous, manipulative or comic figures (Gary Hobbs, David Platt).

- Younger couples: these represent the problems and pleasures of domestic relationships (Ashley & Claire Peacock, Billy and Honey Mitchell, Bradley & Stacey Branning).

- Strong young females: younger women with a mind of their own, independent and confident but not always happy (Ronnie Mitchell, Tina McKenzie).

- Older, interfering person: a nosy individual, often offering unwanted advice (Blanche Morton, Norris Cole).

- A boss character: an authority figure, usually a business person (Ian Beale, Steve Mitchell, Tony Gordon).

Audiences are presented with a number of storylines in each episode, mostly continuing from previous episodes, and each storyline is visited several times during the episode, thus building a narrative mosaic. Incidents or issues raised in one storyline often resonate with another, enabling the audience to identify a web of themes running through the community. A mixture of ages, cultures and backgrounds creates a gallery of characters, some long-running, others imported for specific storylines. At intervals a new family or social grouping is introduced to extend the stock of existing characters or replace those who have departed. Some of the storylines are deliberately comic. More serious narratives sometimes raise issues which are designed to engage sectors of the audience in a more personal way, and links to the relevant supporting agencies are provided for 'those who may have been affected' by the events portrayed.

Occasionally a storyline may 'stray' from the 'everyday' to include more extreme incidents and behaviours usually associated with other types of television production, for example a psychological thriller, crime drama or even an 'action' drama, involving a wider-scale accident or disaster. There may also be a change of location, as characters take holidays or make visits beyond the confines of their own community.

All of the above features have come to be acknowledged as the generic characteristics of contemporary soap opera.

If the content is readily identifiable, so, too, is the form: typically thirty-minute episodes screened in the late-afternoon, early-evening 'family' timeslots, up to five episodes a week, with omnibus editions at the weekends, and/or repeats on digital channels.

Those broadcast on commercial channels usually have one commercial break, preceded by a natural interruption or sub-climax in one of the parallel storylines. The end of the episode will typically reach a suitable 'cliff-hanger', natural resolution to an interim situation, or a major disruption to a storyline, or to the life of a character.

The development of *Coronation Street* as the first serious contribution to the soap opera genre should not be seen in isolation. As noted in Chapter 1, cinema audiences were becoming accustomed in the early 1960s to watching a new wave of gritty, realistic dramas, located firmly in the working class communities and culture of the north of England. These films had largely been based on novels written by northern writers with first-hand experience of the lives of their characters. The generic characteristics of these films exactly parallel those of *Coronation Street*:

- Real-life locations.

- Ordinary working-class characters.

- Genuine northern accents.

- Typical working-class housing.

- Down-to-earth attitudes.

- Confrontational behaviour.

- Marital breakdown.

- Infidelity.

4

- Typical working-class settings – pubs, working-men's clubs, work-places, streets, urban and industrial landscapes, corner shops, narrow alleys.

- Can you identify any other generic characteristics which are common to soap operas today?
- Are there any contemporary films which reflect the ethos of soap operas?

REALISM

One of the key features of soap operas is a great emphasis on realism. The term refers to the process by which media texts create the appearance of reality. While viewers are well aware that any television drama cannot possibly be real, nevertheless they expect from the creators great attention to the details which will make a drama realistic. The process of realism is usually divided into two distinct categories: realism of form and realism of content.

1. **Realism of form:** answers the question 'Does this drama look and sound realistic?' Realism of form is dependent to a large extent on *mise-en-scène* and representation, and on production techniques (camera, sound, editing).

2. **Realism of content:** answers the question 'Is the narrative and its contents a true reflection of real life?' Realism of content deals with narrative and ideology – could this happen/ought this to happen in real life?

In relation to *Coronation Street*, realism of form could be applied to the sets (permanent life-size purpose-built exteriors – houses, pub, factory, street cobbles, pavements, shops; convincing interiors with great attention to the detail of everyday living – domestic equipment, furniture and fittings, shop contents, etc.); representational issues (real-life characters with whom the audience may identify), and technical aspects (naturalistic camerawork, no obvious special effects, diegetic soundtrack).

Realism of content will depend on naturalistic storylines, believable characters and a plausible ethos (attitudes and behaviour).

REPRESENTATION

Representation is the method by which someone or something is presented to an audience. The representation may be one that a majority audience is likely to share, and therefore be regarded as dominant. It may be one that audiences find harder to identify with, and may be regarded as oppositional. It may even be one where the audience is willing to join the debate and see more than one side of the representation, and this is described as negotiated.

There are two key terms central to representation – denotation and connotation. Denotations provide the 'facts'; connotations suggest what those facts might mean and what associations they might have:

- **Denotation** – the simple, face-value description of a person, place, object or event: Sarah Platt is twenty, short, with blonde hair, wide eyes and a round face, a single mother, employed as a hairdresser, wears jeans and casual tops, she also wears an engagement ring…

- **Connotation** – Sarah's blonde hair, big eyes and round face suggest that many would see her as pretty, youthful, sweet. Her job as a hairdresser would suggest to some that she may not necessarily be very intelligent, but her role as a single mother might indicate that she is capable of responsibility and organisation. Her clothes, hairstyle and general appearance suggest she is a fashion-conscious young woman. The fact that she is engaged suggests emotional involvement with, and a level of commitment to her boyfriend, Jason.

By using these two terms we can define representation as the construction of a description *and* a judgement. The 'and' is important, because no constructed image is devoid of the judgement both of its creator and its audience. Every constructed image will be perceived from a particular standpoint. This standpoint will exemplify the ideology inherent in the image. In the case of Sarah Platt, we might say that 'blondes are pretty', 'hairdressers are not bright', 'single mothers might be responsible and organised, but might still be unskilled, fashion-conscious airheads'.

The representation of characters in soap opera could be seen as a carefully constructed balancing act between stereotype and originality. Because an episode does not have much time to develop a character, there have to be immediately recognisable features coupled with unexpected departures to engage the audience's interest. However, the continuing nature of soap opera does allow audiences to build up a familiarity with the characters as their storylines develop. This means that representations may have to change as characters grow older, change occupations and relationships, and wax and wane in importance.

A good example is Ken Barlow. As a younger man and in early married life he tended to follow the hairstyles and fashions of the day, but now that he is a senior citizen, he has opted for the 'comfortable cardigan' look which younger audiences tend to associate with older people. However, his recent (2009) involvement with another woman (Martha) has enabled his representation to change to reflect this development. He receives and wears with enthusiasm a present from her of a boldly designed silk dressing gown, regarded as quite a departure from his 'grey older man' image by both his wife, Deirdre and his mother-in-law, the acerbic Blanche.

It would not be feasible in a study of this scope to make detailed representations of every single character. Instead it is hoped that a gallery of characters from the selected sequence for analysis will present a cross-section of age, class, gender, ethnic background and status.

MISE-EN-SCÈNE

The production style of *Coronation Street* has inevitably undergone many changes in its long history. The early episodes of *Coronation Street* (in black-and-white until 1969) were broadcast live, which meant that cast and crew had to rehearse their lines, actions and moves in advance of transmission and then perform each whole episode in one go, with just two minutes respite for the 'commercial break' half way through. This method of working meant that any slips of dialogue and action had to be covered up and passed over as the programme continued. It also led to some unplanned framing of shots as actors missed their marks. Nevertheless, meticulously planned camera positions did produce some shots which were to become the hallmarks of soap operas for decades to come. Big close-ups on actors' faces started to become a feature, allowing audiences to experience the claustrophobic environments of the tiny houses and gauge the emotions of the characters, especially wordless reactions to situations. The classic establishing two-shot, followed by shot-reverse-shot exchange of dialogue set a pattern for confrontational scenes which is still the staple of soap opera today. Inevitably, some of the camera movements and vision mixing were often slow and cumbersome by today's standards, but some of the sharply choreographed scenes were very striking.

Whereas the early episodes of *Coronation Street* relied on studio sets, much of the street and surrounding area has now been constructed on a purpose-built exterior lot at Granada's studios in Manchester. This full-scale architectural exercise has led to an extremely heightened sense of realism. Real vehicles may now drive along the street. Real weather may now be experienced on the street. Real daylight may now contribute to the lighting design of the street.

Interiors are still studio-bound, of course, but the décor and furnishings of each house are designed to reflect the personalities and backgrounds of the inhabitants, and to match with the external architecture of the exterior set. Every aspect of colour, texture and shape has been designed to represent a real-life setting. For example, Emily Bishop has older, neater, more sedate furniture and fittings to match her age, flair for organisation and kindly disposition, whereas Tony and Carla Gordon enjoy contemporary, up-market décor to reflect their roles as established business professionals. Interiors can sometimes match their owner's personalities in other ways. The Windasses, a recent addition to the street (2009), are represented as a set of benefit fraudsters (the husband is always seen with crutches in public, but is not disabled), with various petty criminal sidelines. The disorganised and chaotic environment they have created within one of the newer houses on the street mirrors the disorganisation of this dysfunctional family.

The lighting design is intended to reflect near-normality. Occasional night scenes have to be more illuminated than normal in order to make images clearer and brighter for the cameras, but otherwise the emphasis is on realism. This means that, for both interiors and exteriors, the lighting may seem flat and somewhat 'home-movie-ish'. Some of the more dramatic storylines have occasionally used starker and more visually striking lighting in order to underline the dramatic significance of a sequence, but this makes the departure from 'normality' all the more effective.

Every aspect of wardrobe, properties and production design is geared to the representation of the real world. Some small concessions to a fictional world are made: for example, The Rover's Return serves 'Newton and Ridley's' beer, a fictional brand. Likewise, magazines, confectionery and food products all have fictional names. In this way the programme will never be a shop window for product placement. Coronation Street is located in Wetherfield, a fictional suburb of Manchester. The names of other localities, such as the 'Red Rec' playing fields, are also fictional. In all other respects, Coronation Street exists in the 'real' world, with appropriate references to real institutions and more distant geographical locations, such as London and other cities throughout the country.

- How far is the *mise-en-scène* of other soap operas similar to that described above?

IN THE FRAME

From Episode 2 – 1960

A dramatic moment during a confrontational scene in the public bar of The Rover's Return is witnessed from the Snug by Ena Sharples (centre) and her friends, Martha Longhurst (right) and Minnie Caldwell (left). At the moment of crisis, their three faces, thrust forward with curiosity and intrigue, are caught in big close-up profile, like the three witches in 'Macbeth', or like three onlookers at a public execution. This framed shot encapsulates their personalities as three stereotyped nosy old gossips to perfection.

Such attention to the detail of the **mise-en-scène** is evidence of the influence of cinema on some of the television directors of the period. It is also evidence of how a popular serial drama could combine a **realist** approach to both **form** and **content** with the deliberate **framing** and **composition** more usually associated with the artificial language of serious film. Remember that this may be 'life', but it's also 'drama'.

- Analyse the televisual style of a current episode, using the techniques in **bold** above. Can you identify features which are similar to, and different from, those described above?

THE TITLE SEQUENCE

The title sequence has always been a very important part of a soap opera. *Coronation Street*'s theme tune, unchanged since the beginning, heralds the start of the programme for those not already watching the TV. The instrumentation, reminiscent of a northern brass band, plays a tune that is initially somewhat mournful, but whose rhythmic double bass and slightly upbeat swing style manages to combine an air of wistful nostalgia with cautious optimism. Its measured, steady pace seems perfectly to capture the hum-drum, the ordinary, the day-in, day-out feel of the environment and its inhabitants.

- Explore the title music to other soap operas. How far does it reflect their atmosphere and environments?

The visuals are equally reflective of a certain perception of northern life – a rain-filled sky, drab uniform houses, the claustrophobia of tight-knit communities – and they make it clear from the outset that our concerns will be with these homes and the people in them, warts and all. The buildings are urban, redbrick, hard-edged, four-square, like the people who inhabit them. In watching the rough, gritty surfaces of the streets and pavements, we are prepared for the gritty realism of the representations in the drama itself.

Compared with some of the more extravagant graphics of some TV shows, then and now, the title sequence seems, too, to suggest a style of documentary realism. (At the end of the very first episodes, the names in the closing credits appeared over shots of the houses where the characters 'lived'.) More recently details have been included to represent more modern developments – aerial views of the newer houses, the factory, and even CGI shots of a metro train passing by on the viaduct. The fact that parts of the title sequence are shot on Granada's permanent exterior lot also suggests something of the 'actuality-heritage-museum' nature of the images.

The title sequence is, and always has been, almost entirely devoid of people. The street, back alleys, back yards; all show virtually no signs of human life, just the occasionally glimpsed figure in the background, and the milk float must be driven by someone, but that's all. It is as though this setting is waiting to be populated by the characters, which then appear in the episode itself, rather like the painted background on a canvas is ready to have the foreground detail added by the artist.

> • What visuals are used in other soap opera title sequences? How far do they
>   reflect the environments in which the soap operas are set?

From early on in its history the sequence has featured a cat (seen below in 2001) – a common symbol of urban domesticity. In fact, the soap's creator, Tony Warren, wanted a cat walking in front of the corner shop as the very first image of the very first episode, but the animal in question would not perform to order for the live transmission. Its easy and comfortable familiarity with its surroundings suggests a welcoming environment where we, too, can feel at home. (Even Shakespeare refers to 'a harmless, necessary cat' in *The Merchant of Venice*.)

> • Can you identify any small but significant details in the title sequences of other
>   soap operas?

The titles themselves, in clear, serif fonts, have a journalistic feel to them, as though the stories are being reported to us in a format resembling a local newspaper.

CAMERA

The early episodes of *Coronation Street* were broadcast live from a multi-camera studio, and the shots were rehearsed in advance, then selected during transmission by the director, and mixed on-air by the vision mixer. The cameras were bulky and made movements difficult to achieve. All the required scenes had to be constructed in the studio, and cameras had to move from one set to another according to the shooting script, which had to be planned meticulously to keep such movements to a minimum.

The confined spaces of the domestic sets meant that camera shots were likely to be restricted. This led to the convention of more close-up shots, concentrating on people's faces, revealing emotions in great detail, and allowing audiences to understand the psychological motives of characters' behaviour. In order to bring the audience into the situation, most shots were from natural eyelines, either standing or sitting. High or low angle shots were kept to a minimum for dramatic effect, and extreme long shots were not generally used. Camera movement was also limited, restricted usually to simple pans and occasional tracking shots.

Even though contemporary technology has resulted in episodes now being recorded in advance of transmission and edited in post-production, many of the early conventions still remain. Only with the occasional high-action dramatic sequences does the director have the freedom to experiment with more adventurous camera angles, movements and positions. In general the cameras are still there simply to record the events of the episode in a semi-documentary fashion, and do not make their presence obvious.

- How far do other soap operas employ the same camera techniques?

SOUND

Apart from the overlapping title and end credit music, almost all of the sound in *Coronation Street* is diegetic, and meant to represent the typical ambient sounds and dialogue of the day-to-day life of the street: people watch TV, listen to the radio, play music, and we hear the soundtrack in the background; cars passing, children playing, birds singing are all present in the mix of ambient sounds.

Dialogue still forms the greatest part of the soundtrack, and is set at levels to reflect anything from a whispered secret in a corner of The Rovers, to a full-scale slanging match on the cobbles. Scenes set in the pub and other more populated places tend to employ 'selective' sound, where we will hear more clearly and a little more loudly, perhaps, the conversations of those currently in shot, than we might otherwise do if we were present. One frequently-used dialogue device to enable audiences to identify and learn about characters is the repetition of character names. Even when members of a family talk to each other, they will frequently address each other by name, perhaps more so than would happen in real life. This is of particular help to new members of the audience, so that they can quickly begin to recognise characters.

Another device employed occasionally is overlapping sound between scenes, when the audio from the following scene begins just a second or two at the end of the preceding scene, before the cut in visuals. Apart from suggesting the continuity of action and time between storylines, the juxtaposition of the soundtrack of one scene against the visuals of another, even for such a short time, can sometimes create a particular meaning for the audience, who might be expected to make a thematic connection between the two scenes.

Apart from these examples, however, all of the sounds are designed to be natural and realistic. Once again, contemporary episodes take advantage of contemporary technology, often employing stereo and even surround sound for many of the ambient sounds, such as cars driving off or footsteps of passing characters and extras.

- Do other soap operas employ non-diegetic sound? What purpose does it seem to be used for?

EDITING

Once the scenes have been recorded in digital video format, they have to be edited into the sequences for a given transmission. Subtracting the length of time required by the commercial breaks, each programme lasts about twenty-four minutes, twelve in each half, for each thirty-minute programme slot. Typically, an episode might contain three separate storylines, each of which is revisited several times during each half, so that some scenes might only last a matter of seconds, while others will have longer to build a progression of action. Part of the editor's task is: to maintain a balance between storylines, some serious, some comic; to keep a sense of pace for the whole episode, and do each of the storylines justice, while bearing in mind that the audience may need to be directed towards certain thematic connections between some stories by a meaningful juxtaposition of scenes.

Editing is also the process by which the pace and tone of a sequence are both reflected and controlled. A leisurely conversation over some drinks in the Rover's Return will require longer shots to reflect the slower pace of such an encounter, but will also control the audience's response to that scene. By contrast, a fast-paced action sequence – an accident or a violent encounter, for example – will need shorter shots to keep up with the speed and urgency of the action, and will take the audience to the pitch of excitement that such an incident is likely to create.

The result, then, is usually a complex pattern of scenes, some seconds long, others running into minutes, with little time to establish character or location. Writers, actors and directors, therefore, have to rely on an economy of dialogue, action and representation, often taking for granted the backstories already present in the memories of the audience. Soap operas spend much of their time building a reservoir of character and backstory knowledge in their audiences, which they then call upon in order to support the progress of characterisation and storylines. In this way they depend on reminding the audience of what they know up to this point, while adding to that store of knowledge as the story progresses – a process not unlike that by which we tend to learn about the real world and our place within it. Editing is one of the key ways by which soap operas enable us to find out where we are, before we are taken somewhere different.

- Explore different types of sequence (e.g. relaxed, tense, confrontational, emotional) and examine how the editing contributes to the overall effect of the scenes.

ANALYSING A SPECIFIC EPISODE OF CORONATION STREET

The episode broadcast on 17 August 2007 contains nineteen scenes relating to six different storylines, although characters from some also appear in others. In order of narrative importance and, arguably, social significance, but not as presented in the episode, they are:

1. The on-going concern surrounding Ashley Peacock's alleged affair with Casey. Ashley's wife, Claire's paranoia over the recent fire at their house has caused her to be mistrustful of everyone, and she has gone to stay with her mother, taking their son, Freddie, with her. Casey, who had befriended Claire, although initially under suspicion by her, has turned her attention to caring for the bereft Ashley, and there have been some intimate moments between them. On one occasion Kevin Webster had arrived for a drink with Ashley, to see Casey coming down the stairs in her dressing gown. Casey had also been seen looking out of the Peacock's bedroom window one morning, having stayed overnight, supposedly to help Ashley out with his son, Joshua. In this episode, Audrey Roberts, who was once romantically linked with Ashley's late father, Fred Elliott, decides to find out what she can about Ashley's relationship with Casey, firstly by asking his friend, Kevin, what he knows, then confronting Ashley himself, and finally comes face to face with Casey herself, who informs Audrey that the relationship has been going on for some months, that this was the reason why Claire has left, and that she, Ashley and Joshua are going to make a family unit. (Six scenes)

2. Although Sally Webster and her husband, Kevin, have tried their best to support their daughter, Rosie, in her education, and are adamant that she should return to the sixth form in September, and then make plans for a university career, Rosie is determined to make a career out of her holiday office job with Underworld. This situation is made worse by the fact that Rosie is actually being very successful in the work, and that her mother, Sally, is one of the machine shop workers. Sally is refusing to accept Rosie's decision. Sally is also studying English literature in an attempt to improve her own educational status. In this episode Sally firstly attempts to obtain her boss, Liam Connor's, support in persuading Rosie to give up any ideas of a permanent career in the factory. She then raises the matter during a family discussion about their forthcoming holiday, to be met by a very determined speech from her daughter, who even threatens not to go on holiday with the other three, and the matter is not resolved to anyone's satisfaction. Sally is not prepared to let her daughter get the better of her. (Three scenes)

3. David Platt continues to create family strife, and Sarah Platt, her boyfriend Jason Grimshaw, Sarah's young daughter, Bethany, and their mother, Gail, are all finding their house too small. David maintains his abusive attitudes towards Jason, the forthcoming marriage between him and Sarah, and his mother. In this episode the rest of his family decide to let Jason and his boss, Bill Webster (Kevin's dad,

and friend of Audrey, Gail's mother) convert their unused garage into a bedroom for David, in order to ease the space problem in their house. David is very angry about this idea, conceived without his knowledge, and accuses his mother of making his exclusion from the family 'official'. The troubled teenager continues to express his hatred for the other members of his family in his usual sardonic and abusive way. (Six scenes)

4. Leanne Battersby is now running her Italian restaurant with the help of trained chef, Paul Clayton, grandson of Jack and Vera Duckworth. It is hard work and Leanne is troubled by staff and financial worries. In this episode, Leanne finally tells Paul about her severe shortage of money, and he tells her to let him see what he might be able to do about it. (Two scenes)

5. After the fiasco of Steve's unfortunate encounter with a transvestite in Malta, captured on photo by Eileen, with whom, as a companion, he had been spending a break away, he has now negotiated a peaceful settlement with his former girlfriend, Michelle, and is enjoying his reprieve. In this episode Steve is beginning to boast about his reconciliation with Michelle, but Michelle, in conjunction with Eileen decides to keep Steve on his toes by continuing to make capital out of his unfortunate mistake while on holiday. She asks Eileen for the incriminating photograph and mounts it over the bar in a frame, much to Steve's disquiet. (Three scenes)

6. David has been very attentive towards Mel Morton, daughter of kebab-shop owner, Jerry, and is angling for a date. He has also been very friendly with Amber Kalirai, Dev Alahan's daughter, who works in his corner shop, and she has taken a great interest in David's romantic endeavours. In this episode David engages Mel in conversation and gets her to agree to a cinema date, although she does not appear quite as keen as he is. Amber contrives to arrive on the scene just as Mel goes off to work. David tells her that things will happen this weekend, leaving Amber not so much just interested in the outcome, but also slightly serious, as though she might be hoping that David would be interested in her. (One scene)

NARRATIVE STRUCTURE

This episode is a very good example of the multi-strand narrative structure of soap opera, because it features a variety of themes: inter-generational conflict, matrimonial disruption, economic difficulties, domestic disputes, relationship betrayals and reconciliations. Some of these are treated with serious melodramatic overtones, others with a level of humour. In this way the seriousness of life is juxtaposed with its comic counterpoints, and the continuum of the human experience is well represented.

The structure of the episode is designed to take us through the different storylines with certain threads leading us from one to another. Scene 1, with the Platts having breakfast, prepares us for both the 'garage conversion' and the 'date' storylines.

[This sequence represents the Platts as both a dysfunctional and a loving family – David and Sarah are constantly at loggerheads; Gail seems unable to communicate with her son, regarding him as arrogant, wilful and devious; Sarah, by contrast, is shown as a caring and devoted mother to her young daughter. The fact that they are having breakfast marks the beginning of the time frame for this episode.]

It also leads neatly to Scene 2, where Gail Platt's mother, Audrey, is having her doubts in the 'Casey & Ashley' strand. The theme 'Troublesome children', starting with David Platt, is continued with the 'Rosie & Sally' story starting in Scene 3.

[Audrey is represented here as both an interfering yet caring member of the older generation; Rosie's manner and mode of address to her mother, Sally, suggest that she is a typical headstrong teenager, whom her mother regards as incapable of making a 'sensible' choice of career. Inter- and intra-generational conflict is another significant generic characteristic of soap operas.]

We return in Scene 4 to two fringe 'Platt' characters, Jason and Bill, who pave the way for Bill's bright idea of the 'garage conversion' theme.

[Bill and Jason work together as builders. Bill is the boss, but he and Jason tend to talk to each other as equals. They are dressed appropriately and exhibit a 'down-to-earth' manner in their dealings with each other and with the world in general. Bill's idea about converting the garage for David suggests a level of calm, common sense amid the turmoil of the Platt family. Bill also acts as a link between the older and younger members of the Platt family.]

Scene 5 continues the 'problem to be solved' theme with Leanne and Paul discussing the restaurant, setting the scene for another 'bright idea', this time hinted at by Paul in Scene 12, but not disclosed in this episode.

[Leanne's dress, serious behaviour and practical common sense suggest that she has progressed well in her role as businesswoman, making a sharp contrast with her former career as a prostitute. Paul's youthful manner, bright appearance and culinary skills make him a good foil for Leanne's older woman. The problem of financing the restaurant is another dramatic device which will enable this storyline to move forward.]

Scene 6 continues another 'problem to be solved': how can Sally prevail upon Rosie to 'see sense' about her education and career? Trying to enlist the boss's help fails, unlike Jason's conversation with his boss, Bill, in Scene 4, leaving Sally at a loss to know what to do next. It is interesting from the point of view of representation that in this scene Sally is very deferential towards Liam because he is the boss, calling him 'Mr Connor', whereas her daughter, Rosie, as an office-based colleague, quite freely calls him 'Liam', much to Sally's annoyance.

> *[In this scene Liam is represented as the young, good-looking boss. He has progressed well as a businessman, rising from market-stall salesman to owner of Underworld and his appearance and manner of address reflect this. Rosie is smartly dressed and speaks with something of an affected accent to reflect her position as an office-worker. Her casual, first-name, mode of address to Liam suggests she sees herself as an equal. Sally, by contrast, is a shop-floor employee of Mr Connor and behaves accordingly, speaking politely to him. As a member of the older generation, her manner and attitudes are at odds with Liam's more laid-back, youthful behaviour. Here are two good examples of characters common in soap operas – the outspoken, feisty teenage girl, and the confident boss-figure.]*

Scene 7, which should really be seen as 7a and 7b, is a good example of a pair of closely linked scenes. Beginning in the salon with Jason anxious to let Sarah in on Bill's idea, and Audrey still anxious to find out more about Casey and Ashley, the action segues from these two parallel sequences into David's 'date' scene outside the salon, by way of Audrey as a central figure in the first section meeting up with her grandson, David, then leaving him to become the significant character in the second section. This overlapping series of events has become a much more prominent narrative device in more recent years, as one set of characters walks into or out of another set of characters' storyline, and we follow either one or the other set.

Scene 8 picks up on Audrey's departure from Scene 7a: having set the scene for her pursuit of the truth about Casey and Ashley, she now visits Kevin Webster's garage. Kevin is Rosie's dad and will feature again in Scene 13. Here, under interrogation from Audrey, he is reluctant to betray Ashley's confidence as a mate, but his serious expression seems to tell her enough, leaving her feeling desperate. At least she feels she has the necessary information to confront Ashley himself. Audrey, as a strong older woman, is both an important focus for representation and a typical generic characteristic of soap operas.

> *[Kevin runs the local garage. At work he appears in the oily overalls of his trade. His hair tends to be unruly and he exhibits the expected demeanour of a workman who gets his hands dirty. He is fiercely protective of his family and his friends, and this shows in his serious and determined facial expressions.]*

Meanwhile her daughter Gail is being persuaded in Scene 9 that the 'garage conversion' idea is a good one. More seasoned viewers may remember the garage as the site of Richard Hillman's imprisonment of Gail, Sarah and David in their car, before attempting

to drive them off to their death in a nearby canal. Such references to previous storylines can serve to provide pleasures for the regular audience by prompting them to draw on their knowledge of the Platt backstory. This is one small example of how an audience can use a detail of their cultural capital with regard to Coronation Street to enhance their understanding and appreciation of the current storyline. Gail is primed to break the good news to David about his new bedroom.

[Gail tends to appear in smart dress, neat hairstyle and exhibits the manner of a middle-aged mother. Her work as a practice receptionist for the local GP also requires her to dress appropriately in office attire. Her expression often appears friendly, but her dealings with David often leave her looking frustrated and angry.]

Scene 10 sees Gail's mother, Audrey, primed to face Ashley with her opinions concerning his behaviour. He is not convinced until Joshua's appearance with a painting 'for mummy', and Audrey's parting comment that he should make sure she gets it, leaves him looking confused, worried and concerned. This is not a cliff-hanger, but is probably enough for the audience to mull over during the advert break. This scene is a good example of how ideologies can be explored in soap operas. In this case some of the dominant ideologies, as presented by Audrey, include: husbands should not be unfaithful to their wives; fathers should place their responsibility to their children before their own interests; decent men should not be led astray by temptations.

[Ashley, the thirty-something local butcher, is usually represented as a caring husband and father. He frequently looks worried and bemused by what's going on around him, and his dress, physical appearance, mode of speech and general demeanour all suggest he is a rather well-meaning but somewhat innocent person. This representation is now at odds with the prospect of his involvement with Casey. Infidelity and betrayal have never been on Ashley's agenda.]

After the commercial break, Scene 11 returns us to a storyline from previous episodes – the reconciliation between Steve and Michelle: Steve has managed to convince her that his mistaken kiss while on holiday in Malta was of no significance. The reintroduction of this storyline, with its good-humoured focus on a couple in love who can weather one partner's supposed 'infidelity' makes a meaningful contrast with the Ashley & Casey relationship, where nothing is good-humoured or lovingly resolved. This storyline also refers to ideologies of relationships and the boundaries which should not be crossed.

[Steve's glum expressions and somewhat clumsy body-language suggest a man who has problems sorting out and maintaining his relationships. His casual dress and apparent relaxed air contrast with the continued uneasiness he feels about his holiday mistake.]

The second visit to Leanne's restaurant in Scene 12 reminds us that Leanne's need for money to repay her backers is a kind of betrayal of her investors' trust in her and the business. Chef Paul has an idea to help her out, but the detail is not disclosed, and audience curiosity is aroused. Part of the purpose of narrative is to conceal rather than reveal narrative details in order to arouse audience expectation and maintain their interest in both plot and character.

Scene 13 features the clash between Sally Webster's idealistic ambitions for her children, even on holiday in Greece, and their desire to have some say in their own futures. When Rosie threatens not to come on the holiday, Sally seems determined to play out a vendetta against her daughter, and waits to see 'who'll blink first'. A different set of ideologies comes into play here as we explore how families ought to behave, whether children should always obey their parents, and how families ought to resolve such confrontational problems.

[This scene is the classic 'petulant teenage daughter versus heavy-handed mother' scenario. Rosie's dress, facial expressions, mode of speech and general manner all present her as a troublesome teenager. Sally's general behaviour presents her as a troublesome mother.]

Following this serious clash of inter-generational personalities, Eileen and Michelle, in Scene 14, brings another glimpse of the 'happy family' that is Steve and Michelle, although some teasing about the photo of Steve and his 'boyfriend' is set to continue.

[Eileen's appearance as a round-faced, middle-aged woman of generous proportions, suggests something of the stereotypical 'larger-than-life', cheery individual, and is put to good use in this up-beat, good-humoured scene.]

After the semi-comic relief of Scene 14, David is told by Gail in Scene 15 about the garage-conversion idea, giving him the opportunity to express his hatred of a family which, in his opinion, already regards him as an outsider.

[David has cultivated a very impressive furious expression to underline the teenage angst and anger he feels towards his family.]

While Gail is struggling once again to understand the bitter behaviour of her son, in Scene 16 Casey arrives at Ashley's house to find him not ready to discuss Audrey's accusations about their behaviour. Although he is preoccupied with Joshua's bedtime bath, Casey seems not to understand his off-hand manner.

[Casey is represented as an attractive young woman, both in her physical features and her dress. Her behaviour and mode of speaking suggest a confident person with a no-nonsense approach to her single-minded purpose of establishing her relationship with Ashley.]

In Scene 17 the more light-hearted banter between Steve, Michelle and Eileen culminates in Steve's discovery of the holiday photo framed and on public view behind the bar, showing him kissing the transvestite, Shania. Michelle declares that she has forgiven him, but is not yet ready to let him forget the incident. This comic 'triangle' has an interesting parallel with the Ashley-Claire-Casey 'triangle', which is picked up again in Scene 19.

Scene 18 features an argument between Sarah and David: this concerns the conversion idea and David's status within the family, and ends on a serious disagreement.

This confrontational atmosphere is maintained and intensified in Scene 19, when Casey arrives at Audrey's salon to deliver some harsh truths, including her fantasy perceptions about her relationship with Ashley and his son. The episode ends on something of a cliff-hanger, as Casey informs Audrey that no one is going to stop her and Ashley being together as a family unit.

[It now becomes clear that Casey's single-minded behaviour is, in fact, a reflection of her obsessive pursuit of Ashley, and the fantasy that he reciprocates her interest in him.]

- Choose a recent episode of a soap opera and break it down into its component scenes in order to discover its thematic structure. Try to identify parallel themes, and how the events of one storyline might mirror another.
- Identify within the scenes some of the theoretical issues outlined above.

CAMERA

The use of the camera in this episode is typical of the shot types to appear in soap operas generally. All of the scenes begin with clear establishing shots, to indicate location and the positioning of key characters. As speakers and conversation groupings are identified, the shots will generally be small grouping shots (two-shot, three-shot).

Once specific exchanges of dialogue are established, the shots become tighter, with a pattern of two-shots, moving to shot-reverse-shot, usually over-the-shoulder shots, in order to track the development of the exchanges. If the mood between the characters needs to become more intense, then the shot-reverse-shot close-ups tighten.

Often scenes need to resolve their visual composition along with their thematic content. In order to achieve this, towards the end of an encounter, shots tend to widen again, finishing with a shot similar to the establishing shot at the beginning of the sequence. A good example of this process is Scene 18 – Sarah and David in their backyard. It begins with an establishing shot of the yard, with David sitting at a garden table. Sarah enters the shot and sits down opposite him. The 'over-the-shoulder' shot-reverse-shot sequence then begins as Sarah attempts to persuade David that the 'garage-conversion' scheme is not designed to alienate him. As each of them becomes more entrenched in their respective positions, the shots tighten to bigger close-ups. When it is clear to Sarah that David has no intention of budging, she brings the encounter to a close and stands up to leave. The shot widens to allow her to go back inside the house, leaving David alone, as he was at the beginning.

There is only one less usual shot in this particular episode. Gail, Jason, Sarah and Bill are seen discussing the conversion of the garage from a camera position inside the open garage itself. As the discussion progresses, the camera tracks forward at a low angle to bring them into a closer shot before the shots then breakdown into the normal dialogue pattern described above. This initial camera position also allows the audience to see the corner shop and a couple of the street's older houses in the background from an unusual angle, thus creating a somewhat different establishing shot.

In keeping with the 'human-scale' of soap operas, camera angles and positions in this episode tend to be 'people-sized', most shots being at character eye-level, whether they are standing or sitting. Higher or lower angle shots merely reflect the relative positions of speakers, and there are very few shots which might be described as 'graphic' or 'dramatic'.

- Select a sequence from a soap opera episode and examine how the use of the camera makes meaning for the audience.

SOUND

All the sound in this episode is naturalistic and designed to create a sense of believable atmosphere and dialogue. Between Scenes 1 and 2, and 2 and 3 there are examples of the overlapping sound technique. At the very end of the Platt's 'breakfast table' scene there is a fraction of a second of car engine noise as, in Scene 2, Bill and Audrey pull up in his car to discuss Audrey's concerns about Ashley. At the end of the scene the engine noise continues as an ambient sound for the opening of Scene 3 with Rosie, Sally and Amber, and then fades as Bill's car moves off.

Another thing to notice about such apparently naturalistic sound is the density of the multi-layered soundtrack as it tries to capture every detail of the sounds that might be heard in any of the scenic surroundings.

- Select a short sequence from a soap opera and try to identify the many different foreground and background sounds which make up the complete soundtrack.

LIGHTING

The lighting design for this episode might be described as 'naturalistic'. Both interior and exterior shots have levels of light which match the environments they depict. The result is that the audience will find the settings and the atmosphere totally believable, and hence be prepared to invest their time and credulity in the storylines as a credible representation of real life.

Since the dramatic date of this episode is August, days tend to begin and end in the light, and there is not much evidence from the lighting set-ups of the passage of time through the day.

- Examine a sequence from a soap opera which uses unusually dramatic lighting effects, and explore how those effects create meaning for the audience.

MISE-EN-SCÈNE

The production design of this episode features most of the environments with which we are familiar:

- Interiors at the Websters, Platts and Peacocks provide the domestic dimension.

- The Rover's Return and Leanne's restaurant are instances of more public spaces, although the restaurant scenes focus on Leanne's personal and financial situation.

- The factory and Audrey's salon are two work-places which are also the setting for more personal confrontations.

- And the street itself, where personal confrontations also have a habit of taking place.

Each of these environments has its expected distinguishing features. Only the pub has an additional item in this episode – the photo of Steve and 'that kiss' – providing an object that is both part of the background design and a key item in the 'Steve & Michelle' storyline.

The appearance of the characters in this episode (dress, hairstyles, make-up, incidental properties) is both typical and familiar to the audience, with one possible exception, which is noted by Dev's daughter, Amber. Now that Rosie sees herself as part of the office workforce at Underworld, she has abandoned her school uniform and 'teen-chic' for smart office dress, which Amber notices with approval and respect.

Objects figure in some of the storylines for this episode:

- The menus in Leanne's restaurant are a jokey pretext for Paul to quiz Leanne on the source of her worries.

- Amber uses a packet of crisps as an excuse to approach David after he has been having a private chat with Mel, in order to find out more about their relationship.

- A picture drawn by Joshua for Claire is used by Audrey as a way of reminding Ashley about his marriage and his responsibilities.

- Steve gives Eileen a little present to represent his good luck in getting back with Michelle.

- The Websters' holiday brochure becomes the focus of a family dispute as Rosie tries to convince them that she is the third adult referred to on the booking form, while Sally is still not prepared to accept her daughter's 'immature' decision about her future career.

- The photograph of Steve in his holiday embrace is the focus of attention for the regulars at The Rover's Return as it reminds him that Michelle may have forgiven, but is not yet willing to forget.

- Analyse the use of objects in a soap opera sequence and explore their significance.

Sarah Platt – Young mum, pretty, girly, sweet, blonde, round youthful face, innocent-looking, not very bright, 'hairdresser', emotional, mean streak, bossy, caring, maternally organised for daughter, supportive to mother, can have a strident, screechy style of speaking:

- Age/gender – sometimes strong young female role, at times vulnerable.

- Ethnicity – white British, reinforced by the 'blue-eyed, blonde' appearance.

- Class – working class.

- Status – employee (shop assistant), daughter, granddaughter, sister, mother, fiancée.

Sarah is represented as a pretty girl with an innocent, youthful face and wide eyes. Her long blonde hair and girly clothes reinforce the perception that she is younger than she is. Her apparent sweetness is belied by the fact that she can be very spiteful, especially towards her brother, David. Her youthful appearance also tends to contradict her role as the mother of a six-year-old daughter, Bethany, whose care she takes very seriously. She is employed by her grandmother, Audrey, in the stereotypical role of a hairdresser. She is determined to marry Jason, towards whom she tends to behave alternately as a loving girlfriend and a bossy fiancée.

David Platt – Spiky hair, scornful and angry expressions, troubled teenager, malicious, spiteful in language and behaviour, untrustworthy, can affect pleasantness, small signs of 'niceness', disrespectful son, has a snidey, sneery manner of speaking:

- Age/gender – youthful/vulnerable male.

- Ethnicity – white British.

- Class – working class.

- Status – student, son, brother, grandson.

David's hairstyle, clothes, physical manner, behaviour patterns and mode of address all mark him out as a troubled adolescent who is continuing to be malicious to everyone in his immediate family. His serious lies and deceitful behaviour have caused considerable anguish to his mother, his sister and his wider family. He uses his old car as a status symbol and a place of refuge from his family. His pathetic attempts to form sexual relationships with Maria and Tracy Barlow, and his current delusion about his 'relationship' with Mel Morton all underline his vulnerable immaturity, and make his self-perception as a smart, mature, knowing young man all the more incredible.

Audrey Roberts – Sixty-something, responsible businesswoman, grandmother, less so a mother by past history, still interested in relationships with men, smart, looks younger than she is, caring for friends, not perceived as overtly nosey, or interfering:

- Age/gender – strong older female role.

- Ethnicity – white British.

- Class – businesswoman.

- Status – shop owner (hairdressers), mother, grandmother, partner.

As the owner of the hairdressing salon, Audrey is clearly successful in business, although her personal life is far less secure. She has either outlived or actively dismissed most of the men in her life. She behaves in a friendly and interested way towards people, but seems to escape the label of 'gossip', and she is able to present the image of one who is genuinely concerned about people's well-being, as she is about Ashley in this episode. Her hairstyle (as might be expected), mode of dress and general demeanour all seem somewhat younger than her age would suggest. She also has a more middle-class manner of speech, and never participates in any of the on-the-street slanging matches and violent encounters which occur between some of the other, more down-to-earth female characters.

Rosie Webster – Maturing young woman, intelligent, well-educated (privately), attractive, dressing the part of smart young businesswoman, single-minded, rebellious, practical, capable, potentially socially mobile, growing too big for her family?:

- Age/gender – strong young female role.

- Ethnicity – white British.

- Class – working class/educated aspiring businesswoman.

- Status – student, employee (office worker), daughter, sister.

Rosie has grown from love-struck, self-centred schoolgirl to self-possessed and self-confident young woman. At a younger age she and boyfriend, Craig, affected 'Goth' clothes, make-up, hairstyles and lifestyles. At school she was always seen in the stereotypical short skirts and blazers of her uniform. Now employed as an office junior by Underworld, the factory where her mother is a machinist, she has chosen to appear in smart and rather restrained 'office dress', and with neat hairstyle and modest make-up. Her private education has enabled her to cultivate a somewhat correct mode of speech. Despite all of this, she can still play the rebellious teenager, especially where her mother is concerned. It is likely that she may be seen as an object of envy by her mother.

Jason Grimshaw – Mid-twenties, young builder, dark hair, good-looking, practical, capable, limited intelligence, unsure of commitment, traditional views, typical builder's clothes, appearance, behaviours (diet, pub, etc.):

- Age/gender – physically strong, but uncertain young male role.

- Ethnicity – white British.

- Class – working class.

- Status – employee (builder), son, fiancé.

Jason's appearance and behaviour both suggest a stereotypical macho young man. His facial expressions tend to make him look permanently bewildered or confused. He has had a string of relationships, and his general manner towards most women has been that of someone 'playing the field', albeit not as confidently as some. His relationship with Sarah makes them a stereotypical couple: strong, good-looking young male with pretty blonde girlfriend. His lack of commitment and interest in their forthcoming wedding both suggest that he is not ready for this kind of settling down, not least because it brings with it a ready-made daughter, and a family unit for which he will have to be jointly responsible.

Amber Kalirai – Sharp, witty, teenage daughter, self-confident, love-hate relationship with father, culturally more English than Asian, quietly interested in boys, reliable, capable:

- Age/gender – rather strong young girl role.

- Ethnicity – Asian.

- Class – working class.

- Status – employee (shop assistant), daughter, friend.

Amber has always been something of a background, behind-the-counter figure in the street. Now that her father, Dev Alahan, is reconciled to his responsibilities as her father, she seems to have grown in confidence and security. Although she has tended to dress in a casual and unspectacular fashion, her interest in David Platt has led her to sport rather more 'feminine' clothes. Neither her appearance nor her manner seems to reflect her traditional ethnic or religious background.

Ashley Peacock – Early-thirties, fair, tousled hair, 'little-boy' looks, caring father, loving husband, perpetually distraught and confused by situations, local butcher running his late father's business, has difficulty with relationships, troubled past, troubled present:

- Age/gender – portrayed as a younger, slightly weak man.

- Ethnicity – white British.

- Class – working class.

- Status – shop owner (butchers), husband, father, friend.

Ashley's strangulated voice and youthful appearance have contributed to his being seen by some as something of a joke on the street. He is portrayed as a loving father for Joshua, who is not actually his, and began as a loving husband for Claire, who was originally Joshua's nanny. Claire's serious depression and paranoia have finally made Ashley less supportive of his wife, and her absence has made it easy for him to be attracted away from his family by the resourceful and deranged Casey. Ashley is always anxious to please and does not appear to possess many resources to cope when things go wrong.

Michelle Connor – Mid-thirties, dark-haired, attractive, sensible, mature, strong caring mother, well-organised, good-humoured, thoughtful, supportive of family:

- Age/gender – strong younger female role.

- Ethnicity – white British.

- Class – working class.

- Status – employee (barmaid), mother, girlfriend, sister.

Michelle continues the tradition of soap operas producing a long line of strong women. Michelle is one of the younger 'anchors' of Coronation Street. Her responsible parenting of her son, Ryan, and support for her two brothers, seem exemplary. The death of her brother, Paul has hit her very hard, but she still maintains security and support for her son and for her other brother, Liam. Her avowed love for Steve is entirely credible and definitely to be valued. Her neat hairstyle, attractive appearance, warm humour and brisk efficiency around the pub all make her a very desirable employee, friend and partner. She is certainly to be seen as a strong contrast with some of the other women in Steve's recent past: self-centred Karen, self-promoting Ronnie and the murderous Tracy. She is also presented as a viable contender for Steve's mum, Liz.

Liam Connor – Early-thirties, dark-haired, good-looking factory boss, organised, capable, supportive of his family, friendly, good-humoured, responsible employer, relates well to employees, has grown into role as successful businessman:

- Age/gender – strong male role.

- Ethnicity – white British.

- Class – working class businessman.

- Status – business owner (factory), brother.

Liam's appearance, manner and generally pleasant behaviour have endeared him to both his employees and his friends. He was devastated by the death of his brother, Paul, and the linked discovery that the girl Paul thought he was dating, Leanne Battersby, was actually working as a prostitute to provide money for an expensive lifestyle and the pretence that she was a successful businesswoman. Liam was strongly supportive of Paul, and has developed his persona as an efficient and responsible businessman from that of a rather dodgy market-trader. Despite his obvious attractions for the opposite sex, Liam has tried to pursue his personal interests in a quiet and generally responsible way.

Eileen Grimshaw – Late-forties, middle-aged mother, blonde, chubby, morose/cheerful in equal proportions, messy life, generally supportive and reliable, a little gossipy, friendly, anxious to be in a relationship:

- Age/gender – strong-ish older woman role.

- Ethnicity – white British.

- Class – working class.

- Status – employee (taxi receptionist), mother, friend.

Eileen's round appearance and kindness towards the temporarily dispossessed make her a supportive individual for many people. She dresses to suit her age and her general manner suits her level of maturity. She was very upset by having to give up the baby she originally thought was Jason's but turned out to be Charlie's. Despite her general pleasantness, she harbours considerable enmity towards Gail Platt, largely because of the way the latter responded when Eileen's son, Todd, finally confessed to his then girlfriend, Sarah Platt, that he was gay and was leaving the street to live in London. Eileen's work as receptionist at StreetCars reflects her willingness to be helpful as well as her ability to maintain the banter that goes on between herself, Lloyd, Steve and Jamie.

- Select some characters from a soap opera and examine how their representations are constructed. Are their representations dominant, oppositional or negotiated?

INFLUENCE

Although not the first soap opera on British television, *Coronation Street* has, nevertheless, been arguably the most influential. It has maintained its high-ranking position in TV drama for nearly fifty years. It has explored a wide variety of social and personal issues, some very controversial, through its storylines and character development. It has produced moments of high tragedy and outrageous comedy. Despite the claustrophobic confines of its setting, it has often challenged the conventions of day-to-day television production styles. It has managed to blur the boundaries between fiction and reality, and create for itself a whole world of character, personality and incident reinforced by magazines, websites and other forms of promotional material.

- Carry out some research into the different kinds of promotional material created to support a soap opera of your choice. How far and in what ways does it try to create an illusion of reality for the audience?

It is impossible to say how far *Coronation Street* influenced, or was influenced by, developments in other forms of drama, but it is probably safe to say that, once established, it did have some effect on the way that television dramatists and their audiences began to represent and perceive the world, in terms of narrative, generic conventions, representation, as well as on the production styles and technology employed to create them.

In the decades since the 1960s, playwrights and audiences have begun, increasingly, to explore more regularly and explicitly the ordinary and the everyday as sites for the discussion of serious issues surrounding the human experience. Our selected episode, for example, is concerned with family relationships, infidelity and betrayal, inter-generational conflicts and personal financial concerns, all weighty and significant matters.

Some key episodes are often followed by public service announcements encouraging those affected by the issues raised to contact the appropriate organisations or authorities for advice and assistance. This 'public service' dimension has become an increasingly common feature of 'serious continuing drama' in recent years. It also plays a significant part in returning broadcasting to its earliest avowed intentions – to inform, educate and entertain.

- Select specific episodes of more than one UK soap opera and make a detailed comparison of their content and structure.

- What features of *Coronation Street* are likely to have contributed to its long-running success?

- Compare some of the earliest episodes with some of the latest. What similarities and differences can you detect?

CHAPTER THREE — *THE SINGING DETECTIVE*

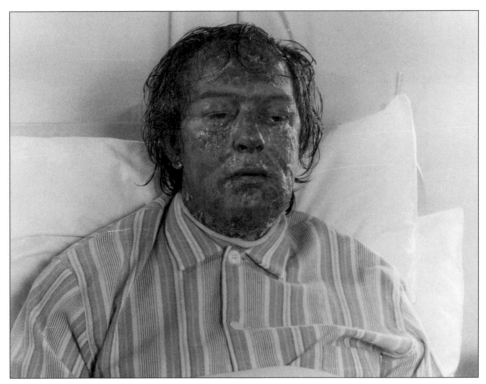

*Michael Gambon
as 'Philip Marlow'*

Dennis Potter was never an 'easy' playwright. All of his work, from the single plays of
the 1960s to his six-part dramas in later decades, explore the darker challenges of the
human experience – sex and sexuality, psychological trauma, repression, dysfunctional
relationships, criminal behaviour, disability and death are all features of his dramatic
output. His work was frequently misunderstood and misrepresented by the press, but he
is nevertheless regarded as the greatest of the television playwrights, not least because
he truly believed in the potentially beneficial power of television as one of the greatest
cultural contributions to all of our lives. 'Turn on, tune in…and grow!' as he was very fond
of saying.

Common threads run through all of his work, many of them seemingly autobiographical:
clashes of social class (Potter was a miner's son from the Forest of Dean who went
to Oxford, stood for parliament, became a journalist and then a writer); physical and
psychological illness (Potter suffered all his adult life from psoriatic arthropathy, a crippling
disease of the skin and joints, as well as enduring the trauma of childhood abuse); the
power of popular music (Potter has described how the popular tunes of his day made
a great impact on him when he heard them on the radio, drifting up the stairs to his
bedroom); the influence of sexual repression, guilt and the betrayal of innocence; the

nostalgia of lost childhood. However, all of his narratives contain many elements that had no place in Potter's own life, and he was very quick to refute any idea that his work is merely a rewriting of his own experiences. In fact, he regarded *The Singing Detective* as hardly autobiographical at all, even though it contains all of the features mentioned above and many more 'Potter-orientated' themes besides.

NARRATIVE

The Singing Detective is a very complex, enigmatic, multi-layered drama, whose non-linear approach to narrative and frequent shifts between time and location have rendered it confusing for some audiences. It could be seen as a huge four-dimensional detective story, constantly visiting and revisiting four separate worlds, until all of the experiences in each world finally come together, rather like the solution in a mystery 'whodunnit'.

There are two 'real-world' narratives:

1. The hero, detective-story writer, Philip Marlow, is in hospital undergoing treatment for a severe skin condition (psoriatic arthropathy) in the present day (mid-1980s). His condition gives rise to hallucinations, delusions, vivid dreams, tricks of memory and fantasies, all common side effects of the illness. He begins to re-write his detective novel *The Singing Detective* in his mind, and later on paper as therapy. One of his fellow-patients, Reginald, happens, coincidentally, to be reading Marlow's original novel, *The Singing Detective*, and his progress through the book mirrors exactly the various stages of the narrative. Marlow undergoes some psychotherapy sessions with Dr Gibbon, whose Scots accent, facial appearance and somewhat domineering manner remind him of his tyrannical class teacher. This part of the drama is constructed and shot as a cross between a serious hospital drama and a medical soap opera/sit-com.

2. The hero is presented as a boy, growing up in the West Country during the Second World War, attending school, witnessing the adultery of his mother with the father of one of his classmates, Mark Binney, defecating on the teacher's desk in his distress, accusing the same classmate of the act and witnessing his brutal punishment at the hands of his class teacher, being sent away to London with his errant mother, experiencing her suicide by drowning in the Thames and returning to his devastated father. This part of the drama is constructed and shot as a serious nostalgic heritage drama.

There are two fantasy narratives:

1. In Marlow's novel, set during the Second World War, a private detective, also named Phil Marlow, is hired by a wealthy businessman, Mark Binney, to investigate the mysterious death of a nightclub hostess with whom he has become involved, and who is possibly connected with Nazi and Russian spy rings. Her body is pulled

out of the Thames near Hammersmith Bridge, as the real Marlow's mother was. Marlow also sings with his band at a local dance hall, hence his title. As his illness takes hold, the real Marlow, confined to his hospital bed, begins to confuse the storyline of his novel with fantasies derived from its plot and characters. This part of the drama is constructed and shot as a *'film noir'* – inspired period thriller.

The 1940s fictional detective scenes employ some of the classic iconography of American *film noir*:

- Trilby, trench-coat and revolver for the detective himself, Marlow.

- Two similarly attired anonymous henchmen.

- Glamorously dressed night-club hostesses.

- Whisky bottles and glasses.

- Enigmatic, slangy, side-of-the-mouth dialogue.

- Dead bodies.

- 1940s dance hall and band.

- Seemingly innocent man lured into a web of corruption and crime.

2. The real-life experience of his illness also causes Marlow to fantasise about his own life, and particularly about the supposed infidelity of his wife, Nicola, whom he imagines as having an affair with an unscrupulous film producer, Mark Finney, who is keen to get his hands on a film script version of Marlow's novel produced some years earlier. Nicola is duped into handing over the script by the promise of a starring role in the forthcoming movie, but is thrown over when an unnamed 'A' list actress is chosen by Finney's American backers. In revenge, Nicola kills Finney and is arrested for murder, although the narrative is not elaborated on further by the fantasising Marlow. This part of the drama is constructed and shot as a contemporary mystery thriller.

All four narratives are inextricably interwoven, with details of one unexpectedly appearing in another, and all of them interconnected by the popular songs of the 1940s, most of them lip-synched by the characters miming to the vocals. This device, already very successfully employed by Potter in his earlier serial drama, *Pennies from Heaven*, produced some eight years previously, is used in *The Singing Detective* to enhance, comment ironically on, or provide bitter-sweet counterpoint to the significant incidents of the four stories, often as they collide in their narrative career.

The complexity does not end there. Running through *The Singing Detective* is another intricately woven strand which lends a high degree of sophisticated intertextuality to the whole work, and goes some way to explaining Potter's purpose in writing the drama as he did.

Scattered throughout the drama is a subtle web of clues, cross-references and reflections of Potter's other television dramatic work. The use of period popular music, as has been noted, is a device Potter employed in some of his earlier works, most remarkably in *Pennies from Heaven*, a story about the desperation of a sheet-music salesman, Arthur Parker, trapped in a loveless marriage, seeking solace in a tragic affair, and ultimately standing trial for the murder of a young girl. Potter also employed other references to popular music and popular culture (*Follow the Yellow Brick Road* (1972) – song-title from the film *The Wizard of Oz* – for example, featured TV advertising as a vehicle to explore the failure of a third-rate TV actor) in many of his single plays.

Autobiographical details were also employed by Potter, particularly his humble origins in the Forest of Dean and his success in later life, and his illness and hospital experiences, in such plays as *Stand Up, Nigel Barton* (1965), *Joe's Ark* (1974) and *Emergency Ward Nine* (1966).

Probably the most remarkable re-working of his earlier material is the casting of the class teacher in *The Singing Detective*, Janet Henfrey. This actor had been cast as the class teacher in one of Potter's earliest plays for television, *Stand Up, Nigel Barton*, where she played a harsh disciplinarian confronting recalcitrant students. Barton himself, like Marlow, is represented as a clever boy who succeeds in escaping from a life in the coal mines by achieving a place at Oxford and thus gaining a passport to a career. A second play, *Vote, Vote, Vote for Nigel Barton* (1965), sees him standing for parliament amid the corruption of local and national politics. A line in *The Singing Detective* seems to be a subtle reference to this, as Gibbon, the psychiatrist, referring to Marlow's physical condition, asks him 'Have you tried standing?' To which Marlow replies 'Who'd vote for me?' We should also note that Potter himself stood as a candidate for election when he was a young journalist.

- Find some examples of Potter's earlier work for television and compare them with *The Singing Detective*. You should explore characterisation, themes, televisual style and dialogue, in addition to representation, narrative, generic features and ideology.

GENRE

Potter tended to describe his 'musical dramas' as 'plays with music'. Such a simple description, however, belies the generic complexity of *The Singing Detective*. The title offers two central clues – it's a detective novel (crime drama) and it's a musical. This apparent clash of genres is neatly resolved in the central character, Philip Marlow, who is, in the 1940s narrative, both private eye and nightclub singer. However, Marlow is also a writer of detective fiction in a present-day narrative, whose stay in hospital makes the work, in part, a medical drama. But Marlow also has a past, seen through the eyes of his eleven-year-old self, making the work a period/heritage/nostalgia drama.

It might be helpful to tabulate the generic characteristics according to the different genres present in the drama.

GENRE	FEATURES
Crime drama	Guns, 1940s clothing (trilbies, trench coats, women's fashions), mysterious men, *femmes fatales*, drink, cigarettes, nightclubs, *'film noir'* low-key lighting, shady locations.
Musical	Popular songs from the 1940s as non-diegetic soundtracks, mimed to by characters, big production numbers, dancing, lavish costumes and props, appropriate lighting design, musicians, instruments, music players (radiograms, radios, CD players, walkmans), microphones.
Medical drama	1980s hospital setting (beds, curtains, corridors, medical staff, white coats, nurses' uniforms, equipment, patients, porters, drugs, tea trolley), visiting times, doctor's rounds, medical treatment, psychiatric consultations.
Period drama	Period (1940s) dress, working-men's club, village school, steam railway, war references, diegetic music (radio, gramophone), dialect dialogue, period shots of London, comics, newspapers.

Genre is not just about labels. Audience expectation also plays a large part in understanding the nature of the drama. So, what had audiences come to expect of a Dennis Potter play?

In his single plays he dealt with issues of illness, death, sexual relationships, complex psychologies, nostalgia, popular culture, identity, religious belief and doubt, and guilt, all of which also feature heavily in *The Singing Detective*. He had also prepared the audience for the innovative use of popular music in challenging ways in his 1978 serial play with music, *Pennies from Heaven*. He had certainly provoked audience and critics alike with his uncompromising approach to human relationships. The tabloid press labelled him 'Dirty Den' for his no-holds-barred attitude to sex.

Despite this unflattering and inaccurate portrayal by the popular papers, the more thoughtful members of his audience were ready to be:

- **Challenged** – because the multi-layered, time-shifting, non-linear narrative was not always easy to follow.

- **Puzzled** – because the shifts between past and present often overlapped and because the multi-layered narratives provided enigmas.

- **Intrigued** – because it was, despite its obscurity, a 'whodunnit'-type mystery which demanded a solution.

- **Provoked** – because there were controversial themes and scenes within the narrative.

They were certainly expecting something they could get their teeth into. The problem with trying to discuss genre in relation to *The Singing Detective* is that it almost defies definition. It certainly was, and arguably remains, the most original piece of drama ever to be written for television. It is certainly Potter's masterpiece.

REPRESENTATION

Great care was taken by Potter himself and by the design team to create accurate representations of the various characters, periods and settings of this complex drama.

Marlow is inevitably a set of complex representations. As a patient in the present-day hospital scenes he spends much of his time in pyjamas and dressing gown. His condition results in much of his body being covered in large, white flakes of skin, suggesting the severity of the disease and its effect on the human body. During one examination by the doctors he appears lying on his bed in just a loincloth, the flaking skin very much in evidence. This is almost religious iconography, as he appears like the crucified Christ.

He is represented as an angry, disturbed and self-centred individual, prone to foul-mouthed outbursts and bitter exchanges with the hospital staff. He can sometimes behave in a more kindly way towards some of the other patients, but this lapse from his normal attitude is rare. His conversations with the psycho-therapist reveal a deep-seated disgust with human sexual behaviour and intense guilt for the betrayal of a classmate.

As a child in the 1940s he is shown as an intelligent boy, small in stature, lonely, bullied, confused and psychologically disturbed by the adult sexuality he witnesses. Despite his mother's working-class London accent, Philip speaks with a broad Forest of Dean accent. However, much of his manner suggests a more mature attitude to life, especially during his monologues to the camera, which are quite philosophical. His natural intelligence enables him falsely to accuse his classmate, Mark Binney, of the act which he himself was responsible for, sensing that the other children would corroborate his story if he made it convincing enough, which they do – '…and I listened as one after another they nailed that backward lad hands and feet to my story'.

Marlow's detective-self appears in the typical trilby-and-trench coat guise of most small-time private eyes. His neat moustache emphasises his brisk efficiency in dealing with cases. He speaks in a mid-Atlantic drawl, using expressions in his dialogue which reveal his hard-boiled cynicism and his world-weary approach to his naïve clients. His gun lets us, his clients and his targets know that he means business. As a nightclub singer and band-leader, he appears in white tuxedos, black bow-ties, and his neat moustache conveys an air of dance-hall chic.

The contemporary scenes in the hospital are recognisably realistic, with all the expected paraphernalia of a medical setting. It is interesting to note that most of the medical staff and patients are not represented as being particularly attractive, either in their appearance or personalities (unattractive, domineering and patronising staff, weak and insignificant patients).

There is one exception: Nurse Mills. She is deliberately represented as a very pretty young woman with a friendly and sympathetic personality, especially in her dealings with Marlow, for whom she has to carry out some quite intimate treatment. Marlow, of course, finds her especially attractive, and describes her as 'the girl in all those songs'. What he means by this is that she is, in his view, the embodiment of all the girls in all the love songs that he heard in his childhood, the love songs that his fictional creation and 'alter ego', the singing detective, croons to his nightly audiences at the local dance hall in the 1940s. This is one of Potter's recurring motifs and a device he uses in many of his plays, both before and after this production.

The other significant character in the hospital scenes is Marlow's wife, Nicola. She, too, is represented as a very attractive woman, with a blazing shock of bright copper-red hair. She is usually dressed in a red coat, and this 'red' theme depicts her, of course, as a flamboyant and potentially dangerous figure. Her role as an unfaithful wife and sexual predator is largely one constructed for her by Marlow's fevered imagination and thus projected onto her character for the audience to consider and judge. Her own behaviour and attitudes do not necessarily support this view of her, and we might conclude that such an interpretation does not ring true.

In the 'childhood' scenes, every attempt is made to construct a period 'feel' through the 1940s domestic and school settings, the wardrobes and physical appearance of the characters, their Forest of Dean dialect, and all of the properties used on-set.

Certain characters are invested with personal characteristics, sometimes exaggerated for effect. The schoolmistress, for example, has a tight hairstyle and employs facial expressions of formidable power and disgust to emphasise her position of straight-laced authority. Her bony, pointing finger not only signifies her control, it also acts as the 'finger of God' attempting to point out the guilty boy.

Philip's father is a tall, lumbering man with a morose expression and a flat, greased hairstyle of the 'short-back-and-sides' variety, whereas Mark Binney's father, who has the affair with Philip's mother, has a cheery expression, free-flying curly hair and an altogether more lively, attractive and open personality.

Philip's mother speaks with a London accent, which marks her out as an 'outsider' with the local folk. She also has a more attractive and more neatly turned out appearance than her neighbours. Her musical skills at the piano also set her apart from the rest of the members of the local miners' club. Her more 'modern' attitudes and manner of speaking tend to antagonise her in-laws, with whom she, her husband and son live. It is not too difficult for the adult Marlow to translate her into the 'Lili Marlene'-spy-'femme fatale' character of his 1940s detective novel, since they both end up dead, his mother by throwing herself in the Thames, the fictional 'dame' by being shot as part of the espionage plot.

IDEOLOGY

Mirroring the complexity of its narratives, *The Singing Detective* speaks to us in a variety of different 'languages' or discourses. This means that it is likely to project a number of different ideologies to its audience.

Once again, a table may help to identify this variety.

IDEOLOGY	DISCOURSE
REAL-WORLD PRESENT-DAY HOSPITAL NARRATIVE	
The medical profession possesses knowledge and power over patients 'for their own good'.	Medical terminology between the senior staff; patronising forms of address to patients. *(Why is it – that – when you lose your health, the entire medical profession takes it as axiomatic that you have also lost your mind!)*
Patients can possess a 'camaraderie' in order to protect their interests.	Friendly repartec between themselves, with subtle rudeness at the expense of the medical staff.
Hospital experience is about life and death.	Matter-of-fact language used by the nursing staff. *(Life is a cabaret, old chum. In here it is.)*
REAL-WORLD 1940s PERIOD NARRATIVE	
Traditional family values in a small rural community.	Language of respect expected in the family setting.
An outsider (Mrs Marlow) can threaten security of family values by her adultery with a village man.	Erotic exchanges during love-making scene in the woods.
Patriotic values espoused by primary school teacher.	Language of victory and triumph. *('It's a Lovely Day Tomorrow' sung as a victory song by children)*

Religious values of right and wrong explored in the enquiry concerning the defilement of the teacher's desk.	Quasi-biblical language used by teacher to force the culprit to own up. *(We are going to ask Almighty God Himself. We are going to beseech Almighty God Himself. He is going to point His Holy Finger. Almighty God will tell us who did this wicked deed. And then we shall know. Let us pray.)*
Issues of truth and betrayal explored in Philip's exposure of the culprit.	Accusatory lies in response to the pressure of the biblical blackmail used by the teacher. *(Mark Binney, miss. It was Mark Binney!)*
FANTASY-WORLD 1940s DETECTIVE NARRATIVE	
Cynical values espoused by both criminals and the detective hired to track them down.	The 'side-of-the-mouth, mid-Atlantic drawl' beloved of pulp fiction crime writers. *(MARLOW: I get the cases the polite guys pass over. I get the jobs the guys who don't sing don't get. I'm the piano tuner who's heavy on the pedal. OK. OK. So what's the story? Who's the dame?' BINNEY: How do you know there's a — MARLOW: There's always a dame.)*
Males are either strong and cynical (criminals or detectives), or weak and manipulated (innocent victims sucked into this dark world, usually by accident and by women – the so-called 'femmes fatales').	*(And you're looking a trifle pale, pal. Like you've been eating fried eggs and green bananas. Who's trying to swing you into this number? And are you as nervous as you seem?)*
Despite the cynicism, the hard-boiled private eye still has fixed ideas about right and wrong, and will take a stand against betrayal, even if the 'rules' need to be bent to achieve it.	

ANALYSIS OF THE OPENING SCENE

The titles appear over the front cover of a paperback book featuring images and typography usually associated with the pulp fiction detective paperbacks of the 1940s (man in trilby hat, raincoat, with a smoking revolver, corpse of blonde woman lying underneath a lamppost, bold lettering, block colouring), and are accompanied by an instrumental version of a popular song of the time, 'Peg o' My Heart'. Peg is a common abbreviation of Margaret, so we should not be surprised to find that Potter's wife is actually called Margaret, as though the drama might be a dedication to her.

The title sequence is simple and relatively short, but its imagery and its music quickly root it for the audience in the two central aspects of the drama – crime drama and musical.

In the very first scene we see a narrow, shadowy passageway. It is a dark and rainy evening. These devices alone would be enough to suggest the air of mystery which pervades the narrative. The only person to be seen is an old busker playing a haunting version of the tune we have just heard over the titles. Some members of the audience might remember a similar busker figure featuring significantly in *Pennies from Heaven*. The image mixes to a shot of railings behind which a flight of steps leads down to a basement club – the name, Skinscapes, picked out in neon above the door. A doorman, in uniform, comes out. As he puts on his cap, he catches sight of a dark smear on the back of his hand (blood? lipstick?). He tries to remove it with his handkerchief as we hear a voiceover, in the style of a smart-talking American private eye from a cheap detective novel, pointing out how the mark may have got there:

> *The doorman of a nightclub can always pretend that it's lipstick and not blood on his hands. But how'd it get there? Let's be economical. Nothing fancy. If he smacked some dame across her shiny mouth, then he's got both answers in one.*

This first speech does seem to hint at the idea that the different threads of the drama could all resolve themselves at the same point, as, indeed, they do.

The voiceover, moody music, dark locations and references to nightclubs, blood, lipstick, dames, all root this opening sequence in the filmic style of a 1940s '*film noir*'. The shot changes back to the dark passageway, at the end of which a smartly-dressed man, Mark Binney, appears in the shadows, and is acknowledged by the busker, who immediately plays a few bars of the German national anthem, and then the man drops a coin into the busker's hat. All of this subterfuge adds an atmosphere of the 'spy-thriller' genre into the mix. The coin turns out to be wrapped in a note bearing the scribbled name of the nightclub we have just seen. This note is received joyously by the 'busker' who now whispers to himself in educated accents ('*Thank you sir. Jolly well done, old fruit.*'), betraying his disguise and identifying him for the audience as an undercover agent. Binney walks down the steps of the club, accompanied by a further voiceover from the unseen private eye.

From the carefully designed *mise-en-scène* of this opening sequence we are expected to understand that the action is taking place at some time during the Second World War

(1940s), involving espionage, secret agents, mysterious assignations, and activities usually associated with the thriller genre of popular film.

Without warning the scene shifts to a contemporary hospital ward. All the trappings of an NHS hospital are present: multiple beds, curtains, medical equipment, tea trolley, personal effects of patients, patients in pyjamas, nurses in uniform. A shot of a patient's notes hanging at the end of an empty bed reveals the occupant to be P. E. Marlow. Readers of detective novels may well recognise the reference: Philip Marlowe was one of the very famous 'pulp fiction' US detectives from the 1940s. Our character seems to have misplaced the final 'e', only to find it now being his second initial.

We see a variety of patients being served tea and cake. The staff nurse in charge, short, brisk, starched uniform, subjects the patients to varying degrees of patronising humiliation as she dispenses refreshment with all the humanity of a reluctant donor to an undeserving charity. One of the patients, Mr Hall, a balding, middle-aged man, is grumbling to his neighbour, Reginald, about the late arrival of the tea. Reginald, a young man with a slicked-back, 'Teddy-Boy' hairstyle, is busy reading a cheap paperback, whose title is concealed from us, but whose content is clearly riveting, to judge by his total absorption. This sequence, with semi-comic dialogue and somewhat caricatured individuals (grumpy old man type and young tearaway type), looks and sounds more like a scene from a situation comedy. The *mise-en-scène* here, with its flat interior lighting, contemporary props and familiar costume, makes a stark contrast with the melodramatic period gloom of the preceding sequences.

We now see the central character, Philip Marlow, for the first time. He is being pushed along a corridor in a wheelchair by a porter. He is dressed in pyjamas and hospital gown, and is sitting in a hunched and withdrawn position. It is clear from his face that he is suffering from a serious skin condition. He is talking to himself in voiceover, narrating the story of the wartime sequences we have already seen. As he does so, we cut back to the nightclub scene. Binney enters and approaches the bar. The barman asks for his order, and then bends forward suddenly, wincing with pain. We cut quickly back to Marlow in his wheelchair, also wincing with pain as the porter carelessly jolts him. In this way we are expected to make the now very clear connections between the wartime and present-day sequences. We begin to understand that Marlow is a writer, and the wartime sequences we have been watching are dramatisations of the novel he is re-writing in his head. We return immediately to the nightclub, where Binney is being chatted up by one of the resident hostesses, Amanda, who is ordering expensive champagne on his bill.

Back in the ward, Marlow is being delivered to his bed. Unable to stand, the porter lifts him and helps him slip off his robe, to reveal the full extent of his skin lesions. He is horrified by what he sees and Marlow screams at him to pull the curtains for the sake of his privacy. Alone and temporarily shut off from the world, he struggles to combat his pain and then rages against his disease and his fellow patients, announcing 'Bastards! I'll wipe you out! Don't you know who I am? I'm the – *(chuckle)* – I'm the Singing Detective'.

In the ward Staff Nurse White is busy patronising an Asian patient while continuing to deliver the tea. She then finds Marlow lying on his side, attempting to reach his pyjamas, and infuriates him with her patronising tone. She is outraged by his sarcastic swearing, so he reverts ironically to the manner of a timid little boy using baby-speak to get his message across. His desperation and frustration are comically mirrored by Mr Hall's exasperated outbursts concerning the late arrival of the tea. When the tea does arrive, Mr Hall reacts with ingratiating timidity, prompting Reginald to tell the nurse what Mr Hall really thinks about the service. Hall's angry and embarrassed asides to Reginald, urging him to shut up, are met by further comments from Reginald. This leads to Hall embarrassing the nurse still further by blurting out that she is 'very welcome in his bed, whichever way she turns'. This comic *double entendre* and the banter that precedes it continue to mark the hospital sequences as belonging to the situation comedy/soap opera genres.

There is then a quick cut to a starkly contrasting scene. It is barely light on the River Thames by Hammersmith Bridge. Two policemen in a launch are lifting the body of a young woman out of the black water, while the soundtrack repeats the exchanges between Binney and Amanda, implying it is her body. We see the policemen covering the body with tarpaulin and then a cut back to the bridge reveals only one spectator – a younger, fresher-faced Marlow, dressed like a stereotyped movie private eye, trench coat and trilby, watching the recovery of the body with what looks like a professional interest. This is clearly his 1940s detective persona.

In this way this opening sequence sets the pattern for the remainder of the first episode and the rest of the drama – constant shifts between the different levels of narrative, each sequence in some way commenting on, contrasting with, or providing explanations of the scenes that precede or follow it. The complexity of the dramatic structure thus reflects the complexity of the narrative strands.

- Select another sequence from *The Singing Detective* and write an analysis which incorporates technical codes as well as aspects of genre, narrative, representation and ideology. Try to find one which covers more than one of the narratives and show how they interlink and cross-reference each other.

SUMMARY

The Singing Detective may be summed up as follows: the contemporary Marlow, coming to believe that his current medical condition is in some way the result of his guilt at implicating an innocent classmate as the perpetrator of a disgusting act. The act was actually carried out by himself as a disturbed response to the discovery of his mother's adultery with the father of the same classmate. Marlow is using his re-working of a 1940s-set detective novel to explore the psychology of infidelity and betrayal, not just by himself and his mother, but also, as he irrationally perceives it, by his wife. Each of the interconnected narratives has an appropriate production design to reflect theme, period and character. Potter, in turn, uses the entire work to revisit his own complex dramatic output, reflecting characters, themes and styles from previous work.

CHAPTER FOUR – CLOCKING OFF & STATE OF PLAY

Philip Glennister (left) as Mack, pivotal character of ensemble drama, Clocking Off.

CLOCKING OFF

In keeping with the long established tradition of setting substantial television drama in the north of England, Paul Abbott's Manchester-based serial drama, *Clocking Off* (BBC1, 4 series: 2000–3), uses the backdrop of a textiles factory to tell the personal stories of some of the employees. Each episode in the series focuses on one character, with the stable of regulars providing support until it's their turn to be in the spotlight. Each episode fills a one-hour slot and the episodes were screened weekly for the duration of each series.

Mackintosh Textiles is owned and run by Mack (Philip Glenister), ably assisted by his secretary, Trudy (Lesley Sharp), but not always supported by his unfaithful wife, Katherine Mackintosh (Christine Tremarco). Mack and Trudy are ongoing characters throughout most of the episodes, acting as a kind of anchor for some of the other more transient characters. The names might have significance – Mack, a garment offering protection, and Trudy = true, in the sense of loyal, faithful.

Abbott chose this setting because he had once worked in a textiles factory and recognised that the layout, the activity and the big, bright colours of the fabrics all created a visually vibrant environment, against which to play out the private, sometimes comic, often tragic stories of the workers, their relationships and their desperate attempts to contend with the realities of their lives. It is also, of course, a very appropriate location, since the textiles industry is one of the defining institutions of the Industrial Revolution and the northern working class.

The title refers to the end of the working shift, when the workers 'clock' their timecards before going home. Because the timecards are supposed to be a record of hours worked, workers are expected to 'clock off' whenever they leave the factory. In many of the episodes people seem to absent themselves from the factory for a variety of personal reasons, so 'clocking off' seems to mark the transition from work to home-life. However, the storylines frequently blur the boundaries between work and home, with members of the same family encountering each other in the work-place. 'Clocking' is also a slang term for 'taking notice of, watching or observing', and we are aware of the interest taken by some members of the workforce in their colleagues' private business. To 'clock' someone is also slang for hitting or beating them, and now features in contemporary teenage slang, meaning 'to catch someone out'. The term also sounds similar to the slang expression, 'copping off', a reference to people who become casually sexually involved with others, a situation frequently encountered in the stories. Finally, the sound of the title is not too far removed from the harsher sounding expression 'fucking off', which happens in all its interpretations throughout the stories.

One of Abbott's intentions in *Clocking Off* was to explore the personal crisis moments of ordinary people who do not always receive the support of friends or family, but are left alone to sort out their own messes. Loose ends and unanswered questions are often not resolved in *Clocking Off* – audiences and other characters on the periphery of the story are left to speculate on what happens, as the series moves on to the next story.

GENRE

Clocking Off belongs to a genre of TV drama series which uses the workplace as its ongoing setting (for example, police: *The Bill*, *Holby Blue*, *Heartbeat*; medical: *Casualty*, *Holby City*, *The Royal*, *The Chase*; educational: *Waterloo Road*, *Teachers*, *Grange Hill*). It differs from many such series, however, in that its central focus for each episode is one character's personal life, rather than a continuing story of the factory and the people who work in it. Although an individual's story may impact on other workers, and may be referred to in later episodes, it does not form part of a continuous narrative. A typical episode of *Clocking Off* shines a bright and scrutinising light on one character or set of characters, while leaving others largely in the dark, only tangentially involving them in the central narrative. This approach to the dramatisation of a community is reminiscent of Alan Bleasdale's seminal work, *Boys from the Blackstuff* (see Chapter 1).

Audience expectation is both reinforced (by familiarity of setting and the realistic representations of characters) and subverted (by unpredictable character behaviour and the originality of the storyline). In this way it foreshadows *The Street* (Jimmy McGovern – BBC, 2006–present), a similarly-structured series, which uses a typical working-class northern street as the setting, and focuses on the stories emanating from the individual households. Just as with *Clocking Off*, other residents may play marginal roles in the central story, and then appear as the protagonists in their own stories. Once again, the stories in *The Street* are hard-hitting, gritty, no-holds-barred, dissections of the personal lives and relationships of their central characters.

NARRATIVE

The stories are told in strictly linear fashion, but the pace of the narratives is fast and elliptical – audiences are expected to understand the transitions and fill in the gaps. As far as possible the narratives represent real life, but there is inevitably much condensing of time and space in order to move the story along and to fit it into the standard episode length of fifty minutes.

Todorov's theory of narrative disruption is much in evidence in *Clocking Off*, although it should be noted that there is not usually much of an equilibrium to begin with. The narrative disruption, some kind of personal crisis, is usually contained within the first minute or so of the action, with suggestions of what the equilibrium might have been following on. Towards the end of the crisis, there is sometimes a resolution of sorts, but for some of the characters at least there is precious little equilibrium to look forward to.

Propp's ideas are also useful because these stories are strongly character-driven, and the themes of marital infidelity and betrayal, criminality and corruption lend themselves well to the identification of quests, heroes, helpers, blockers and false heroes. Nearly all of them are usually found within the families themselves.

REPRESENTATION

Although Paul Abbott worked for several years on *Coronation Street*, he believes that the British working class are not always represented accurately or sympathetically, writers and producers often resorting to stereotypical and formulaic representations.

Bearing in mind these concerns about working-class stereotyping, we are likely to find some interesting examples of a strongly realist approach to representation. The shop-floor employees of Mackintosh Textiles mostly wear uniform work-clothes, blue and white in colour, although the lorry drivers and goods handlers wear all-blue uniforms. One of the few exceptions seems to be Kev Leach, whose fanatical devotion to Manchester United leads him to turn up in red football shirts on occasion. There do not appear to be any seriously unconventional appearances among the work-force. Hairstyles and make-up also reflect the ordinary fashions of the late 90s.

Although the men are keen to present themselves as traditional males and predominantly sexist, many of the women, too, are deliberately depicted as very strong, no-nonsense types in their late thirties or early forties. This representation of 'strong' women has much in common with soap opera. Despite these potential stereotypes, both men and women are shown to be very vulnerable in times of extreme crisis, suffering degrees of emotional breakdown.

Speech patterns are carefully constructed to reflect the vocabulary, turns of phrase and modes of address prevalent among the industrial working class. Obviously, for much of the audience, the Manchester accent lends a high degree of authenticity to this environment, and the overall effect is very convincing.

> * What representational features would need to be changed if this series were to be set in, for example, London? Or New York?

AUDIENCE

The audience for a drama like *Clocking Off* tends to be varied. Some will have seen some of Abbott's earlier work and be keen to make the re-acquaintance. Others will have fond memories of work-place drama from another era (*Boys from the Blackstuff, Auf Wiedersehen Pet*). The age range is likely to be that of the main characters – there are very few younger parts. Some will be attracted by the actors who have been seen in other TV drama. Still more will be fans of realist drama in any setting.

The 9.00 pm post-watershed slot on the BBC is often a guarantee of quality drama with an uncompromising approach to theme and character – another example of the institution's remit to 'inform, educate and entertain'.

INSTITUTION

The series was made for mainstream TV, to be shown at 'prime time'. It was made by an independent production company and sold to the BBC as a complete package. Although independent companies might be regarded as having more lavish budgets, it must be remembered that the BBC is constrained in its expenditure by the revenue obtained by the licence fee. Nevertheless, the BBC is prepared to invest in high quality programming and can often factor in sales to other countries and income from DVD and other related sales. The BBC is not a commercial television channel, but is still able to work commercially with others for both its profit and theirs.

IDEOLOGY

The central setting of an industrial company firmly locates *Clocking Off* in a capitalist manufacturing environment, and 'Mack' is undoubtedly 'the boss'. However, he seems to be a genuinely supportive 'boss', and his manner of speech and general behaviour place him closer to his shop-floor colleagues than many another suited managing director. It is suggested that his workers generally get quite a good deal by working for him.

Within the personal lives of the workers, great emphasis is placed on responsibility to family, especially children. Nevertheless, many of the crises in the stories arise from varying types of infidelity and betrayal. Such behaviour, while sometimes understandable, is always condemned, either internally by other characters, or externally by further developments in the plot. The first episode of Series 1 is a good example of this device. Even within narratives of this kind, where situations do not always develop in logical or consistent ways, the overriding moral ethos ensures that those who transgress will be brought to account in one way or another.

ANALYSIS OF THE OPENING SEQUENCE OF SERIES 1, EPISODE 1

The title sequence of *Clocking Off* is a fast-paced montage of the working textile machinery at Mackintosh's factory. It is bright, multi-layered, swiftly-moving and multi-faceted. It is accompanied by an old-style rhythm-and-blues soundtrack, featuring harmonica and guitars. The music suggests the steady rhythm of the working machinery, while the blues element reflects the emotional landscape inhabited by the workers. The overall effect of the sequence is to suggest the driving urgency, yet steady rhythmic pace of the working environment, coupled with a haunting and wistful mood of melancholy. The melancholic mood is reinforced by occasional incidental music in a similar style, with the harmonica's mournful tones or plangent blues guitar riffs often reflecting the current state of mind of a character.

An establishing shot of the textile factory quickly sets the industrial context of what is to follow. Workers are seen entering the factory, suggesting a thriving working environment, but not necessarily promoting an ethos of 'the happy worker'. The name 'Mackintosh' seems appropriate, suggesting a garment to wear when it's raining (life is full of troubles), but designed to protect the wearer from the worst of the 'weather', as though the factory is something of a refuge from the problems of the outside world. Mack's supportive and paternal manner would seem to support this view.

This is followed by a series of cross cuts between Martin Leach supervising the unloading of lorries and his older brother, Stuart, travelling on a tram, walking along a busy street and finally arriving at his home. Both have short hair and are early to mid-thirties. Martin has a youthful, bright, somewhat cheeky appearance; Stuart's expression tends to be more serious. Martin is 'clean-cut', while Stuart is shown here as unshaven, and his clothes show a rather unkempt appearance. As we discover later, they both speak with a working-class, Manchester accent.

There are some deliberately parallel shots – the front of the tram is seen moving uphill and rising up the screen, and a delivered load is seen being lifted up by a fork-lift truck; the bustle of the streets is paralleled by the bustle at the factory. Both of these sequences appear to reflect a typical, day-to-day normality.

Letting himself into his house, Stuart enters the kitchen to make a drink. His behaviour is natural and he is clearly familiar with the environment, except for one small detail – the cup is not quite where he expected to find it. This is a well-decorated, well-appointed house, bright and clean, from which we are expected to understand that the family that lives here is proud of its environment, caring, well-organised and domestically orientated. In northern working-class terms this usually means that the house is run by a reliable and efficient woman.

Stuart turns to see his young son observing him curiously from the doorway. The boy is about eight or nine, small in stature, and looks nervous. He does not speak at first. Stuart's friendly expression and casual demeanour suggest to the audience nothing out of the ordinary. The boy then startles him by running out in a panic, shouting for his mother, Sue, who is in the garden, hanging out the washing. She is in her mid-thirties, with neat, short blonde hair, and has something of a careworn expression. She enters, is confronted by her bemused husband, and is thrown into a state of shock by the sight of him standing in the kitchen. These extreme responses are not yet explained, and leave Stuart completely perplexed. This is clearly the narrative enigma posed at the opening of the story, leaving the audience as much in the dark as Stuart is, and the narrative disruption which disturbs the equilibrium of Sue's domestic life.

In this opening sequence of scenes there are also cutaway shots of a third brother, Kev, a material cutter, who shouts out sexist remarks to the female employees. He's dressed in his Manchester United red shirt, and is squatting on the cutting table. He is represented as a younger man in his mid-thirties, a short, wiry, quick-moving individual, with a sharp and cheeky expression.

Back at the factory the boss, Mack, is trying to sort out a matter of business with his assistant Trudy. Some jokey banter, involving Mack swearing a lot and being made to put money into the 'swear box' by Trudy, is interrupted by a phone call from a panic-stricken Sue, asking to speak to Martin about his brother's obviously unexpected arrival. Trudy, a blonde woman in her early forties, appears to be a very reliable and efficient secretary of long-standing service; Mack is clearly a relaxed and good-humoured employer, something of a rarity, we are meant to think. He's in his mid-forties, looks uncomfortable in a suit and tie, but his friendly appearance belies a bluff, no-nonsense personality.

Martin is seen running from the factory and driving directly to Sue's house. He enters without knocking, as though familiar with the house and very abruptly comes face-to-face with Stuart, still looking bewildered by everybody's reactions to his presence. Sue calls to Martin to get Stuart out of the house, because he is frightening them both. Martin's familiarity with the house and Sue's reliance on Martin to resolve this situation lead the audience to understand that theirs is a close relationship.

In the front garden Martin informs his brother that he has been missing for thirteen months, believed dead. Stuart claims to remember nothing of this, but believes that

he has been coming home as normal. He is also puzzled by the fact that his wife's first instinct was to call his brother, setting up a suspicion in his mind about the relationship between the two of them, thus confirming our earlier understanding. Martin and Stuart return to Martin's flat, where Martin shows him a very neatly-kept scrapbook of local newspaper articles detailing his 'disappearance' and presumed death.

Later, they meet their brother, Kev, and after an emotional reunion, Kev becomes very aggressive, suspecting that Stuart is shamming his condition. They go off to the pub, where Martin and Kev plan to get Stuart drunk in the hope that his memory will return. They return to Martin's flat, where a very drunk Stuart vomits over the sink, and Martin spots a recently stitched injury to Stuart's lower back. Stuart claims to have no recollection of

this either. A visit to the hospital confirms that he has had a knife wound recently, and has received a blow to the head, but is otherwise medically fit. The doctor suggests a visit to a psychiatrist to explore his amnesia further. The audience is now in possession of several key facts which lead to a greater understanding of Stuart's situation, and from which deductions could be made about Stuart's life during the last thirteen months. One of the audience's central pleasures in watching drama is to have the opportunity to second-guess the storylines and make predictions about outcomes.

Stuart claims to remember part of a Sheffield phone number, but cannot complete it, and has no idea what it means. It is now up to Martin to follow the clues in his quest to find out what happened to Stuart during his missing thirteen months. This has now set up the direction and purpose of the narrative for the rest of the episode. It has also positioned the audience to follow the narrative through Martin's eyes.

[*As the mystery unfolds, it seems as though Stuart had actually planned his disappearance thirteen months before. He deliberately abandoned his Mackintosh lorry by the docks, leaving people to believe that he may have drowned himself. In fact, he had already developed a relationship with another woman in Sheffield, whom he subsequently married and with whom he had a child, and was working as a lorry driver for another firm. It is this firm's telephone number that Stuart partly remembers. A chance encounter with a Mackintosh driver revealed his identity, and he was attacked by his new wife's brother, stabbed, knocked out and lost his memory. His only thought then was that 'he wanted to go home'. This prompted him to travel to Manchester and return to his real home and family, totally unaware of the 'family' he was leaving behind in Sheffield, and left only with scraps of memory of half a phone number and some nightmare visions of being attacked. As he puts it to Martin, 'I just wanted to go home. Wrong home.' Without the loss of memory, he wouldn't have made the mistake of coming back to Manchester. In the closing scene, he is shown being arrested by police, presumably for bigamy.]*

The editing of this sequence is a combination of some fast-paced cuts within some scenes and longer shots during the more reflective moments of the narrative. The editing does seem to follow the basic principles of classic continuity editing within scenes. Cuts from location to location tend to create an elliptical sequence which does not always orientate the audience before each scene begins. Although it is not difficult to follow the action, this style of editing does replicate to a certain extent the confusion that Stuart's unexpected arrival has caused.

Camerawork is a combination of hand-held immediacy and more static sequences during the expository parts of the narrative. Framing tends to be conventional, although close-ups at more significant moments within the narrative foreground the emotional context of the characters.

- Select some other sequences and explore the use of technical codes and how they create meaning for the audience.

STATE OF PLAY

Stephen Collins (David Morrisey, left) gets his point across to Cal McCaffrey (John Sim) in State of Play.

In 2003 Paul Abbott created a six-part drama serial, *State of Play*, dealing with political corruption and the power of the press. Apart from these topical themes, it is also a convoluted murder mystery involving one victim at the very centre of the political world it describes, and one who appears to be an innocent bystander.

Unlike *Clocking Off*, *State of Play* is a linear narrative played out over six episodes, with a disruption occurring at the beginning of Episode 1, and a resolution to that disruption and the fall-out from it occurring at the end of Episode 6, with other disruptions along the way.

Stephen Collins is a mid-level politician of some importance, because he chairs the energy committee. His PA, Sonia Baker, falls in front of the tube train he is travelling to work on, and is killed. In another part of London, a young black man, Kelvin Stagg, is shot to death in what looks like a drug-related killing. However, his family insist that he had absolutely nothing to do with drugs. The police insist otherwise and a post-mortem report is changed to show that his body did in fact contain drugs.

Journalist Cal McCaffrey, an old friend and campaign manager of Collins, follows up Stagg's story and discovers from his brother, Sonny that he did the odd handbag grab, in the hope of getting money for the return of valuables, but never did drugs. On the occasion he was killed, he had stolen a metal briefcase, believing it would contain valuables. Sonny arranges for Cal to meet an unnamed girl who could sell him the case that Stagg had left with her. Cal further learns that Stagg was shot because he had stolen the case and examined its contents before passing it to the girl for safe-keeping. He also discovers from a contact at the hospital where the post-mortem was carried out that Stagg's body contained no drugs of any kind, except some steroids for his asthma.

Cal pays the girl for the case and takes it to the offices of his paper, *The Herald*. The editor, Cameron Foster, decides to pursue the story after it emerges that Collins had been having an affair with Baker, and was planning to leave his wife, Anne.

Cal works alongside Herald journalist, Della Smith. With other colleagues, they investigate the two deaths. During the course of the investigation, Cal begins an affair with Anne Collins, and Della joins unofficial forces with DCI Bell in order to swap vital information.

It turns out that Baker had been planted as Collins' PA in order to find out secret energy committee information for a large oil conglomerate, but she had fallen in love with Collins and had even become pregnant by him. All of this pointed to a possible hit by the energy company who would have no further use for her. When McCaffrey and Smith find out that Baker was 'recommended' as Collins' PA by senior politician, George Fergus, it looks as though the whole affair involved both government and corporate corruption. This idea is reinforced by the discovery that Baker had initially been recruited by city wheeler-dealer, Dominic Foy, who had been paid handsomely for his trouble by the oil firm concerned.

Considerable pressure is put upon *The Herald* not to continue with the story, supporting the idea that people at the highest levels of government and industry were involved with the corruption.

Collins stays with McCaffrey in an attempt to keep a low profile and also discover the extent of the corruption which appeared to be leading to his political downfall. However, McCaffrey deduces from a throwaway remark by Collins that he knew about Baker's double-dealing. Light finally dawns for McCaffrey when he learns that the police likeness of the black man's killer, matches CCTV footage of a man seen on the tube platform near to where Baker was standing before she fell, and further matches that of a freelance electrical contractor employed by Collins, Robert Bingham.

At the conclusion, we learn that Collins himself had contracted Bingham, an army-trained marksman, to kill Baker because of her double-dealing. He, in turn, had to shoot the black man who had got hold of the incriminating case, and also attempted to kill a passing motorcyclist who had witnessed the young man's shooting. Collins is arrested and Cal returns to the paper to observe the next day's edition, carrying the whole story, being printed.

GENRE

State of Play belongs to the genre of drama usually known as a political thriller. Typical content of such a genre might include:

- Corrupt practices at very senior levels of government and law-enforcement agencies.

- Specific crimes, such as murder and fraud, are common.

- One individual, or a small group, outside the web of corruption, acts to expose the crimes and the criminals, often at great personal expense.

- Contract killers are employed in order to distance the central figures from actual criminal behaviour.

- The police do not always seem to be in control of situations, but are frequently pressurised by higher authorities.

- Some form of romantic/sexual liaison serves to complicate the action.

- The media become involved as they report events.

- Innocent bystanders can be swept up in the fallout from such action.

- The action tends to touch people at many levels of society.

- The action usually involves betrayal of both innocent and guilty individuals.

- Cynical viewpoints are common on both sides.

- Resolutions are not always tidy; good does not always prevail.

Generic production features might include:

- Urban settings (Houses of Parliament, industrial complexes, newspaper offices, city offices, police stations, luxury hotels, lavish apartments, restaurants, bars, city streets and other iconic landmarks, run-down areas, bleak estates, poor housing).

- Expensive cars, luxury travel in boats, trains or planes.

- Expensive clothing and accessories.

- High alcohol consumption.

- Appropriate weaponry (sniper rifles, automatic guns with silencers).

- Constant telephonic communication.

- Appropriate stationery and office items (briefcases, emails, handwritten notes, newspapers, answer phones, folders, files, computers, disks, classified documents).

- Significant objects (important items lost or found, objects of quest).

- Large amounts of money.

Generic behavioural features might include:

- Secret meetings (in cars, car parks, abandoned buildings, public parks, anonymous bars, at unsocial times, alone).

- Threatening behaviour and intimidation.

- Violent confrontations.

- Professional arguments between colleagues.

- Sexual relationships between protagonists.

- Lying and deception.

- Choose a selection of sequences and identify examples of the generic features they contain. Explain how those features create meaning for the audience.

REPRESENTATION

Stephen Collins – Male, late thirties, politician, middle class. He is of smart appearance, with neat hairstyle, smart business suit, briefcase, papers. He has an educated northern accent because he represents a Manchester constituency. He is a family man, with a wife and two children. He has a secretary and, until the story begins, a researcher. He is clearly successful – he chairs an Energy Committee and is tipped for a cabinet seat.

Cal McCaffery – Male, late thirties, journalist on *The Herald*, liberal middle class, casual appearance, casual clothes. He has a lower-middle-class northern accent. He's single, brash, independent-minded, dedicated to his job. He tends to have a cheerful expression, but it can quickly become world-weary in the face of reality. He's good at his job (chief reporter) and is respected by his colleagues. Can become verbally and physically aggressive under pressure, but only with what he would regard as good reason.

Della Smith – Female, late twenties/early thirties, journalist on *The Herald*. Strong, educated Scots accent, she tends to wear long, shapeless coats and skirts with short, dark hair, worn in a neutral style. Always wears a serious expression, hardly smiles. A sharply intelligent reporter, economic of speech, and can appear brusque and unfeeling, but becomes upset at the killing of a detective sergeant, a fellow-Scot, with whom she built up a rapport. Her tears, however, are more of anger and frustration at her helplessness than deeply emotional.

Anne Collins – Female, late thirties, businesswoman. She is the wife of Stephen. Short, dark hair in a neat bob and fringe style; attractive, intelligent, tends to wear smart clothes. She is independent of spirit, passionate. Less pronounced northern accent. Plays the devoted wife in public, but expresses anger at her husband's infidelity. She has strong emotions and becomes attracted to McCaffrey after she has left her husband and gone to ground in his house.

Cameron Foster – Male, late forties, newspaper editor. He is of smart executive appearance and educated London accent. Very intelligent and worldly-wise, with a sharp, sardonic tongue, but can also appear laid-back. He is passionate about his work and defensive of his staff.

IDEOLOGY

State of Play raises a number of important ideological issues and positions the audience very clearly in support of Cal McCaffery's campaign to expose the corruption at the heart of the Government's handling of a scandal involving one of its rising stars.

The central issue is the thorny question of the freedom of the press and the protection of sources. The press, in the form of *The Herald* (a fictional paper), is shown to be investigating the murder of a young black man and the death of a House of Commons researcher. The police have constructed the first death as a drug-related killing, and the second as either suicide or an accident. The paper has evidence that the killing of the young man was not drug-related but actually connected to the death of the researcher, which, it suspects, was murder.

- Does *The Herald* have the right to withhold evidence from the police while it pursues its own investigation? Is it the role of journalism to investigate crime in this way?

During their private investigation, Cal, Della and their colleagues commit a number of criminal offences, including kidnap and intimidation (of Dominic Foy), withholding of evidence and obstructing the police in the course of their investigation. The audience is positioned to support the journalists' activities in the face of the corruption of Government officials.

- How is the audience made to feel that the journalists are in the right to act illegally in this way? Are such actions ever justified?

Apart from the issues of criminality raised here, *State of Play* also explores sexual morality. Stephen Collins is unfaithful to his wife, Anne, by committing adultery with his researcher, Sonia Baker. After Anne has decided to leave Stephen, she embarks on an affair herself with Cal McCaffery. Stephen and Anne have two children who are shown struggling with the infidelities of their parents.

- How does *State of Play* position the audience with respect to the issues of infidelity and betrayal mentioned above? Consider aspects of representation and the outcome of the narrative.

During the course of the narrative various Government ministers and officials are shown to be involved in a number of corrupt practices. These include fixing the appointment of Sonia Baker as Stephen Collins' researcher, despite better candidates being available; preferment of some companies over others in securing government contracts; covering up the tracks of their corruption.

- How is the representation of Government officials used to encourage the audience to view their actions as corrupt? Consider the manner in which such actions are conducted, including dialogue, behaviour and relevant settings.

Once the police are involved in the investigations, two officers, including a DCI, establish informal relationships with Della Smith, one of the journalists, the ostensible purpose of which is to exchange relevant information.

- How far are these relationships shown to be acceptable practice? Is there any evidence that either side has overstepped the mark by doing this?

The title is also a clue to some of the ideological issues raised in the drama. The phrase 'state of play' is often associated with sport, and particularly cricket, and is used to describe the score, the progress of the teams and other data. Cameron and his investigative team meet regularly to discuss the progress or 'state of play' of their investigations. Cameron's suave upper-middle-class manner suggests that he could easily be a cricket fan.

In English, the phrase 'it's not cricket' suggests an action which is morally unacceptable, an action that an English person could not be conceived of as doing. It is often regarded as an expression more likely to be used by upper-middle and upper-class males, from independent school/Oxbridge backgrounds. Just the backgrounds usually associated with senior political figures, like George Fergus, whose sober suits, silver hair and educated accent represent him as such a figure.

The 'state', of course, is another word for 'country' or 'political entity', here referring to the UK government. Perhaps 'play' in this context suggests that the business of government is just like a game of cricket for its top-ranking practitioners, with its own unwritten rules, teams or cliques, insiders and outsiders. Cricket also reflects parliament in that one 'team' (the government) is batting, while the other team (the opposition) is trying to get them out.

Finally 'play' is a word sometimes used in the phrase 'playing away', meaning to commit adultery and be unfaithful to a partner, reflecting the actions of both Stephen and Anne Collins.

- Explore ways in which the production design and representational processes contribute to the construction of realism in these two dramas.

- Consider other ways in which the titles might reflect the content and issues raised by the dramas.

- Select other dramas and explore how their titles suit their themes and content.

CHAPTER FIVE — CASUALTY & HOLBY CITY

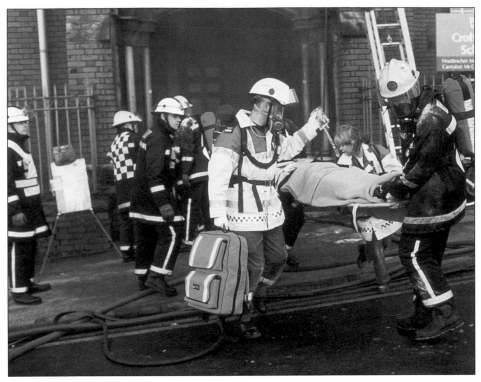

Another day at the office for the emergency services in Casualty

The practices of medicine and medical environments have long held a fascination for television audiences. In the 1950s ITV played doctors and nurses in a long-running medical soap called *Emergency – Ward 10*. Even before this, BBC radio had featured a long-running afternoon soap called *Mrs Dale's Diary*, written from the perspective of a GP's wife and family. The BBC continued its interest in things medical with *Dr Finlay's Casebook*, as well as presenting a series of groundbreaking documentaries, *Your Life in their Hands*, which showed viewers for the first time real surgical operations in graphic black-and-white.

The home-grown product suffered something of an onslaught from the US in the 1950s and 60s with such glossy, high-quality products as *Dr Kildare* and *Ben Casey*, a tradition continued to this day with *ER*, *Grey's Anatomy* and *House*.

In 1986 the BBC aired the first episode of a serial medical drama set in the accident-and-emergency department of a big city hospital. The city chosen was Bristol, the hospital was located in the fictional suburb of Holby, and the drama was called *Casualty*. Its beginnings were modest. A small team of nurses, a couple of doctors and the department manager held the fort against the invasion of medical emergencies, the complications of personal relationships and the intrusion of evermore restrictive government policies.

The pattern was set from the very first episode: a fixed location with a permanent team, whose interrelationships form an ongoing focus for maintaining an audience base; and 'guest' stories making a one-off appearance and providing a changing foreground to maintain audience interest. It seems clear that the success of this type of television drama is largely due to the clever combination and exploitation of the soap opera and single drama formats.

The incidents that provide the subject-matter for each week's storylines tend to be shot on location, whereas the hospital sequences are studio-bound. In the earlier series, the standard video specifications, flat studio lighting and multi-camera production techniques of the day provided the typical 'TV-studio' look to the images, which did not always compare well with the higher quality film-based US productions. More recent series are now shot on HD video with more 'dramatic' lighting schemes which enhance the visual aspects of the episodes considerably, and give them a filmic quality.

Despite a greater investment in the technology, the major emphasis of *Casualty* and its mid-week spin-off, *Holby City*, is on a high degree of realism. Great care is taken to ensure that all the medical procedures are in line with current practice, and that the details of those procedures are accurate. Considerable use is made of prosthetics to represent injuries and operations, and the medical environments all contain a vast array of the necessary equipment and materials in order to present a convincing portrayal of a contemporary hospital.

EPISODE STRUCTURE

A typical episode now begins with a fast-moving title sequence featuring a montage of the central characters and other medical iconography (machines, equipment and locations), accompanied by the title theme, a brisk, and somewhat strident synthesised melodic sequence suggesting urgency and efficiency. This theme has been used since the first episode in 1986, and serves to create familiarity and continuity for the audience.

This is followed by the almost statutory 'previously on' sequence, allowing the audience to 'catch up' with the inevitably complex relationship and incident issues concerning the resident staff, arising from recent previous episodes. Sometimes a 'guest' storyline will carry over from the previous week, but usually such storylines are self-contained weekly events. Some 'fringe' characters, connected with or related to the main staff, sometimes have a longer 'shelf-life'. The purpose of these levels of complexity is to construct a web of interrelationships and interactions which reinforce the realism of the drama, and provide further levels of interest and engagement for the audience.

The 'previously on' sequence is then followed by the opening scenes of the new story, accompanied by an appropriate title which will have resonances for many of the characters, both 'guest' and resident, throughout the episode. The title is sometimes a quote from a popular song or a proverb, or some other familiar saying, and its layers of meaning can be designed to provide a 'moral' for, or at least a connection with, all concerned.

The opening scene is often, though not always, located at the site of an imminent major incident which will provide the focus for the 'guest' narrative of the episode. Seemingly everyday happenings at this location may be intercut with similar scenes at another, apparently unconnected location, and then by scenes back in A&E, allowing the audience to witness some possible new developments in ongoing 'resident' storylines. However, such mundane occurrences are quickly disrupted by a significant accident, disaster or other major event which usually links the opening scenes. This disruption usually precipitates the arrival of a paramedic crew and ambulance. Some of the initial drama may be played out at the scene and then continued back at A&E, where the arrival of the victims provides a disruption to the routine of the resident staff.

The rest of the episode is concerned with the playing out of the 'guest' story or stories (there may be more than one, and they may be coincidentally connected). At the end of the episode, some of the loose ends may be resolved, but not everything is concluded tidily. A fractured family may be reunited, a fractured arm may be treated, but, equally, an unexpected death may occur, or an unexpected cure be found. Some of the characters may learn a little more about themselves, their loved ones, or the world in general; some may act on that knowledge, some may not – just like real life, in fact.

ANALYSIS OF A SEQUENCE – TWO-PART STORY, BROADCAST 02 & 09 AUGUST 2008

The title, 'The Mess We're In' appears over a shot of Maggie, one of the A&E doctors, lying on her back in the doctors' rest room. She is looking tired and worried. The backstory is that she is facing an appearance at an inquest into the death of a patient, for whom, it is alleged she failed to order a crucial test. She has maintained her innocence, and many of the staff support her. The audience are aware that her notes have been tampered with by a male nurse in charge of a private ward in the department, with the connivance of a hospital administrator anxious to promote the ward. Another doctor, who suspects this, has been blackmailed by the administrator, who threatens to reveal what she knows about this doctor's affair with a married consultant, whose wife works as a nurse in the same department.

The next scene shows a man talking to a girl in bed. A small boy is seen in a kitchen surrounded by piles of unwashed dishes, discarded food and the general detritus of a household where no one is seriously in charge or in control. The boy is searching for food in the fridge, on the door of which is a photograph of the boy, the girl and their father. Next to the photo is a drawing of 'mummy'. It appears that the family may have been abandoned by, or have lost, the mother.

[Later in this storyline the boy attempts to shoplift in a local supermarket, is chased by a security man, and falls from a high wall, suffering injuries as a result.]

In the A&E department a hysterical young mother is accompanying her sick baby to the resuscitation unit. Although the baby is attended by two other doctors and a whole nursing team, it is Maggie who successfully intubates the infant and restores breathing. This is greeted by a series of silent looks from her colleagues, some recognising that this might be her last day as a practising doctor, one the blackmailed member of staff, acknowledging her own potential guilt in Maggie's downfall.

Intercut with scenes of the hospital staff getting ready to accompany Maggie to the inquest and further conspiratorial behaviour between the administrator and her crony are scenes of illegal immigrant workers in their caravans who are waiting to be chosen for work by an unscrupulous quarry owner. The father of a young daughter is chosen, along with a young married couple.

[Later in this storyline the corrupt and illegal activities of the quarry owner are revealed – he has sexually assaulted the wife of the couple, and has employed and is exploiting all of the illegal immigrants contrary to the law – followed by an accident at the quarry involving the father and one of the paramedics.]

Charlie, the nursing manager, is very outspoken about what he believes to be the management corruption surrounding Maggie's case, and it is clear he will fight her corner all the way.

[The resolution of this storyline involves the revelation by the blackmailed doctor to the inquest that the administrator and her nursing assistant had tampered with the patient's notes in an attempt to undermine Maggie's authority and professional competence. As a result, Maggie's name is cleared and the guilty parties are facing criminal proceedings. Clearly the blackmailed doctor decided to 'do the right thing', even thought it resulted in her affair with the consultant being made public, much to the distress of the consultant's wife who was also present in the coroner's court to hear the case and support Maggie.]

MISE-EN-SCÈNE

The *mise-en-scène* of these opening sequences has been very carefully designed to provide immediately recognisable 'short-cuts' to the meaning of each scene for the audience:

- The doctor's rest room is darkened and basic (it is not meant to be a place of sleep and refuge for long periods of time).

- The untidiness and lack of hygiene of the kitchen show both the lack of care available for the children and the potential health hazards of their sad lives.

- The A&E department is bright, brisk and business-like, where the focus is on saving lives and alleviating sickness; the patients brought there also provide a site for the playing out of dramas connected with the staff, their central positioning forcing staff to confront each other quite literally across the emergency bed.

- As Maggie and her colleagues prepare for the inquest, more formal dress codes are adhered to.

- The scene in the immigrants' encampment conveys something of the transient and impoverished lifestyle they endure, and the desperate hopelessness of their economic plight as they vie with each other for work.

- The scenes at the quarry suggest the disordered and slapdash arrangements: few amenities for the workers, lack of organised working practices at the rock-face, a squalid and untidy office occupied by the unscrupulous boss.

- The scene in the coroner's court is depicted by the formality of dress of the main characters, the sobriety of the furnishings and décor, and the strict layout reflecting the importance of the legal proceedings taking place there.

Despite this attention to detail, the lighting and other aspects of the visual design are intended to represent an accurate portrayal of the reality of these environments, rather than as constructed settings for dramatic incidents. Mood and atmosphere are conveyed more by the dialogue and performance of the characters than by an over-emphasis on production design.

SOUND

All of the sound in these sequences, and, indeed, for most of the episodes is diegetic and further reinforces the realism of the drama. Each environment is depicted with its expected soundscape (hospital equipment, background talking, internal and external ambient sounds – room noises/traffic/industrial equipment). There is some over-emphasis of specific sounds (dialogue that needs to be heard above ambient sound, the noise of an important item, e.g. a ticking clock, impact sounds accompanying an accident), but even this tends to replicate the ability of the human ear to filter unwanted noise and focus on important or relevant sound. There is generally no non diegetic 'mood' music, apart from the more recent use of popular music soundtracks to close an episode. This feature seems to have been borrowed from US series such as *House* (see Chapter 9).

GENERIC CHARACTERISTICS

The cutting between parallel storylines, a distinctive feature of the soap opera genre, is a common characteristic of this type of serial drama, but such dramas should be distinguished from soap operas by their reliance on one-off 'guest' stories as a major part of each episode. Nevertheless, *Casualty*, *Holby City* and other dramas in this genre do share many of the generic characteristics of soap operas:

- Permanent and ongoing characters in fixed locations.

- A mixture of ages, genders and ethnic backgrounds are represented.

- A group of strong female characters (Tess, Maggie, Zoe, Connie Beauchamp, Lola Griffin, Jane Grayson, Jac Naylor).

- Younger, less experienced but sexually confident women (Donna, Kelsey).

- Older, paternal male figures (Mark Williams, Rick Griffin, Elliot Hope, Charlie Fairhead).

- Vulnerable characters (Percy 'Abra' Durant, Joseph, Alice, Ruth, Toby).

Although the setting for such medical dramas does not give the audience a sense of 'family' (a major aspect of all soap operas), there are, or have been, several family relationships in place among the main characters:

- Rick and Lola were once married.

- Tess' son, Sam, worked on reception.

- Mark's daughter, Chrissie, worked as a sister, and his late wife was also a nurse.

- Joseph's late father was a visiting consultant, and his mother is a trustee of the hospital.

- Connie and Sam Strachan have a baby daughter from their earlier relationship.

There are, of course, the inevitable less formal relationships common to many work-places, and too complex to detail here.

Different areas of the hospital also give rise to 'family' groupings of an unrelated kind, for example:

- Charlie (senior nurse) and Maggie (A&E doctor) form a kind of 'parent' pair for some of the younger staff (Abs, Toby, Ruth, Alice).

- Mark takes some of the younger staff under his wing (Maria, Fay, Daisha), as he had once done for his daughter.

Such pseudo-families provide typical problems of inter-generational conflict and gender-divides for some of the staff storylines, as well as featuring some occasional positive aspects of such relationships.

IDEOLOGY

From the first episode, *Casualty* has always courted controversy. One of its first storylines involved a clash of medical staff and management over the financing of the emergency department, and the issue of patients before money, or vice versa, has been one of the central moral and material concerns ever since.

Early medical dramas tended to promote ideas of medical infallibility – the doctor as a pillar of the local community and saviour of mankind. Issues of corruption, negligence and incompetence were not often dealt with, and if such themes were addressed, the central characters were usually peripheral to such narratives.

Casualty and *Holby City* now seem to revel in issues which have generated such storylines as:

- Alcoholism of central medical characters.

- Marital infidelity between doctors and nurses.

- Allegations of medical and surgical incompetence.

- Proven instances of medical and surgical incompetence.

- Corruption concerning medical supplies on the part of senior consultants.

- Tampering with medical records to protect professional reputations.

- Inappropriate relationships between staff and patients.

- Complex webs of deceit surrounding central staff characters.

- Conflict between private and NHS services.

- Euthanasia.

- Violence between staff and patients.

- Serious moral dilemmas concerning patient confidentiality.

- Major financial concerns affecting departments.

The list would appear to be almost endless. While doctors and nurses are no longer seen as gods and goddesses, however, the worthy still seem eventually to triumph over the corrupt.

A number of ideological issues are explored in the opening sequences of this episode. Some of them deliberately relate to more than one storyline.

In the 'Maggie' story, we see a female doctor under great stress, her career threatened by the corrupt practices of some of her 'colleagues'. Although she is blameless, the hospital management need a scapegoat to explain the death of a patient. She does her best to maintain her position of innocence, but is portrayed as an emotionally upset and distraught woman. Her distress is highlighted and played on by the counsel for the dead patient's family, suggesting that her behaviour under stress in court could possibly mirror her alleged wrong actions under stress while dealing with the patient. At this point Maggie looks close to breakdown under such pressurised questioning. An angry male colleague, Charlie, speaks out on her behalf. His impassioned and articulate plea makes a strong contrast with Maggie's emotional state. Once again, it could be argued, a man has to come to the aid of an upset female.

However, in a neat ideological twist, it is actually Zoe, Maggie's A&E colleague, who rescues the situation by producing the forged hospital records, accusing the hospital administrator and her nursing associate of corruption and blackmail, and revealing her affair with the orthopaedic consultant, even though their careers are threatened by her action. Charlie's rhetoric is impressive but powerless. Zoe's factual account, by contrast, has the power to right the wrong which was about to be committed.

Corruption of a different kind is brought to light by the storyline concerning illegal immigrants and their exploitative employer. A member of the paramedic team is already involved with her fellow-countryfolk by trying to help them in their plight. The accident at the quarry brings her into direct professional contact with her friends. One of the young married women is reluctant to accuse her employer of sexual harassment for fear of losing jobs for her and her husband, and revealing their illegal status to the authorities. The story presents these immigrant workers in a sympathetic light, portraying them as hard-working, caring towards their families and eager to do an honest day's work. They are also shown as exploited by the quarry boss and constantly in fear of discovery and exposure. As the story progresses the woman finally accuses the quarry boss of attacking her, and he is arrested for assault and illegal employment, leaving the immigrant workers unemployed. As with Zoe's revelations in the 'Maggie' story, a final willingness to tell the truth on the part of the wronged wife, places the blame where it really belongs. Both stories highlight women prepared to face personal hardships in order to secure a just resolution to the circumstances in which they are involved.

A frequently occurring feature of many storylines is the so-called moral dilemma. A central character is faced with alternatives, one of which may resolve a situation, while the other may place a patient or colleague at risk. In so doing information must be passed on and truths revealed which will prove traumatic and life-changing. We have seen this operating in the two above stories:

- Zoe may keep her knowledge about the forged hospital records quiet, ruin Maggie's career, but save her own, or reveal the truth and put her own career and private life on the line.

- The female immigrant may say nothing about being exploited by her boss, and save the jobs and identity of herself and her fellow-workers, or reveal the truth and place her fellow-workers at risk of unemployment and exposure to the authorities.

An unspoken 'what-would-you-do?' question is put before the audience, which places their own moral standpoint under self-scrutiny.

HOLBY CITY

Following the success of *Casualty*, *Holby City* was first aired as a spin-off in January 1999. *Casualty* is set in the pressurised atmosphere of a busy A&E department; *Holby City* focuses on the rest of the hospital, dealing with patients and staff on the wards, in operating theatres and in management offices.

The mid-noughties incarnation of the core Holby City *cast*

Although there have been occasional crossovers, the two strands remain largely discrete, sharing neither staff nor storylines.

Like *Casualty*, *Holby City* features on-going storylines with a group of permanent staff, and 'guest' stories which are usually resolved within one hour-long episode. There are sometimes two-parters, which allow a more complex set of stories to be developed over a longer transmission time, matching that of a cinema feature film.

The show is scheduled for transmission on a weekday evening, at the time of writing normally a Tuesday, at prime time 8.00–9.00 pm.

In common with *Casualty*, the show features a large quantity of medical detail: examinations, diagnoses, operations, after-care. There is great emphasis on realism by employing high-tech medical equipment and highly realistic body prosthetics, which allow any procedure, from simple wound stitching to full-scale heart surgery, to be seen by the audience. Blood, intestines, organ transplants, broken bones and diseases of every kind are very much the norm in *Holby City*; so are moral problems confronted by both patients and staff.

The following analysis highlights to what extent the audience are meant to understand the current episode in the light of what has gone before. This involves not just incidents but also the complex interrelationships of the permanent staff.

HOLBY CITY – EPISODE BROADCAST 02 JUNE 2009 OPENING SEQUENCE

The opening sequence of this episode follows the current convention of featuring a montage of relevant narrative images accompanied by a relevant popular song as the soundtrack, dubbed by some commentators a 'songtage'.

In this example, the images refer to four separate storylines: the murder of Doctor Maddy Young, the birth of a child to a seriously ill mother, the on-going relationship between Joseph and Fay, as observed by Jac, and the health of Elliot's daughter's husband, Ben.

The sequence opens with a respirator which is breathing for an anaesthetised black female patient. The array of hi-tech medical equipment signifies the hospital environment and the seriousness of the case. The titles are superimposed over this image. This episode is called 'What Will Survive of Us', and is taken from the last line of Philip Larkin's poem 'An Arundel Tomb': 'what will survive of us is love.' This line is quoted later in the episode by Elliot Hope, with reference to his late wife and his daughter's recent marriage.

We hear a baby cry and understand that it has just been born to the anaesthetised woman by caesarian section. The slow and reflective piano and vocal introduction to a song begins on the soundtrack. It is 'This Woman's Work', written and sung by Kate Bush.

From the outset our emotions are being manipulated by the smooth, slow, deliberate movements of the camera, the poignant images of life and death, and the plangent tones of the vocalist on the soundtrack.

We see the baby being handed to its father, a black African. We cut to a shot of a memorial table, set up in the hospital foyer. On it are flowers, a book of condolence and a large framed photograph of an attractive young woman, smiling at the camera. It is Doctor Maddy Young, who was murdered in the previous episode. A nurse is signing the book. The appearance of the table, the flowers, the photograph and the mournful nature of the music are all designed to elicit an emotional and sympathetic response from the audience. They also remind us that Maddy was a popular colleague, with a positive career ahead of her. We are witnessing the aftermath of a young life cut tragically short.

We cut to a shot of Jac Naylor, one of the surgeons, looking serious, as though moved by the death of her medical colleague. She turns to see Joseph Byrne, a surgeon with whom she is in love, and his fiancee, hospital sister Fay Morton, come through the door. She turns away and makes for the lift as Fay places flowers on the memorial table. Jac has played a long game of pre-marital disruption with the other two, because of her feelings for Joseph, but now has to face the prospect of their imminent wedding. For this reason we are expected to understand that her expression of distress has more to do with this than with the death of a colleague.

We cut to a shot of Connie Beauchamp, consultant surgeon, walking along a corridor towards us, reading the local paper. She is looking upset. We are expected to think that this is an unusual emotion for the arrogant, self-confident and frequently dismissive Connie. Cynics might be forgiven for thinking that she is more upset by the paper splashing the news of Maddy's murder across its front page, thus broadcasting concerns about hospital security.

The lyrics of the song begin at this point, and the images are cut to the meaning of the lyrics:

Pray God you can cope.

I stand outside this woman's work.

Connie tosses the paper onto a chair and we see a close-up of the headlines referring to the murder and a large photo of Maddy. There is also an article about hospital security, obviously related.

We cut to a shot of Connie studying an x-ray. Two women, one whose work is now sadly over, the other needing to get on with the serious business of saving lives. On a monitor we can see the out-of-focus image of the open wound of the caesarian operation ready to be closed. This image is repeated a few seconds later. It might suggest the raw, open emotional wound that is Maddy's death:

This woman's world.

This line is sung under the shot of Connie going about her work, and reminds the audience of her strong and steadfast personality as she promotes her position as a senior consultant within the hospital. The camera pans left to discover the father holding the baby:

Ooh, it's hard on the man,

Now his part is over.

It is then taken away from him and placed in a cot. The lyrics reflect very closely the action on screen at this point:

Now starts the craft of the father.

The husband bends over to kiss his unconscious wife. We see the cot wheeled away. Once again we see the monitor image of the open wound being closed. The woman's survival is by no means certain, but her husband is convinced she will pull through. The words of the song seem to articulate his thoughts as he watches both his wife and his child:

I know you have a little life in you yet.

I know you have a lot of strength left.

The mood changes as we cut to Elliot Hope, another consultant surgeon, walking towards us along a corridor, speaking on his mobile. We hear his conversation over the song. He appears to be arranging a meeting with someone:

I know you have a little life in you yet.

I know you have a lot of strength left.

He glances out of the window to see his daughter, Martha, entering the hospital, carrying a bunch of flowers. Cut back to him looking thoughtful. We have understood from previous episodes that Elliot has been concerned about his daughter's recent marriage to Ben, who has been found to have a serious illness, and is now worried about his sight.

Many of the details in the scripts of on-going serial dramas such as Holby City rely on a regular audience in order to give extra meaning to scenes such as this – Elliot's anxious expression can be read in the context of his earlier concerns. The following line of the lyrics seems to refer both backwards to Elliot's feelings, and forwards to the next shot:

I should be crying, but I just can't let it show.

We cut to a shot of the memorial table, someone signing the book, and Maria, a nurse, standing in the background, watching all of this and looking very distraught. Maria's script at the end of the episode, when she tries to say something about Maddy at her memorial gathering, closely reflects the line quoted above. We know, from the previous episode that it was she who found the stabbed Maddy, a close friend, in the toilets, already dead. Over the next few lines of lyrics, the camera slowly arcs around a close-up of the memorial table and then around Maria, now in medium close-up.

Once again, viewers familiar with Maddy's story will understand Maria's state of mind at this time. The slow movement of the camera, as Maria stands helplessly watching others paying their respects to her dead friend, together with the following song lyrics, contribute hugely to the pathos of this scene:

I should be hoping, but I can't stop thinking

Of all the things I should've said,

That I never said.

All the things we should've done,

That we never did.

All the things I should've given,

But I didn't.

We cut to a medium close-up of Linden Cullen, a surgeon, sitting at his desk, staring at his computer screen. He, too, is looking at a photograph of Maddy, with whom he has worked very closely on the wards. Regular viewers will know that theirs was a working relationship: Linden is in love with Fay, although he has never revealed this fact to her. Linden is also a strongly religious man, and Maddy's unexpected and inexplicable death has obviously shaken him very badly:

Oh, darling, make it go,

Make it go away.

We hear a phone ringing as another nurse, Daisha, enters with a cup of coffee for Linden:

Give me these moments back.

Give them back to me.

He thanks her and she goes to answer the phone, but he tells her it's all right, and answers the phone. All the small details of this scene – the office environment, the computer screen, the coffee, the phone ringing – are there to remind us that, despite the tragedy, everyday life goes on and has to be faced.

We cut to a shot of Martha placing the flowers on the table and approaching Maria, and her friend, Donna, another nurse. Martha tells them that she's sorry, although she didn't know Maddy well. It is as though Martha stands in for all of us who did not know Maddy very well, but are saddened by her death:

Give me that little kiss.

Give me your hand.

I know you have a little life in you yet.

I know you have a lot of strength left.

The song fades out as Donna leads Maria away for a coffee.

This whole sequence is a very good example of the marrying of a non-diegetic music track with the montage of images, so that each informs and reinforces the other. It therefore shows how meaning within a media text is created by the careful juxtaposition of sound and image. Some would argue with Barthes that a specific text, in this case the song, anchors the meaning of the visual image, but it is equally arguable that such anchorage actually produces something which transcends the simple denotation and even the connotations of each of the individual components.

REPRESENTATION

I have selected the central characters who appear in this opening sequence:

Connie Beauchamp – A senior consultant surgeon, specialising in cardio-thoracic procedures. She power dresses in order to impress her colleagues with her position, but there are many examples of her using her sexuality to advance and consolidate her status within the hospital. She has an attractive face, neat hairstyle and a battery of facial expressions which modulate from the sweet, good-natured colleague to the brusque, no-nonsense adversary, whom others cross at their peril. She has an educated, upper-middle-class accent, and a manner of speaking which is often sarcastic, cynical and brooks no contradiction.

Elliot Hope – A senior consultant surgeon, the antithesis of Connie. An overweight, bearded, middle-aged, scruffily dressed father-figure, Elliot has the air of the absent-minded professor. A thinning mop of unruly hair, narrow spectacles perched on the tip of his nose, a permanently bemused expression, a penchant for junk food, and a liking for 60s rock music (he also plays guitar) all contribute to this persona. He conveys the impression of always being totally disorganised. He is a warm, friendly man, always going the extra mile for his patients and his colleagues. He is a widower, losing his beloved wife, Gina to cancer, when he accompanied her to Switzerland for her assisted suicide.

Joseph Byrne – A young surgeon, tall, well-spoken. He is the son of the late Lord Byrne, a renowned consultant, and comes from a very well-to-do family. Joseph is always immaculately turned out, with neat, dark hair, clean-shaven and smartly dressed. He tends to have a somewhat shifty, downward and sideways gaze, and even his smiles are fleeting and furtive, as though he is always embarrassed. When he first joined the hospital, he appeared to suffer from OCD, being obsessed with order and personal hygiene, which revealed itself in his habit of carefully re-arranging surgical instruments which had already been carefully laid out, and his need to wash his hands with the utmost precision. He is constantly unnerved by the presence of Jac Naylor, who is in love with him, and for whom he seems to have feelings, despite his being engaged to Sister Fay Morton. His nervous movements, even in the operating theatre at times, seem to suggest a lack of confidence. Nevertheless, he has displayed great kindness towards Fay and her autistic son, Archie.

Jac Naylor – A young, female surgeon. She has a gaunt, drawn appearance, and her expression is usually grim and serious. She is tall and thin, and she tends to wear her long auburn hair in a rather plain, straight cut, which lends her face a somewhat severe look. Out of her surgical garb, she often wears dark clothing. Her speech, while clear and educated, is often brusque and to the point. Her troubled relationship with Joseph has left her making barbed and sarcastic comments to both him and Fay at every opportunity. Her black motorcycle gear gives her an air of sinister mystery, and some of her secret actions have allowed the audience to form an opinion of her as a malicious, manipulative, almost sadistic woman. Her accident, which left her with a limp supported by a walking stick, turned her into a female equivalent of the cynical, grumpy, limping US medic, *House* (see Chapter 9).

Maria Kendall – A young, female nurse. She wears the standard, blue nurse's uniform. She has a shock of ginger hair, usually worn up, but wears it free-flowing on social, non-work occasions. She has a pale complexion. She often has a bemused, puzzled expression, as if things do not always make sense, but in this sequence her serious and thoughtful expression betrays the devastation, grief and guilt she is feeling for the death of her friend, Doctor Maddy Young. She is very nervous at the thought of addressing her colleagues at Maddy's memorial gathering, becomes very upset and is supported by her good friend, Donna.

Linden Cullen – One of the senior ward doctors. A man in his mid-thirties, tall, clean-cut, with dark hair and glasses, he has the air of a reserved and detached academic. His whole manner is that of a person who does not wish to reveal his thoughts or his feelings, but, as he stares blankly at his computer monitor and answers his phone on auto-pilot, it is clear he is deeply affected by Maddy's death. His unshaven appearance and weary demeanour suggest someone who has not slept well and is clearly upset. Regular viewers will also know that much of Linden's troubled expression is not helped by the fact that he is in love with Fay Morton, but has not yet revealed this to anyone.

- Compare *Casualty* and *Holby City* with other current hospital-based dramas from both the UK and US. Concentrate particularly on their production design, including technical codes, and issues of representation. What are the similarities and differences? How can you account for these?

- Try to find examples of earlier TV medical dramas and make similar comparisons.

- If you have had recent experiences of a hospital environment, have a go at constructing a short dramatised sequence based on them.

CHAPTER SIX – DOCTOR WHO

The revitalised
and regenerated
Doctor (Christopher
Eccleston) is
reacquainted with
his old adversary,
the Daleks

BEGINNINGS

On 23 November 1963 children (and some adults) hid behind the sofa for the first
time in response to a new Saturday teatime sc-fi series called enigmatically *Doctor Who*.
The BBC had been looking for a programme idea aimed at both younger viewers and
an older audience to plug the gap between Saturday afternoon sports coverage and the
early-evening pop music programme *Juke Box Jury*.

The original idea for the series involved a mysterious old man, The Doctor, who is found
by two schoolteachers and one of their teenage pupils. They discover that he is an alien
with no clear idea of his identity (Doctor *who*?), who travels in a large, defective spaceship
miraculously housed inside an ordinary (for 1960s Britain) blue police box.

- Read the planning note on pages 104-5 and explore in what ways the current
  series (2005 onwards) is similar to, and differs from, the original programme ideas.
  Refer to *mise-en-scène*, technical codes, narrative, representation, genre, audience
  and ideology.

- Using the original storyline proposal, consider how the story might be developed
  if it were to be made now.

This is an extract from an original planning document for the show. It is available for download via the BBC website (see Bibliography)

BACKGROUND NOTES FOR 'DR. WHO'

CE Webber and Sydney Newman outline the format for the new 'Doctor Who' series in a BBC document written in 1963

"DR. WHO" General Notes on Background and Approach

A series of stories linked to form a continuing serial... Within the overall title, each episode is to have its own title. Each episode of 25 minutes will begin by repeating the closing sequence or final climax of the preceding episode; about halfway through, each episode will reach a climax, followed by blackout before the second half commences (one break).

[Handwritten note from Sydney Newman: "Each episode to end with a very strong cliff-hanger."]

Each story, as far as possible, to use repeatable sets. It is expected that BP [abbreviation for 'back projection'] will be available. A reasonable amount of film, which will probably be mostly studio shot for special effects. Certainly writers should not hesitate to call for any special effects to achieve the element of surprise essential in these stories... Otherwise work to a very moderate budget.

CHARACTERS

BRIDGET (BIDDY) A with-it girl of 15, reaching the end of her Secondary School career, eager for life, lower-than-middle class. Avoid dialect, use neutral accent laced with teenage slang.

MISS McGOVERN (LOLA) 24. Mistress at Biddy's school. Timid but capable of sudden rabbit courage. Modest, with plenty of normal desires. Although she tends to be the one who gets into trouble, she is not to be guyed: she also is a loyalty character.

CLIFF 27 or 28. Master at the same school. Might be classed as ancient by teenagers except that he is physically perfect, strong and courageous, a gorgeous dish. Oddly, when brains are required, he can even be brainy, in a diffident sort of way.

DR. WHO A frail old man lost in space and time. He seems not to remember where he has come from; he is suspicious and capable of sudden malignance; he seems to have some undefined enemy; he is searching for something as well as fleeing from something. He has a "machine" which enables them to travel together through time, through space, and through matter.

QUALITY OF STORY Evidently, Dr. Who's "machine" fulfils many of the functions of conventional Science Fiction gimmicks. But we are not writing Science Fiction. We shall provide scientific explanations too, sometimes, but we shall not bend over backwards to do so, if we decide to achieve credibility by other means. Neither are we writing fantasy: the events have got to be credible to the three ordinary people who are our main characters, and they are sharp-witted enough to spot a phoney...

Granted the startling situations... we should try to add meaning; to convey what it means to be these ordinary human beings in other times, or in far space, or in unusual physical states. We might hope to be able to answer the question: "Besides being exciting entertainment, for 5 o'clock on a Saturday, what is worthwhile about this serial?"

OVERALL CONTINUITY OF STORY.

Besides the machine [the Tardis] we have the relationship of the four characters to each other. They want to help the old man find himself; he doesn't like them; the sensible hero never trusts Dr. Who; Biddy rather dislikes Miss McCovern; Lola admires Cliff... these attitudes developed and varied as temporary characters are encountered and reacted to. The old man provides continuing elements of Mystery, and Quest.

He remains a mystery. From time to time the other three discover things about him, which turn out to be false or inconclusive. (i.e. any writer inventing an interesting explanation must undercut it within his own serial-time, so that others can have a go at the mystery). They think he may be a criminal fleeing from his own time; he evidently fears pursuit through time… But also, he is searching for something which he desires heart-and-soul, but which he can't define…

While his mystery may never be solved, or may perhaps be revealed slowly over a very long run of stories, writers will probably like to know an answer. Shall we say:-

The Secret of Dr. Who: In his own day, somewhere in our future, he decided to search for a time or for a society or for a physical condition which is ideal, and having found it, to stay there. He stole the machine and set forth on his quest. He is thus an extension of the scientist who has opted out, but he has opted farther than ours can do, at the moment. And having opted out, he is disintegrating.

[Handwritten note from Sydney Newman: "Don't like this at all. Dr Who will become a kind of father figure - I don't want him to be a reactionary."]

The Second Secret of Dr. Who: The authorities of his own (or some other future) time are not concerned merely with the theft of an obsolete machine; they are seriously concerned to prevent his monkeying with time, because his secret intention, when he finds his ideal past, is to destroy or nullify the future.

[Handwritten note from Sydney Newman: "Nuts"]

…By the third story we could first reveal that [the Tardis] is a time-machine; they witness a great calamity, even possibly the destruction of the earth, and only afterwards realize that they were far ahead in time. Or to think about Christmas: which seasonable story shall we take our characters into? Bethlehem? Was it by means of Dr. Who's machine that Aladdin's palace sailed through the air? Was Merlin Dr. Who? Was Cinderella's Godmother Dr. Who's wife chasing him through time?

[Handwritten note from Sydney Newman: "I don't like this much - it reads silly and condescending. It doesn't get across the basis of teaching of educational experience - drama based upon and stemming from factual material and scientific phenomena and actual social history of past and future. Dr. Who - not have a philosophical arty-science mind - he'd take science, applied and theoretical, as being as natural as eating."]

When the first episode finally aired on that now-legendary winter evening, much had changed. The pupil had become The Doctor's teenage granddaughter, Susan Foreman, one of the school's 'star' pupils, described by the title of the first episode as 'An Unearthly Child'. Two of her teachers, Ian and Barbara, are intrigued by her apparent genius, particularly in science, and decide to follow her home to talk to her grandfather, a doctor, about her potential, even though she has been reluctant to disclose her address. They arrive at a junkyard, with the name 'Foreman' painted on the gates. Once inside, they find a blue police box which they discover appears to be vibrating as though it is alive. They are confronted suddenly by an old man who aggressively demands to know what they want. They accuse him of keeping their pupil, Susan, captive in the box, and threaten him with the police. At this point Susan emerges from the box, although her grandfather attempts to prevent her. Ian and Susan push their way into the box, only to discover that its interior is very much larger than its external proportions.

Giving up all pretence of concealment, The Doctor and Susan try to explain their origins and the nature of their ship, the Tardis (Time and Relative Dimension in Space). Ian refuses to believe them and attempts to unlock the door by pressing buttons on the central control console. The result is to activate the ship's drive mechanism and it 'takes off', transporting them all back to the Stone Age, at the point where, as we discover in subsequent episodes, humankind is about to discover fire, with a little help from their mysterious visitors.

At the beginning of the second episode there occur the only two occasions when the title phrase 'Doctor Who' is mentioned. Ian begs 'Doctor Foreman' to open the ship and let them out, to which The Doctor mutters under his breath 'Eh? Doctor *who*? What's he talking about?' Once they have left the ship to explore the barren landscape to which they have come, Ian tells Barbara that they have no idea of the old man's identity, 'Doctor? Doctor *who*? If only we knew his name…'

So began, rather modestly, a television phenomenon which was to last, with breaks, for forty-five years, and still thrills millions at Saturday teatime.

A GALLERY OF DOCTORS

The first Doctor was played by William Hartnell, a character actor better known at the time for his appearances in UK films of the 40s and 50s, and as a comic sergeant-major in an ITV sitcom of the 1950s, *The Army Game*. His casting as The Doctor, initially a bad-tempered, professorial, grandfather character, seemed, therefore, to be something of a departure from his previous acting roles. His long, dark coat and white flowing hair lent the role a period feel and presented The Doctor as something of an authority figure. His intellectual and scientific curiosity were often to place his companions at risk, but his general manner and appearance fixed the identity of The Doctor as a serious seeker-after-truth and an enigmatic time-traveller of great wisdom and universal knowledge. All of his successors have demonstrated some or all of these characteristics, and always for the greater good of the Universe, as might be expected of the Time Lords.

Hartnell's characterisation of The Doctor seems to have fitted the current public perception of the 'eccentric scientist' – a popular image in the 1950s and early 1960s, no doubt relying in part on some of the scientific geniuses who supported the war effort (code breakers and bomb designers), and some of the intellectuals who were beginning to appear on television as 'experts' in a variety of discussion programmes.

After three years in the role, the actor playing The Doctor, William Hartnell, decided to retire, leaving the BBC with a problem. The solution was inspired, and has been used ever since, as the next Doctor appears to replace the old – regeneration! This simple process, a change of shape and appearance, allows the next actor to step into the part with an already established continuity, but with the opportunity to expand and develop the role. The actors who followed Hartnell each stamped their own individual identity on the role.

Patrick Troughton played The Doctor for four years (1966–70) as what he described as a 'cosmic hobo', much quirkier and lighter than his older and more irascible predecessor. His somewhat unkempt hairstyle, scruffier clothes – large jacket, baggy trousers and floppy bow tie – and whimsical expressions all suggested a Chaplinesque tramp character. He chose to play the recorder which, together with his clothes, lent him something of the 'pied piper' air of an eccentric musician or artist. It was during his occupation of the role that audiences were first introduced to the concept of the 'Time Lords'.

Troughton's Doctor was a timely reflection of a major shift in popular culture towards the end of the 1960s – extravagant fashion, the cult of youth, peace and love, the hippy phenomenon.

In 1970 The Doctor went into colour and was regenerated by John Pertwee as an Edwardian dandy, with luxurious velvet jackets, extravagantly frilly shirts, an exuberant shock of white hair and a flamboyant personality to match. His Doctor spent more time on our Earth, linking up with UNIT (United Nations Intelligence Taskforce) and aided by an array of technological gadgets to fight aliens sent to invade the planet by one of

The Doctor's perennial enemies, The Master. Pertwee's Edwardian image was another reflection of the popular fashion of the day, continuing the free-wheeling approach of Troughton, but developing it to provide the explosion of colour, ubiquitous in the early 1970s, which arrived just in time to benefit from the new TV technology.

The first three Doctors – l r: Troughton, Pertwee and Hartnell

In 1974 the role was taken over by Tom Baker who was to remain in place for seven years. His storylines allowed him to travel the universe as something of a swashbuckling adventurer, complete with curly dark hair, lively expression, broad-brimmed hat, long coat and even longer, legendary scarf. His most celebrated companion was actually a small robotic dog, K9. Baker brought an inventiveness and exuberance to the role, which made his Doctor 'larger than life'.

Baker has been judged by many to be the quintessential Doctor, combining humour, authority, a friendly personality, an air of enigma, and something of a rebellious streak. Although his appearance could still be interpreted as a hangover from the hippy era, his behaviour tended to reflect the edgier mid-1970s, when the UK was not enjoying the best of times socially or politically.

He was followed by a much younger actor, Peter Davison. He adopted the guise of a more sedate Edwardian cricketer, sporting jumpers and jackets to match. It was during his spell as The Doctor that a twentieth-anniversary show, featuring all five Doctors, was aired.

Davison's retro/vintage appearance seemed to suit a period in UK history when the Thatcher era was trying to restore the country to a post-1960s ethos of the successful individual rather than a mutually supportive society. The Edwardian era had been a time for the self-made man – perhaps Davison's Edwardian Doctor was the original yuppy.

The comparative calm of the Davison era was shattered by the next incumbent, Colin Baker, who brought a garish, unpredictable and, at times, violent characterisation to the role. His clashing patchwork jackets and unruly hair seemed to underline the contrasts in his character. He played The Doctor more as a temperamental artist. This darker, roguish Doctor did not seem to appeal so much to audiences in the mid-1980s and the series was given a rest from February 1985 until September 1986, while alternative ideas were sought.

Despite Thatcher's insistence on a particular kind of reactionary Conservatism as the salvation of the UK, the 1980s were troubled times, and Colin Baker's loose cannon of a Doctor exactly matched the uncertainties of the decade.

Baker returned for a brief spell, but audience figures did not improve. One last chance was given to The Doctor, but BBC1 controller, Michael Grade, insisted on a new actor for the role.

In 1987, Sylvester McCoy, an experienced comic actor, brought an up-beat, light-hearted feel to the role, using his skills in physical comedy and his talents for circus-style performance to emphasise the enigmatic side of The Doctor's character. His jumper, decorated with question marks, and an umbrella with a question-mark handle, helped to underline the 'Who?-ness' of the role.

As his 'period of office' developed, his character became more serious, more manipulative, and in 1989 the show finally came to an end.

An attempt was made in 1996 to revive the show, with a pilot, US-backed, movie, starring Paul McGann, but it was not successful and the idea for a series was shelved. Loyal 'Whovians' had to wait until 2005 to see a triumphant return of the last of the Time Lords, with Christopher Eccleston taking up the reins, and an initially very down-to-earth Billie Piper as his companion, Rose Tyler.

DOCTOR WHO 2005–PRESENT

The latest incarnations of The Doctor (Christopher Eccleston, David Tennant and Matt Smith) have opened up the character to even more interpretations. Both of them became pin-ups with sex appeal, and their relationships with their assistant, Rose Tyler, have hinted at more than mutual friendship. At the close of the summer 2008 series, Rose and an alternative, cloned Doctor appear to have gone off to be together in Rose's parallel universe, while the original Doctor is left, once again, alone.

The more recent versions have both adopted more contemporary, almost 'normal' dress and appearance. Eccleston favoured the close-cropped hair, black leather jacket and relaxed dress code more suited to the young city professional than inter-galactic traveller. Tennant on the other hand employed pin-stripe suits, ties and long coats, together with red basketball boots and black-rimmed spectacles to create the impression of an older-looking, casual sixth-former or student.

They have also been able to enjoy the full benefits of the latest television technology (see 'Settings, Locations and *Mise-en-scène*' below), and the full force of contemporary, cross-media marketing. Current merchandise includes any number of variants of the Sonic Screwdriver, Dalek helmets with built-in voice distorter, books, magazines, action figures, models of the Tardis, stickers, DVDs, ringtones, games, working Daleks, cufflinks, keyrings, clothing, caps and very much more. The original series spawned toy and model spin-offs, but nothing like the variety available from 2005.

The latest series has also given rise to its own spin-off, the anagrammatic *Torchwood*, a futuristic series set in near contemporary Cardiff. A group of dedicated scientists, led by Captain Jack Harkness from *Doctor Who*, seeks to protect the world from the accidental invasion of aliens who arrive here through a rift in the time-space continuum. There are many intertextual clues linking the two series, but *Torchwood* has been left to forge its own identity and sphere of action.

At the time of writing (mid-2009), the world waits for the arrival of the next Doctor, played by young actor, Matt Smith, early indications suggesting that he may play The Doctor as a darker figure.

- Investigate the marketing of the *Doctor Who* brand and its impact on the audience perception of the programme.

- Study the various incarnations of The Doctor on YouTube. What similarities and differences do you detect?

Recent storylines have included a rich mixture of the historic (Queen Victoria, Agatha Christie, Charles Dickens and Ancient Romans from a real school Latin course have all made appearances), the futuristic (the Slitheen, the Ood, the Sontarans, the Face of Bo, the Adipose), the traditional (the Daleks, Davros, the Cybermen, the Master) and the mysterious (The Empty Child, The Library, Blink).

Compared with the stories in the earlier history of *Doctor Who*, the current crop have featured some very complex and sophisticated concepts of time, space, reality, altered states, existence, historical responsibility, moral dilemmas, life, death, the universe (and everything!). Despite these levels of sophistication, the basic themes are still very much the same – the Earth/the Universe is threatened by alien and malign forces, and it is The Doctor's responsibility to save it from domination and/or extinction. This he can do only with the assistance of his companions and other, very few, agents for good: Captain Jack Harkness, Harriet Jones, Sarah-Jane, Mickey, Rose's mum, Donna's grandfather.

REPRESENTATION

The major representational features of the Doctors themselves have been described above.

The assistants began with everyday appearances (the first being very soberly dressed schoolteachers and a not very trendy schoolgirl – The Doctor's granddaughter). As the popularity of the series increased, the wardrobe and hairstyles of the assistants became more extravagant, reflecting a cross between current fashions and the wilder excesses of glamour magazine kitsch. As the audiences represented a wider age range than the original target age group, the female costumes in particular became sexier, tighter, more revealing. This in turn created an assistant-type, depicting an attractive young woman at the mercy of an alien attack and needing to be saved by The Doctor. While the younger fans identified with the heroics of the protagonists, older viewers (usually male) enjoyed the 'damsel-in-distress' fantasies generated by this type of assistant.

SETTINGS, LOCATIONS AND *MISE-EN-SCÈNE*

Starting from the known and the familiar, *Doctor Who* took its audience to a very wide variety of places and times. Its creators were keen to link its entertainment function to the BBC's intention that programmes should also be informative and educational; a remit applied to the Corporation by its legendary founder, Lord Reith, since its inception. By allowing The Doctor to travel through time and space, science, history, astronomy and geography could all find a place in the storylines. *Doctor Who* could also capitalise on the growing interest in space travel and the latest developments in science and technology which marked the 1960s as a period of change and progress.

The very first story (1963) began in a school, to which every single member of the audience could relate. The location of The Doctor's spaceship in a junkyard, and its appearance as a police box, employed very familiar British iconography. Blue police (public call) boxes were a common sight on city streets in the 1960s. It was from these recognisable settings that, just like Ian and Barbara, the viewer was transported to strange new worlds and unknown times.

The earlier series were constrained by the limitations of studio sets and multi-camera recordings. It didn't help the 'other-ness' of distant worlds that they all had to be represented in black-and-white. Special effects were also somewhat limited, especially without colour. Nevertheless, *Doctor Who* drew audiences of millions. As TV technology improved, The Doctor was able to go 'on location', increasing the 'realism' of the programme and providing a greater variety of environments.

The movements in space and time meant that set-designers could experiment with alien worlds as well as with the effects of huge periods of time on more familiar territories.

Central to the design is the interior of the Tardis. Originally conceived as a futuristic, laboratory style space with a central control console housing a vertically moving core, the current interior has been designed to look more organic. The central console is still in place, but its core and appurtenances have grown in size and complexity. The interior walls have taken on a less angular, more 'natural' style. There is something of the 'art nouveau' about the flowing shapes and colours, as though today's Tardis is more a fashion and design statement than a spaceship. Some think it is redolent of the design for the futuristic submarine Nautilus in Walt Disney's *20,000 Leagues under the Sea* (1954). Fans have suggested that the Tardis can change with its owner's moods, and that its latest incarnation is meant to represent an almost living creature.

Such conscious design contrasts even more strikingly with its modest exterior. Two non-functioning features of the original ship have been retained throughout all the series. The Tardis has a defunct 'chameleon' circuit, which no longer allows its exterior to camouflage itself by fitting in with any surrounding context. Its time and space controls continually malfunction, leaving destinations unknown and largely un-programmable. This second feature has sometimes been overridden by The Doctor in the more recent series.

As the developments in television technology became even more sophisticated, digital video editing and CGI, together with an increase in budget and production values, have enabled the latest series (2005+) to provide audiences with cutting edge spectacle and excitement on a cinematic scale.

The original brief contained an instruction that there should be no Hollywood-like 'bug-eyed monsters'. Instead, The Doctor was challenged by a very inventive selection of adversaries, the best-known of whom were the Daleks. Their robotic appearance, behaviour and speech patterns immediately endeared them to audiences, and playgrounds throughout the land soon resonated to shouts of 'YOU-WILL-BE-EXTERMINATED!' Their inability to climb stairs and steps was initially overcome by the extensive use of lifts and ramps in the futuristic sets of the early series. In their latest reincarnations, they are now able to hover and even 'fly', thus making them more convincingly invincible. The inspiration for their innovative appearance and movement patterns is not clear, but their slow, silent glide and broad-based, cumbersome shape, not to mention their optical equipment mounted in a single, lensed 'arm', are all reminiscent of the large, heavy, pedestal-mounted studio television cameras in use at the time. The cameras also shared the Dalek's need for perfectly flat, level surfaces on which to move from shot to shot.

It was some time before it was revealed that these metallic forms actually housed life forms. These were conceived as weak, vulnerable, deformed, octopus-like mutants, the result of exposure to atomic radiation, following nuclear war. Their apparently invincible metallic shells afforded protection and provided them with weaponry and a means of transport. This image of a soft and vulnerable entity enclosed in protective armour is not too far removed from humanity living in the hard shells of houses, moving around in all forms of metallic transport and protecting itself with heavy artillery.

GENRE

Science fiction has a long literary history – even the earliest Greek myths were replete with monsters, alien worlds and fantastic adventures, as mortals pitted their strength against the 'other'. One of the obvious influences on the time-travelling dimension of *Doctor Who* was undoubtedly H G Wells' novel, *The Time Machine*, originally published in 1895, and usually claimed to be the inspiration for all time-travelling stories that followed it. It was filmed twice, in 1960 and more recently in 2002.

Another significant influence on the development of *Doctor Who* will have been the earlier TV sci-fi productions: *The Quatermass Experiment* and *Quatermass and the Pit*. BBC radio had also produced sci-fi dramas in the 1950s, notably *Journey into Space* and *Orbiter X*, partly in response to the presentation of *The Adventures of Dan Dare – Pilot of the Future* by the English-language service of Radio Luxembourg, beamed to the UK from Europe.

Much of the this sci-fi boom on radio and television was also fuelled by the glut of 1950s sci-fi movies, many made in black-and-white on very low budgets, a style that early television found easy to emulate.

The films themselves, with their concentration on attacks by hostile aliens determined to annihilate the human race, the world, the universe and everything, definitely found inspiration in the very real threat of exposure to nuclear radiation during the cold war atmosphere of the late 50s and early 60s. It is no coincidence that the earliest threat from an alien force in *Doctor Who* came from the Daleks, a life-form mutated by exposure to nuclear radiation, and bent on the extermination of everyone and everything that stood in their way. They first appeared in December 1963 and have been pursuing The Doctor ever since.

Other monsters and alien life-forms soon followed, each developing loyal audience followings of their own and adding to the growing canon of '*Doctor Who*' lore. More recent narrative and representational strands have included ancient Pompeii, Victorian Britain, Second World War scenarios, as well as visits to the far-flung corners of the Galaxy. These developments have added generic features from period and historical drama, action-adventure films, as well as elements of self-referential comic drama to the mix.

With the increasing technological sophistication of film in the 1970s, two blockbuster movies had a considerable influence on the development of the genre: *Star Wars* (1977) and *Close Encounters of the Third Kind* (1977). *Star Wars* depicted a universe where human life-forms could peacefully co-exist with all manner of alien beings, even if the usual good-versus evil ideology still informed the major storyline. *Close Encounters* took the idea of peaceful co-existence one step further by demonstrating that aliens could be entirely benevolent and, indeed, a positive influence for good both for humans and the universe in general. Multi-culturalism and movements for world peace in the 1970s were clearly having an effect on the genre. *Doctor Who*, though, must inevitably feature scenarios involving threats to a peaceful world-order, in order to provide The Doctor with every opportunity to save the universe. It should, however, be remembered that The Doctor himself is the ultimate friendly alien.

GENERIC CHARACTERISTICS

The following list is wide-ranging but not exhaustive.

General sci-fi characteristics:

- Spaceships.

- Aliens.

- Other worlds.

- Time-travel.

- Threats to the Earth.

- Heroic figure/figures that defend the Earth.

- Death resulting from aliens/uncontrollable forces (viruses, etc.).

- Battle set-pieces between good and evil forces.

- Alien landscapes.

- Futuristic scientific/industrial settings and locations.

- Government conspiracies/cover-ups.

- Personal stories told against the broader sci-fi canvas.

- Religious/spiritual allegories explore man's place in the universe.

Specific to *Doctor Who*:

- The Doctor is an enigmatic figure, possessing a vast array of scientific knowledge and experience. His personal history is mysterious, although certain details are well-known – he is a Time Lord, originates from Gallifrey, is thought to be the last of his kind, can regenerate into a completely different physical appearance, has possessed at different times a daughter and granddaughter.

- He travels through time and space in a ship which employs advanced alien technology and whose interior reflects the 'other-ness' of its origins, while its exterior is mundane, familiar and unthreatening.

- The stories feature alien life-forms, almost all of which have hostile intent towards each other, humankind and/or the universe in general.

- These alien life-forms display a variety of appearances – humanoid, robotic, reptilian, mutant, hybrid, monstrous, invisible, viral, insect-like, fantastic (in the true sense of the word).

- Life-threatening and potentially catastrophic clashes with aliens always result in victory for The Doctor.

- The Doctor is accompanied by an assistant/assistants, often human, sometimes robotic (K-9, the robot dog), frequently female and young, often the focus for alien attack.

- The Doctor possesses scientific devices to aid him against the aliens, most notably the sonic screwdriver (not a weapon).

- Visual characteristics include: alien worlds (desert/rocky landscapes, hi-tech futuristic urban environments), expanses of space (skies, stars, planets, moons), techno interiors (metallic industrial/laboratory/spaceship), period settings (ancient Italy, Shakespearean/Dickensian London, Stone-age Britain), special effects (weaponry, alien monsters, alien locations, explosions).

- Aural characteristics include: appropriate electronic/technological sounds to represent the working of alien machinery and equipment, music which is strident, martial, triumphal and majestic, or moody and threatening, dialogue in alien languages, the iconic sounds of the Tardis materialising and dematerialising, the instantly recognisable theme tune developed, appropriately, by means of electronic sound generators in the BBC Radiophonic Workshop.

In the original planning note of 1963, *Doctor Who* is described as an 'adventure-science fiction drama series for children'. However the series creators take pains to point out that *Doctor Who* is 'neither fantasy, nor space travel, nor science fiction'. Even at the planning stage, the intention seems to have been to create a generic hybrid, thus leaving the way clear to include features from other genres. Even the most recent developments have not shifted the show substantially from its 1963 generic parameters.

ANALYSIS OF OPENING SEQUENCE

DOCTOR WHO – 11 APRIL 2009 EASTER SPECIAL: 'PLANET OF THE DEAD'

The pre-title sequence opens (*mise-en-scène*) with an establishing aerial shot (camera) of central London. It is night. Iconic images (Big Ben, London Eye, South Bank, The Thames) are illuminated. *These quasi-tourist images provide a ready-made lexicon for international audiences, and possibly a reassuring and familiar one for UK viewers.*

Having clearly located the narrative, we cut (editing) to the more immediate setting (*mise-en-scène*) – the exterior of the columned front portico of the International Gallery, its classical architecture and imposing façade *identifying it as a building of prestige and*

importance. A red London bus, *another instantly recognisable icon of London,* is seen in the background turning a corner behind the building. Majestic, strident orchestral music with a militaristic flavour accompanies these opening images (sound), *presenting the audience with a soundtrack reminiscent of stock adventure movies. We can expect some extreme incidents, possibly criminal, certainly full of action sequences.*

We cut to an interior gallery every bit as grand and imposing as the exterior. Four armed security guards are marching along the marble floor, their heavy footsteps joining the music on the soundtrack, their uniforms and the precision with which they move *all reinforce the militaristic nature of the situation* (editing & sound). The atmosphere created by the music, the action, the uniforms and weapons, the low-key gallery lighting and

the fixed expression on the face of a fifth guard is one of serious intensity – *an event or situation of considerable importance is taking place here.* The music stops abruptly just as the men halt behind the fifth guard, *suggesting a shift in the action.* They are now standing facing a golden goblet mounted on a pedestal – *clearly the object of their carefully structured ritual.* The order 'Positions', given by the fifth guard is followed by a resumption of the music and the movement of the men, one to each of four metal pillars standing at the corners of a space which surrounds the pedestal. The iconography here is reminiscent of tall candlesticks flanking a ceremonial coffin at the lying-in-state of a dignitary (*mise-en-scène*). This goblet is no ordinary museum artefact. *We are led to believe that a huge amount of time, effort and money has been expended in order to protect it.*

As the men take up their positions facing outwards from each corner, there is a close-up of the fifth guard keying in a security code on a keypad. *The high-tech security is intended to make a sharp contrast with the artistic, historical overtones of the gallery and its obviously priceless, very old exhibit.* We hear the beeps of the keypad as the code is entered, and then the heavy 'clunk' of a master switch thrown by the guard (sound). *These electronic and mechanical sounds are also designed to be reassuring – this object is totally secure.* They are followed immediately by a series of blue illuminated rays passing around the four pillars and rising to their tips, entirely surrounding the object on display (special effects). The security rays are accompanied by a high-pitched electronic whistle, indicating the functioning of the security device (sound). *We are meant to understand that the enclosed space is impenetrable, and the space that surrounds it is under close and continuous scrutiny.* With a cheery 'Goodnight, boys,' the fifth guard leaves his colleagues to mount a nocturnal vigil over this valuable object. This casual valediction seems at odds with the formality of what we have witnessed so far. *Perhaps we are meant to believe that, despite the plethora of technology surrounding this object its ultimate protection is still at the mercy of ordinary, fallible human beings.*

The music softens and varies, juxtaposing the orchestral stridency with controlled electronic drumbeats and atmospheric sounds from a synthesiser. *This combination of contrasting musical styles seems to reflect the contrast between old-style men-with-guns security and the state-of-the-art technology employed to provide a belts-and-braces solution for the protection of this unique object.*

The camera tilts up to show a small aperture in the dome above the exhibit, which now opens to reveal a tiny figure. *Given the security overkill at ground level, this must be the only way in.* The figure is masked in classic balaclava style, *protecting the anonymity of the criminal and evoking images of terrorists.* It looks down to check out the scene. There

are cutaways (editing) to close-ups (camera) of the guards' faces, all looking serious and vigilant, *providing us with the dramatic irony of knowing what's going on, while they remain in ignorance.*

The music plays on relentlessly, *building suspense.* The masked figure, dressed in black, lets itself down on wires to the level of the goblet. As it does so, the camera, shooting from below, slowly rotates, *mimicking the spiral of a screw and the twirling of an object suspended on a string.* The descent sequence is intercut (editing) with shots of the goblet – predator and prey. Some swishing string passages in the music, *reflecting the wires supporting the figure,* accompany this descent (sound). In a swift second, the figure seizes the goblet, replaces it with a bag, which itself is removed to reveal another object which is left in place of the exhibit, *no doubt to ensure that the sensors continue to detect an object on the pedestal.* This last action is seen in long shot (camera) *so that the object cannot immediately*

be seen. Simultaneously the figure activates a button command on a keypad, *in true Batman style,* to enable the wires to lift it back to the aperture in the dome. It is at this point that one of the guards turns to see what is making a small squeaking sound – we see a close-up of a small mechanical cat figure waving one paw. *Since cats tend to move silently and maintain an aura of mystery and enigma, this seems to be a very appropriate choice of figure. Cats also, proverbially, get the cream.*

- The first part of this analysis has been annotated with references to the technical codes: camera, sound, editing, *mise-en-scène,* special effects. *Sentences in italics* provide analytical explanations of what we are seeing and hearing. Annotate the remainder of the analysis for yourself in the same way.

We now see the shadowy figure of the intruder running along the galleries in order to escape. At the end of one of them, it stops and removes its mask to reveal a close-up of an attractive young woman with long dark hair smiling in breathless excitement. She is dressed in a leather jacket, tight black ski-pants and black leather boots and is carrying a backpack. She has clearly enjoyed every minute of this dangerous adventure. During this last sequence the music has become ever more intense and urgent, with percussion and brass figures emphasising the triumphant nature of this escapade. This whole sequence is designed as an homage to the Mission Impossible films, with a nod to French thriller, *Rififi* (1955), the Pink Panther films, James Bond films, *Topkapi* (1964), and all the heist movies which involve stealing valuable objects from under the scrutiny of the highest security.

The triumph and the enjoyment are short-lived as security bells, sirens and lights are triggered by her presence in this part of the gallery. In exasperation she makes for the nearest emergency exit and finds herself in a side alleyway. It is still dark and she is not

seen by the police arresting a man at the end of the alley. His face is being pressed against the roof of his sports car. As she speaks to herself out loud the words 'Sorry, lover', we understand his identity as her accomplice in the robbery. We also understand in this brief phrase her ruthless exploitation of those who help her.

She turns and runs in the opposite direction along the alley, and the camera keeps her in shot as she runs beneath it, turning right over to create an upside-down shot of her at the other end of the alley. This kind of action shot is reminiscent of such action-adventure movies as *Spider-Man*, *Catwoman*, *Wonder Woman* and *Batman*, thus suggesting that the young woman might have supernatural powers. This could also be an intertextual reference to the actress' (Michelle Ryan's) previous role as *The Bionic Woman* in the US series of that name.

The continuity editing of this whole sequence is designed to keep pace with the action – slightly longer shots for the slower details of the security guard and aerial robbery scenes, shorter and faster cuts for the escape scenes. Nevertheless the shots do tend to move the viewer constantly from detail to detail, from long-shots to close-ups, in order to provide variety of image and pace of action.

The music stops momentarily as the woman attempts to lose herself in the evening crowd. Police sirens and the scream of traffic suggest the frenetic pace of the hunt for the burglar, spearheaded by a somewhat panic-stricken young police officer who directs operations at fever-pitch level.

The woman spots a red double-decker bus, one of the classic icons of London, and jumps aboard in order to escape her pursuers. In a very well-educated upper-class accent she asks if she can pay with her 'lobster' card. The bemused driver, working-class, middle-aged, bearded corrects her error. In fact, she has no cash or card of any sort, so she offers her diamond earrings instead. With a very firm 'works for me' from the driver, the bus is about to depart when a figure in a long coat, only partially seen, boards the bus, swipes his card and moves towards the seats. This figure's feet have already been glimpsed below

the bus, and an audience familiar with the appearance of The Doctor will have already identified him as the mystery passenger. One or two other passengers are glimpsed as the figure slides into shot into the seat next to the young woman. He proffers an Easter egg with a cheery 'Hello! I'm The Doctor. Happy Easter!'

Cut to familiar titles and music.

After the title sequence, we cut back to the chaotic street scenes as the detective spots his quarry on the bus and he issues orders to 'follow that bus!' The remaining credits are superimposed over this sequence. We cut to the scene in the bus. The Doctor chats to the girl about Easter, pointing out how difficult it is for a time-traveller to pin it down, since its date moves from year to year. He also mentions the fact that he was present at the very first Easter. The girl's expression suggests a cross between boredom and the slight suspicion that her travelling companion might be ever so slightly mad. The Doctor gives her the egg and takes out a small electronic flashing device with a tiny aerial dish. This spotted by a young man sitting opposite. The Doctor bemoans the fact that the aerial is not working and fiddles with it, chatting incomprehensibly all the while. A black middle-aged couple notice The Doctor's odd behaviour and share a puzzled look.

The bus, still being pursued by police cars, enters a tunnel, its movements tracked by traffic surveillance cameras. This sequence cuts continuously between the bus and its pursuers, and the police road block establishing itself at the other end of the tunnel. One officer informs his boss by radio that the tunnel is sealed and 'there's no way out.' The detective in pursuit is now convinced that they've run the girl to ground.

Interior shots of the bus in medium long-shot reveal a middle-aged woman sitting at the front, and the other three passengers sitting further back. The Doctor is still fiddling with his gadget and the girl is still looking bored. To humour him, the girl asks if the device can detect a way out. We now cut to a shot of the black couple. The woman is concerned that she can hear voices calling. The Doctor's device becomes more agitated – the aerial is now rotating and the lights are flashing. Its noise irritates the female passenger sitting at the front. The Doctor jumps up, moving to the front, asks the girl her name (Christina), and then shouts to all the passengers to 'hold on tight!'. There now follows a chaos of sound and light, accompanied by the increasingly dramatic music, as the bus appears to crash. There is the sound of smashing glass and we can still hear the woman shouting out that she can hear the voices. The screen dissolves into blurred white light as confused images flash across it, ending with more smashing glass and breaking sounds. The bus appears to have crashed. The music stops and we cut to the police roadblock. An officer reports that there is no sign of the bus, and his boss informs him that it just disappeared right in front of him in the tunnel. A series of forward-and-reverse tracking shots inside the tunnel underline the fact that there is no sign of the bus. The final reverse tracking shot of the tunnel dissolves to a big close-up of The Doctor's right eye staring

 straight ahead. Random shots around the bus reveal the passengers recovering from the crash. They look puzzled, staring out of the windows. The Doctor makes his way to the exit. Exterior shot of the bus door reveals The Doctor steps off the bus into a desert of golden sand ('End of the line.') An aerial shot of the bus tracks back to reveal a wide-

angle shot of the bus marooned in a vast desert landscape. We cut to a shot of an alien screen. The arrival is being viewed by what appears to be an alien being, whose mode of communication is a clicking noise, reminiscent of insect life.

The recent resurgence of interest in the *Doctor Who* strand provided audiences with a complete 'Whovian' world, supported by TV programmes such as BBC3's *Doctor Who Confidential*, *Torchwood*, fan magazines and other literature, and an extensive and wide-ranging Internet presence. Merchandise is plentiful and constantly in demand, and DVD sales provide the BBC with considerable additional income.

- Explore the wide range of *Doctor Who* spin-off materials. How far do they support the fiction of The Doctor's world, and how far are they just a merchandising opportunity?

CHAPTER SEVEN — PERIOD DRAMA ADAPTATIONS

The Dedlocks (Timothy West, background; Gillian Anderson, foreground), whose mystery lies at the heart of Bleak House

BLEAK HOUSE

One of the major features of contemporary television is the need to challenge existing programme conventions, and in so doing, bring new audiences to innovative productions. The BBC, one of the cornerstones of world television, has, over the last fifty years, established a global reputation for making the highest quality 'classic' serial drama. Through BBC2 and, more recently, BBC3 and 4, it has also been recognised as an innovator in the art of television production. Combining traditional elements with contemporary televisual techniques is never easy; making the monumental, multi-layered complexity of a Charles Dickens novel accessible to and enjoyable for a modern audience might seem a challenge too far.

Bleak House, originally published by Dickens as a serial novel in 1852–3, looks a daunting prospect for both a twenty-first-century audience and a twenty-first-century production team. It is a long, highly detailed narrative, whose myriad twists and turns are traced through the ever-increasing interactions of plot and character. The obscurity of its central theme, the impenetrable maze of the mid-nineteenth century judicial system and its impact on both practitioners and victims, reinforcing a rigid class-and-power structure and the inflexibility of social and cultural values, do not appear to guarantee record viewing figures one hundred and fifty years later. A careful analysis of the novel's many dimensions, however, might prompt a different view.

So what is *Bleak House*?

- A serial, multi-layered narrative – modern soap operas follow a similar pattern.

- A detective story, arguably the first piece of detective fiction (complete with the first Detective Inspector – Inspector Bucket), concerning true identities, tragic deaths, a murder and a missing will – such details are the staple fare of modern crime drama.

- Three romances involving the central characters of the narrative – love stories are a common thread in most contemporary dramas.

- A rich gallery of characters, some tragic, some evil, some good, some comic – again, soap operas abound in such characters.

- An exposure and critique of social ills: poverty, debt, class prejudice, lack of healthcare, injustice, inequality, corruption, abuse of power – all of these issues, have been and remain the core of much television drama.

- An evocation of the atmosphere of life in London for both rich and poor using powerful descriptions of realistic settings and locations – much contemporary drama relies on such a high level of realism.

Looked at like this, *Bleak House* might seem an obvious choice for dramatisation. This does not mean that there were no obstacles. The novel is a very long and dense narrative. The central story is told in two ways: Esther Summerson's narrative, told in the first person, and a conventional third-person narrative. Although the story was originally serialised by Dickens in nineteen monthly instalments, the episodes contain much of his extensive trademark description and reflection which does not always lend itself easily to televisual interpretation. It is also recognised that today's television audience has become more and more attuned to faster-paced, bite-sized styles of presentation. A single episode of a soap opera might contain dozens of very short scenes, some without dialogue, some only a few seconds long.

It has often been said by less serious students of the media that, if Dickens had been alive today, he would be writing for *EastEnders*. We cannot know this, nor is the speculation helpful. Dickens is a product of his time, as all writers are, and it tells us nothing to consider what he might have done in another. The quote, however, could have been a useful starting point for the creators of the recent television adaptation of *Bleak House*. Previous adaptations of Dickens' novels have often been serials in weekly episodes of thirty minutes, screened late on Sunday afternoons, a traditional slot for 'classic' serials. Some, by contrast, have taken over two-hour prime time slots to allow greater space for the development of story and character.

Bleak House did neither. Instead, confining itself to the thirty-minute format, it was scheduled for twice-weekly, early evening, i.e. soap opera, slots, so that the audience could keep up with the detail and the momentum. This viewer-friendly approach was further reinforced by the imaginative casting. Big names from television drama in both the US and the UK (Gillian Anderson, Timothy West, Charles Dance, Ian Richardson, Pauline Collins, Alun Armstrong, Warren Clarke, Phil Davis) were supplemented by more surprising additions from other television genres (Johnny Vegas, Alistair McGowan, Charlie Brooks, Liza Tarbuck) and a group of younger actors (Burn Gorman, Carey Mulligan, Anna Maxwell Martin).

At the centre of the narrative is the long and tortuous lawsuit, known as Jarndyce and Jarndyce. The resolution of this interminable action over wills is expected to be a large inheritance for two young wards of court, Ada Clare and Richard Carstone. However the proceedings appear to have been going on for decades, and there is no obvious end in sight. Men have died in pursuit of their claims; the case has disrupted and ruined the lives of all who have become involved in it, except, of course, the lawyers, who grow fat on the costs that arise from it.

Ada and Richard are protected by their guardian, John Jarndyce, who seems to have kept clear of the lawsuit whose name he bears. He has also engaged a young orphan, Esther Summerson, to be Ada's companion, and they all live together at Bleak House. Ada and Richard fall in love, but John Jarndyce wants Richard to make a career for himself. Unfortunately his expectation of the inheritance unsettles him, and he is unable to apply himself seriously to any of his chosen professions, medicine, law or the army. Finally he gives himself up entirely to the pursuit of his claim in the case, exploited by the unscrupulous Mr Skimpole and his mercenary lawyer associate, Mr Vholes, until his health is ruined and he tragically dies, having just married Ada, who has supported him unwaveringly throughout, and is now pregnant. As the narrative progresses it becomes clear that John Jarndyce has also engaged Esther to be his housekeeper and, ultimately his wife, despite the great difference in their ages. It further transpires that he has been unobtrusively supporting her interests from her earliest orphaned childhood, possibly with this end in view.

One of the big names among the lawyers, and one of the most feared, is Mr Tulkinghorn. He conducts business connected with Jarndyce and Jarndyce for a minor aristocrat, Sir Leicester Dedlock, and is intrigued by the extreme reaction of his wife, Lady Dedlock, to the writing on a legal document he has brought for their perusal. As a result he becomes interested in the activities of the law writer who copied the documents, a mysterious and uncommunicative man, called Nemo (Latin for 'no one') who lodges at a curious rag and bottle shop called Krook's. The law writer dies of an opium overdose before Tulkinghorn can pursue the matter further with him.

A law clerk, called Guppy, who has fallen in love with Esther, although not she with him, believes there is something in the mystery of the law writer which connects him with Esther. Tulkinghorn, meanwhile, is convinced that the law writer is in some way connected with Lady Dedlock, and is determined to get to the bottom of the mystery. He makes his suspicions known to Lady Dedlock, but before he is able to pursue the mystery to its conclusion and reveal what he knows, he is unexpectedly shot and killed. Because of the many people he has ruined through his legal practice, he is reputed to have many enemies. The case is taken on by Inspector Bucket (arguably fiction's first detective). In another interesting turn of events, Krook, the dead law writer's landlord, dies in mysterious circumstances attributed to alleged spontaneous combustion. His shop and possessions are appropriated by Smallweed, a moneylender, who discovers a batch of letters sent by Lady Dedlock to the law writer many years before.

In the course of investigating the murder of Tulkinghorn, Bucket uncovers a web of information and intrigue. It turns out that Esther is the illegitimate daughter of the law writer, a Captain Hawdon, and Lady Dedlock. Esther does have a brief and poignant meeting with her mother, who insists that they must not meet again for fear of discovery. Lady Dedlock, fearing exposure and the condemnation of her husband, makes her way to London to visit the cemetery where her lost lover, Hawdon, is buried in a pauper's grave. Illness and harsh weather overtake her at the gates of the cemetery, where she dies in the arms of her daughter who has followed her trail with the help of Bucket.

Towards the end of the story, Smallweed also discovers at Krook's shop a will which proves to be the last and incontestable will, which will settle the case of Jarndyce and Jarndyce once and for all. Ada and her late husband, Rick, are indeed the beneficiaries, but the case has dragged on for so long that whatever legacy there was has been eaten up by all of the legal costs, and, consequently, Ada inherits nothing. However, during the course of the story, Esther has formed a close relationship with a doctor, Allan Woodcourt. It was undermined by his mother at one point, and he believes that Esther does not return his affection and goes to serve as a doctor in the navy. While he is away, Esther contracts smallpox and is left with a pock-marked face, whose scars gradually fade but not completely. On his return he confesses his love and the two are married. John Jarndyce has purchased a large cottage, renamed *Bleak House*, for Esther and her husband, and the story ends happily enough.

There are many other incidental stories and sub-plots contained in the novel, some of which were retained in the adaptation.

COMPARISON OF OPENING OF *BLEAK HOUSE* (TV) AND THE NOVEL

TELEVISION VERSION

After a set of calligraphed titles, containing images from the narrative which float across the screen, accompanied by a simple, almost non-melodic, theme, the episode opens with dramatic, strident, urgent orchestral music as the soundtrack to some fast-moving, somewhat chaotic images of pouring rain, an inn, a coach and horses, luggage, a woman in a hooded cloak boarding the coach, the coach taking off, the young woman removing her hood inside the coach, the coach making good speed through the rain-swept countryside. The identity of the young woman, her purpose in making this coach journey, its origin and destination all remain obscure and enigmatic. The dark skies, pouring rain, gloomy coach interior and hooded cloak all contribute to the enigma.

We cut to scenes in the Court of Chancery, presided over by the Lord High Chancellor. We are very quickly plunged into this unfamiliar world, with no real clue regarding its meaning. The courtroom is equally gloomy, with dark-panelled woodwork, black-gowned lawyers and the impenetrable fug of the law in its due process. The matter of Jarndyce and Jarndyce is announced and one of the lawyers is able to explain a little of the case.

Cut to a large and rather forbidding country house, pouring rain, and dialogue from an older man commenting on the weather and the lack of action in Jarndyce and Jarndyce. This is echoed by his younger wife, who stands by the window watching the rain and comments under her breath how bored she is with everything. The dark, cheerless interior exactly matches the detached communication between the two.

Back at the court the Chancellor announces that the two young wards-of-court, Richard Carstone and Ada Clare, are themselves present, and that a companion for the female ward is on her way. The young wards seem daunted and confused by this crowded and oppressive environment, as indeed we are expected to be. This is a game whose rules we do not know and cannot begin to guess at. The Chancellor notes the presence of Mr Tulkinghorn, who appears to be controlling other lawyers' contributions by the nod of his head. Although the legal profession is exclusively male, there are women claimants present, including Miss Flyte, an eccentric busybody, who takes a kindly interest in the 'wards in Jarndyce' as she persists in calling Richard and Ada.

Cut to further scenes of the coach rushing through the countryside on its way to London. The harsh weather continues to reinforce the dark mystery of this coach journey, although the identity of the young woman (who appears to be reflecting upon an unhappy childhood) may now be assumed to be that of companion to the female ward. Another cut to a street near the Court, where a young clerk is waiting for the coach's arrival. It is a London street, and its atmosphere exactly matches the drab darkness

we have already witnessed in the other scenes. The coach arrives and the clerk helps the young woman down, introducing himself as Guppy and addressing her as Miss Summerson, our first introduction to the passenger. His somewhat hypnotised look suggests he has been emotionally affected by her manner and appearance. As they make their way towards his offices, a long-haired and bearded man in his mid-forties bumps into her and they exchange lingering glances, as though some note of recognition passes between them. He is certainly struck by her appearance. This exchange adds another layer of mystery to this story from the outset. Then the man moves off and Guppy takes Miss Summerson to the offices of Kenge and Carboy's, solicitors, where we learn more about the case at the centre of this story.

Miss Summerson is taken before the Chancellor by Mr Kenge to meet the young woman she is to be a companion to, and the young man in the case, and learns that they are all to go and live in Bleak House with the couple's cousin, John Jarndyce. Despite the dreary appearance of these scenes, this news brings some cause for optimism.

Notice how the separate scenes begin to build on each other and help to develop the narrative complexity. The first, unexplained, scene of Esther boarding the coach is followed by the complete contrast of the first Court scene, equally unexplained. The one does not seem in any way connected to the other. But, when we hear about a companion on her way to London to join the wards, and then cut back to the passenger making her coach journey, matters now make more sense. When we then see Guppy waiting impatiently for the coach, our conclusions about the young passenger and her expected arrival in court are confirmed. When the unknown man bumps into Esther, the exchange of looks and the sudden slowing of the narrative pace suggest that this is a meeting of some import. (Later, of course, we shall discover the poignancy of this one meeting between a father and his daughter, each unknown to the other.) The delivery of Esther by Guppy into the offices of Kenge and Carboy's leaves no doubt about her identity or Guppy's growing affection for her. With that narrative trail established, we return to the court to witness Tulkinghorn plying his trade. Here is an important lawyer connected to the case, and therefore with some of the characters we have already met.

The cut to Chesney Wold, the country house of the Dedlocks, introduced another unexplained location and set of characters. But their references to Tulkinghorn and Jarndyce and Jarndyce now anchor them into the growing complexity of this story. When Esther and the wards are introduced to the Chancellor, who explains what will happen to them, and these initially disparate scenes now become connected.

These swiftly-moving opening scenes, around 12 minutes of screen time, cover the first three chapters of the book, some twenty-six pages of the novel.

CAMERA, SOUND AND *MISE-EN-SCÈNE*

In accordance with the weather, all of these scenes, even the interiors, are shot in low light, with much use of shadow and low-key lighting. A combination of the visual gloominess, the erratic, hand-held camerawork and the melodramatic music serves to create an atmosphere of mysterious uncertainty, as though the whole story is steeped in the same degree of obscurity as the law suit itself. An editing device between scenes serves to highlight the urgency and mystery of the narrative. At the beginning of many of the scenes there is a swiftly-cut three-shot sequence, where the camera appears to move instantaneously from long-shot to close-up still images. This effect is emphasised by a harsh musical percussion sound at precisely the point where the shots change. It is as though we are having the new scene thrust abruptly in our faces. It certainly serves to move us at lightning speed from scene to scene.

The overall *mise-en-scène* conveys the strong impression that everything was shot in real locations and real interiors. Dark panelled woodwork, big heavy doors, the wooden sound of footsteps on bare boards, meticulous attention to costume and hairstyles, and dialogue spoken in spaces with heavy reverb all emphasise a high degree of realism.

THE NOVEL

While Dickens obviously constructed a work of fiction, we must be aware that many of his locations either were, or were based on, real places. Two sites in St Albans, for example, lay claim to being the inspiration for *Bleak House*, and there were many brickworks in the St Albans area in the mid-nineteenth century. Many of the legal sites in London which he referred to actually existed, and Dickens and his audience would have known them well.

Surprisingly, the novel begins with as much abbreviated suddenness as the adaptation. The two opening paragraphs contain no main verb – they are just collections of statements describing the city, the second containing the famous description of a London fog:

'Fog everywhere. Fog up the river, where it flows among green aits and meadows; fog down the river, where it rolls defiled among the tiers of shipping and the waterside pollutions of a great (and dirty) city. Fog on the Essex marshes, fog on the Kentish heights. Fog creeping into the cabooses of collier-brigs; fog lying out on the yards, and hovering in the rigging of great ships; fog drooping on the gunwales of barges and small boats. Fog in the eyes and throats of ancient Greenwich pensioners, wheezing by the firesides of their wards; fog in the stem and bowl of the afternoon pipe of the wrathful skipper, down in his close cabin; fog cruelly pinching the toes and fingers of his shivering little 'prentice boy on deck. Chance people on the bridges peeping over the parapets into a nether sky of fog, with fog all round them, as if they were up in a balloon, and hanging in the misty clouds.'

The ingredient missing from the opening of the television adaptation is obviously the fog. Clearly Dickens used the London fog as a striking and highly appropriate metaphor for the impenetrable judicial processes at the centre of the story. It also presages the secrecy and mystery surrounding Esther Summerson and Lady Dedlock.

The adaptation chooses to use a combination of persistent rain, dark and gloomy environments and a catalogue of enigmatic exchanges between unknown characters as metaphors for the obscurity of this narrative. It also uses a visual device which serves several purposes. Many of the images are shot through or partly obscured by out-of-focus foreground objects (for example, banister rails, door frames, curtains, a vase of flowers). This device conveys the impression that the audience is glimpsing events and exchanges between the characters which are not meant to be on public view. It also further reinforces the obscurity of the narrative by concealing rather than revealing some of the detail of a shot. This leads to the construction of shots which seems to challenge the accepted conventions of shot framing and composition. It is as though the audience is picking up many of the narrative details by accident, overhearing secret exchanges, eavesdropping on private occasions, being made to feel almost unwelcome.

REPRESENTATION

The rich gallery of Dickensian characters are a gift for production designers, and for students of representation:

Esther Summerson – A young woman, caring, selfless, intelligent, mature. She has a soft, pleasant face and dark hair. The sober and proper plainness of her dresses and hairstyle underlines her unaffected modesty. She exudes goodness. Her steady and controlled facial expressions suggest calmness and composure, whether she is confronting the abrupt and unexpected proposal of marriage from Guppy, the astonishing effrontery of the selfish and manipulative Skimpole, the deceptive legal chicanery of Vholes, the feckless impetuosity of Richard, or the altruistic generosity of her guardian, John Jarndyce. Few things shake her composure: coming face to face with her disfigurement following the attack of smallpox; the death of Richard and devastation of Ada; the thought of having lost a chance of happiness with Woodcourt; and, most of all, the trauma of her one and only meeting with her mother, and having to conceal that knowledge for ever; and finally the death of her mother in her arms.

She is played by Anna Maxwell-Martin, whose stage career includes the award-nominated role of Lyra in the National Theatre's production of Philip Pullman's *His Dark Materials*. Before *Bleak House* she had appeared in an episode of *Doctor Who* and the period drama *North and South*. After *Bleak House* she secured the role of Sally Bowles in the stage musical *Cabaret*.

Lady Honoria Dedlock – A mature woman of forty-plus, attractive (once stunning), emotionally drained, distracted, withdrawn; she maintains an air of aristocratic repose and quiet dignity. Her dress is simple and unaffected, although elegantly restrained, sometimes coincidentally reminiscent of Esther's appearance. She tends to wear her hair pulled tightly against her head, as though reflecting the repressed and private nature of her character. She is quiet and, for the most part, uncommunicative. She has a habit of gazing into the middle distance, with an expression which could be interpreted as thoughtful or vacant.

She retains a secret attachment to her earlier relationship with Captain James Hawdon whose love letters she has kept for over twenty years. Despite this secret, she has remained faithful to her husband, who has treated her with the utmost kindness and respect, and to whom she shows a studied, grateful affection.

She maintains an aristocratic and somewhat haughty bearing towards most of her inferiors, and a studied distance from others. Because of the emotional vacuum in her life created by the loss of her illegitimate daughter, she forms a close attachment to a young girl of nineteen, Rosa, and employs her as her personal maid. She treats the girl with kindness and sympathy, especially when she learns that she has formed a romantic attachment to a young man, whose father does not regard her with favour.

When Lady Dedlock is informed by Tulkinghorn of the death of her former lover, Lady Dedlock becomes obsessed with finding his grave. She is clearly a very emotionally troubled woman, and her gaunt and grave demeanour reinforces this aspect of her personality for the viewer. In fact, her expression barely wavers, even when told of Hawdon's death by Tulkinghorn.

She is played by Gillian Anderson, best known for her role as Dana Scully in the long-running US sci-fi series *The X-Files*. Before *Bleak House* she played the leading role of Lily Bart in Terence Davies' film *The House of Mirth*, a period drama set in the nineteenth century. She has also had many roles in US TV and film.

Mr Tulkinghorn – A middle-aged lawyer, tall, imposing, soberly attired, with a learned and gentlemanly bearing. His manner towards others is cold and terse. He is universally feared by all who know him, and he seems to take pleasure in the power this gives him. It is difficult to gauge his thoughts and opinions – his face tends to appear devoid of emotion, except the occasional smug and self-satisfied smile. His white hair, clean-shaven face, small, steel-rimmed spectacles and almost immoveable expression lend him the air of an inscrutable academic. However, when he begins to pressurise his hapless victims, his eyes narrow and his facial expression takes on a hardness which suggests he will brook no opposition. He has an air of self-possession and self-control which both suggests the extent of his power over others, and prevents him from revealing anything either about him or about the matters that concern him.

His whole appearance suggests that his existence is entirely concerned with the law – he is not seen to have any other form of life. He is always seen wearing the dark frock coat and stiff collar shirts that traditionally betoken his profession. As the narrative progresses, the depth of his insensitive cruelty is gradually revealed. He is overheard interrogating Jo, the crossing sweeper, about Nemo. He threatens Sergeant George with eviction if he fails to produce an example of Nemo's handwriting. He is obsessed with the desire to discover but conceal Lady Dedlock's secret, presumably to protect the honour of his client, Sir Leicester Dedlock. His air of detachment, however, prevents us from understanding the real motives behind any of these actions.

He is played by Charles Dance, an actor with a long and distinguished career, earning an OBE for services to drama. He came to the attention of a wider audience in the leading role of Guy Perron in Granada's period (1940s India) drama *Jewel in the Crown* (1983). Since then he has worked extensively in theatre, film and television.

John Jarndyce – An educated, middle-aged gentleman, of modest appearance. His mode of speech and educated accent place him as a member of the landed upper-middle class, and his house, the size of his staff and his lifestyle all suggest considerable wealth. This is also attested by the remarks of Mr Kenge to the Lord Chancellor, who is anxious to know of John Jarndyce's character before entrusting the wards to his care.

He is a genuine philanthropist whose altruism benefits all who come into contact with him. He affects the need to retire to his 'growlery' when he claims to be feeling out of temper, but, in reality, the extent of his disquiet is expressed simply by his mild-mannered observation that the 'wind is clearly in the east', by which he means that he is upset by a circumstance or a person, but pursues the matter no further. The raising of his hand to his forehead is the only outward sign of his feelings. Despite his friendly, outgoing behaviour towards his guests, he still wears, from time to time, an air of long-suffering, which he no doubt attributes to the wearing nature of the lawsuit which has involved his family for so long, and to the demands made on his generosity by the parasitic activities of such as Mr Skimpole.

He has an open and honest expression, and exudes an avuncular warmth towards Esther, Rick and Ada. He always acts in a kindly manner towards his household staff.

He is prepared to support Rick's wavering ambition and warms to the growing relationship between him and Ada. Any earlier reluctance he shows in this respect is due entirely to his concern for them both. Later in the narrative we learn that he has become romantically attached to Esther.

The theme of a much older man attracted to, and sometimes marrying a young woman is one that Dickens uses in other novels and is thought by some to reflect his own secret relationship with his young mistress, an actress called Nelly Ternan. John Jarndyce, therefore, could be seen as a portrayal of Dickens himself as the kindly guardian angel of the young people in his charge. Jarndyce is keenly aware of Esther's love for the young doctor, Allan Woodcourt, and, through his continuing generosity and selflessness, they are able to celebrate their marriage and begin a new life in a new *Bleak House*.

Richard Carstone – One of the two young wards of court. Richard looks generally smart, high-collared and young. He is good-looking and well-spoken, clean-shaven and dark-haired. He is cheerful-looking, bright-eyed and optimistic when the narrative begins. As his attempts at becoming a doctor, a lawyer and a soldier all fail, and he becomes more and more embroiled in the lawsuit in which he is a claimant, his appearance and manner change. He pays less attention to his personal appearance – his hair is unkempt, he is unshaven and his dress is more dishevelled. He deteriorates as the pressures of the case and his lack of money induce an exhausted physical and emotional breakdown. This in turn exacerbates a bout of pneumonia, leading to his death. During these last scenes, he appears deathly pale, wracked with pain and perspiration.

Ada Clare – Ada is the other ward of court in the Jarndyce affair, cousin and fiancee to Richard. She is a light-haired, pretty, chaste, sweet young woman. She is always modestly dressed, well-spoken and feminine. She usually has a friendly, innocent expression, but, in times of stress, can have an air of quiet sadness. Whenever Richard's more feckless behaviour is mentioned, she can wear an expression of fierce loyalty to him. She is easily moved to tears by the plight of the poor brickworkers, by Esther's illness, by the death of young Jo, the crossing sweeper, and, naturally, by the death of Richard.

Mr Guppy – A young law clerk working for Kenge and Carboy's, the solicitors representing Richard and Ada in the Jarndyce case. He is a sharp, ambitious and inky-fingered young man, with a bluff, rueful expression. He wears the dark coat, narrow trousers and winged collars of his profession, but his dark hair is always long and untidy, suggesting a disorganisation of his personal affairs. He speaks in a lower-class accent and his body language suggests great deference in the presence of his betters, especially Lady Dedlock, bowing clumsily and backing out of her presence with an over-elaborate show of courtesy and submission. However, he can affect an air of casual confidence in the company of those he regards as his inferiors, such as the waitress in the inn where he lunches, or Mr Krook. He is besotted by Esther Summerson on whom he bestows the wistful looks of a devoted dog; his manner towards her changes, however, when he encounters her after her illness. His shifty, downcast expression, as he attempts to avoid looking at her scarred face, betrays his disgust and horror at witnessing the destruction of what he had come to regard as perfection, thus revealing the superficial nature of his affection for her. By contrast, he can maintain a tight-lipped and fixed-gaze determination when confronted by the machinations of Mr Tulkinghorn, or by the obsequious condescension of Mercury, Lady Dedlock's footman.

GENRE

The television adaptation of *Bleak House* belongs to the familiar genre of classic or period drama. Two sub-sets of this genre are: adaptations of classic novels (*I, Claudius, Pride and Prejudice, Middlemarch, Brideshead Revisited, Little Dorrit, Bleak House, Cranford*); and series written especially for television (*Upstairs Downstairs*, *The House of Elliot*, *Edward and Mrs Simpson*). In more recent times some period dramas have taken their inspiration from a literary work, but have included storylines developed and extended by contemporary writers, such as *Lark Rise to Candleford*.

Television has also played host to dramatisations of novels belonging to the genre of historic romantic fiction or of contemporary historical novels (the Catherine Cookson novels, *Tipping the Velvet*, *Fingersmith*, *Lillies*, *Sharpe*). In addition, there are hybrid productions, such as *Lost in Austen* (see Chapter 10), which mixed contemporary comic drama with period drama and an element of science fantasy time-travel, or *Life on Mars* (see Chapter 8), which blended crime drama with science fantasy time-travel to produce a 1970s-set period piece. *Ashes to Ashes*, its sequel continues the theme by locating its characters in the early 1980s. Arguably the long-running and very successful 1960s-set police series, *Heartbeat*, located in rural North Yorkshire, is as much a piece of period nostalgia, as it is a cop drama.

Once again, it is important not to apply too strict generic rules, since one of the major features of contemporary drama is to bend the genres in order to present innovative material to its audience.

The most common generic features of period drama include:

- Period costume.

- Period hairstyles.

- Appropriate settings and locations, often based on a specific community, such as a town or village (large country houses, London slums, country estates, palaces, rural scenes, market towns, villages).

- Period interiors (furniture, fittings, paintings, domestic equipment).

- Depictions of different levels of society (upper classes, lower classes, landed aristocracy, self-made men, the poor and destitute, the criminal class, the professional class – lawyers, doctors).

- The arrival of a newcomer, often a young professional male (doctor, engineer) or a young aristocrat renting a local property.

- External threats to the community from events or developments which will change lives forever (railways, medical progress, political upheavals, modernisations of all kind).

- Relationships which defy the class and age barriers, usually when the male is older and upper class, and the female younger and lower class.

- Thwarted romantic relationships, usually where a male is constrained by a variety of different circumstances to leave a community, thus abandoning the woman with whom he is romantically involved.

- Tragic deaths of all ages, classes and genders, by accident, illness or crime.

- Select a typical period drama and identify as many of the generic features as you can from one or two specific scenes.

LITTLE DORRIT

Tom Courtenay as the deluded William Dorrit

Following the success of *Bleak House*, screenwriter Andrew Davies adapted one of Dickens' less familiar novels, *Little Dorrit*. Once again he adopted the shorter episode, serial style of its predecessor. Although it did not capture the imagination of audiences to the same extent as *Bleak House*, it still bore all the hallmarks of the classic period drama serial. It was transmitted in the late autumn of 2008, and its central themes of debt, financial corruption and the changing fortunes of families high and low struck a resonant chord with the economic circumstances of the time.

Like *Bleak House*, its central heroine is a young woman of modest origins, whose family connections form part of the core mystery of the story. Like *Bleak House*, which Dickens wrote to throw a harsh critical light on the judicial practices of his day, *Little Dorrit* was written to expose the cruelty and injustice of being imprisoned for debt, as Dickens' own father had been, the inefficiency of the civil service departments which stifled the creativity and productivity of the country, and the corrupt practices of unscrupulous financiers and businessmen who brought ruin to the ordinary people of Victorian England by embezzling their modest investments. Like *Bleak House*, *Little Dorrit* is also told from two perspectives: the affairs of the Clennam household, and the story from Little Dorrit's point-of-view.

Similarly, the production featured very well-known and established actors (Tom Courtenay, Alan Armstrong, Judy Parfitt, Robert Hardy, Bill Patterson, John Alderton, Ron

Cook, Sue Johnston, Amanda Burton, Eddie Marsan, Andy Serkis, Pam Ferris, James Fleet), younger actors who had already established themselves in film and television (Matthew MacFadyen, Eve Miles, Freema Aygeman, Russell Tovey) and a complete newcomer in the title role of Amy Dorrit – Clare Foy.

The novel had been filmed some twenty years earlier, also featuring a string of famous actors, such as Derek Jacobi, Alec Guinness, Cyril Cusack, Joan Greenwood, Patricia Hayes and a young newcomer in the title role – Sarah Pickering. The distinctive feature of the film was the fact that it was, in effect, two films – *Nobody's Fault* and *Little Dorrit's Story* – each three hours long, with many of the central events being seen from two different and contrasting perspectives. The television adaptation approached this idea by using the multi-layered narrative structure familiar from soap operas. In this way all of the connected storylines could be kept running side by side.

STORY OUTLINE

Amy Dorrit is twenty years old. She was born in the Marshalsea debtors' prison in south London, where her father, William, has been an inmate for twenty-five years, and she continues to live there, looking after him. His son, Edward, older daughter, Fanny and his brother, Frederick, visit him frequently.

Arthur Clennam is in his late thirties and has returned to London from China, where the family textiles business had a branch, managed by his father until his recent death. While travelling home, Arthur befriends the Meagles, and especially their daughter, Minnie, who are also returning to England. They all encounter a mysterious English woman, Miss Wade, who seems unusually interested in them and their business.

Amy begins working as a seamstress for Arthur's mother, a lonely old woman, living in a dark, ramshackle old house, and tended by an old servant and business partner, Flintwinch and his down-trodden wife, Affery.

Arthur returns to the family home to tell his mother that he wishes to leave the family business, work he has always hated, and set himself up in his own lodgings. He also brings her a watch, with an inscription 'Do Not Forget' on the watch paper in the case, which his father handed to him on his deathbed. He asks her for its meaning and is met with strong disapproval for his intentions and a refusal to discuss the matter further. He also notices Little Dorrit and later asks Affery who she is and why she is working for his mother. Affery has no idea why she is there. Mrs Clennam instructs Flintwinch to destroy private family papers relating to Arthur, but he decides to keep some of the important ones in a secret box which he entrusts to his twin brother.

A French criminal, Rigaud, arrives in London, chances upon the twin brother and murders him for the contents of the box which he judges to be of monetary value by threatening to reveal the contents to Arthur if Mrs Clennam does not pay him one thousand pounds.

Arthur befriends the Dorrits, and especially Amy, whom he wishes to help. Amy's father is grateful for Arthur's gifts of money, but Amy is anxious that Arthur should not yield to her father's requests for charity. Nevertheless, Arthur secretly settles a debt incurred by Amy's brother, Edward, so that he might be free of the prison. Amy guesses who might have paid off the debt and visits Arthur at his lodgings. She is beginning to fall in love with him, and is most anxious to thank the man who has set her brother free. Arthur pretends not to know of Edward's release and tells her how pleased he is to hear of it.

Amy is friendly with some of the residents of a poor lodgings quarter, called Bleeding Heart Yard, and visits there often. The landlord, Casby, is acquainted with the Clennams, Arthur having been engaged to his daughter, Flora, until his mother put a stop to the relationship and sent him to join his father in China. Casby's rent collector, Pancks, is engaged by Arthur to investigate the Dorrits' circumstances, in the hope that he might help them out of their position of debt.

Arthur meanwhile meets up with the Meagles, is invited to stay with them, and is introduced to an engineer, Doyce, with whom he goes into partnership. He is also introduced to Henry Gowan, who, it turns out, has just become engaged to the Meagles' daughter, Minnie. The Meagles disapprove of Gowan, and express their wish that Arthur should become their son-in-law. Arthur is certainly much attracted to Minnie, but she has placed her affections elsewhere. Arthur also meets Harriet, a girl adopted by the Meagles but treated like a servant by them. In her frustration and anger at her treatment she runs away to stay with Miss Wade. It turns out that Miss Wade was once engaged to Gowan, jilted by him and now seeks revenge.

Amy's sister, Fanny, is a dancer at the music hall, where their uncle, Frederick, plays the clarinet. She has formed a relationship with Edmund, the impressionable step-son of a wealthy financier, Mr Merdle. Edmund's mother seriously disapproves of this relationship and proceeds to buy off the girl with a bracelet and a dress from her couturier.

Mr Merdle is very highly regarded in the banking world and large numbers of people are encouraged to invest heavily in his financial schemes, including Doyce and Clennam, who are persuaded by Pancks that the investment is entirely sound. Doyce is encouraged by Arthur to pursue their business interests abroad, and Doyce leaves for Russia.

Pancks discovers that the Dorrits are heir to a large estate in Dorset, and Arthur delights in telling Amy and later her father the incredible news. Once his wealth is established, William Dorrit no longer wishes to associate with Arthur, despite protestations from his brother and Amy. They travel to Italy, where they encounter Mrs Merdle and her son, and Minnie, now married to Gowan, who is setting himself up as a painter. Fanny, determined to repay Mrs Merdle for her earlier insult, renews her relationship with Edmund and she marries him in order to spite his mother. Amy corresponds with Arthur, despite her father's refusal to acknowledge him as a friend of the family.

On his return from Italy, William Dorrit decides to invest his fortune in Merdle's bank. This guarantees his entrée into polite society, but he gradually loses his grip on reality as memories of his former life in prison begin to affect his thoughts and behaviour.

Merdle commits suicide when his financial schemes collapse, leaving hundreds of people in debt, including Arthur, who finds himself a prisoner in the Marshalsea, where the turnkey, Chivery, allocates Mr Dorrit's old room to him. William Dorrit returns to Italy to join Amy and his brother, but he becomes ill and subsequently dies, followed shortly by his brother. Amy returns to England to discover that all of the family's wealth has also been lost in the Merdle fiasco. She hears of Arthur's imprisonment and collapse into ill-health. She comes to look after him, pledging herself and her undying love to him, but he sends her away, unwilling to commit her to a life with a pauper.

After many intrigues, Rigaud confronts Mrs Clennam with the documents he has found in the box, especially a will which names Amy Dorrit as the benefactor of Arthur's grandfather's estate. The box also contains a letter from Arthur's real mother, a dancer who lodged with Frederick Dorrit and with whom Arthur's father had an affair which resulted in Arthur's birth. Mrs Clennam hounded the poor girl to an early death because of her husband's infidelity, and Arthur's grandfather, by way of reparation, willed his money to a child born in the Marshalsea on the same day that Arthur's real mother died. That child was Amy Dorrit. Mrs Clennam, however, kept the money which was left to Amy. It was this secret which Arthur's father insisted that his wife should 'not forget'. Amy learns of this from Arthur's mother who, miraculously, regains the power of movement, leaves her house to find Amy, begs her forgiveness and then collapses and dies, just as her old house also collapses, burying Rigaud and Flintwinch in the rubble.

Amy visits Arthur to tell him of his mother's death and finds him reading his real mother's letter from the box which has been given to him by the adopted ward of the Meagles, Harriet, who has run away to stay in Miss Wade's house. Miss Wade was asked by Rigaud to look after the box while he negotiated his price with Mrs Clennam. Amy reveals to Arthur that she is no longer rich, and that she wants nothing other than to spend the rest of her life with him. They are finally together, although Arthur is still a prisoner. Unexpectedly, Doyce appears, having returned from his business venture abroad to announce that he has been so successful that the profits will easily pay off Arthur's debts and re-establish their business in London, closed by the losses created by Merdle.

Arthur is released, and he and Amy are married.

GENRE & MISE-EN-SCÈNE

Little Dorrit conforms to the generic characteristics of period drama quoted above. The production design takes great care to reproduce the atmosphere and environments in which the action takes place:

- The Clennam household is dark, gloomy and seriously dilapidated. Frequent groans and creaks from the woodwork, and clouds of dust falling from the ceilings all indicate a house on the verge of collapse. Its inhabitants are dressed in dark, austere clothing, reflecting the tight-lipped, puritanical attitude of Mrs Clennam. Despite the supposed wealth of the family textiles business, there is no sign of warmth, comfort or a lavish lifestyle.

- The Marshalsea Prison for debt is equally gloomy and run-down, an image reflected by its impoverished inhabitants. In many ways it mirrors the Clennam household.

- The Meagles' household in Twickenham is, by contrast, a large, bright and sunny establishment, reflecting the good-natured generosity of the family.

- Bleeding Heart Yard is a collection of poor houses, workshops and stables inhabited by impoverished families and run-down businesses, rented by their occupiers and owned by Mr Casby. The rent is collected by his ruthless agent, Pancks. The overall appearance of the place is one of squalor and degradation, although some of the poor families do try to make the best of their lot.

- Casby's house, on the other hand, is refined, beautifully decorated, reflecting the wealth he accumulates from his exploited tenants. His injunction to Pancks: 'You're paid to squeeze, so squeeze them to pay' explains his whole philosophy.

- The Merdle's house is a vast monument to the wealth of the Merdle business empire. Extravagant decoration, expensive furniture, exquisite tableware, excessive staff all support the notion that the Merdles are at the very pinnacle of society.

- The hotels and fine houses inhabited by the newly-rich Dorrits, both in London and Italy, provides an opportunity to reflect the wealth and status of the family as people who enjoy a very high social status.

In common with *Bleak House*, *Little Dorrit*'s screenplay has been 'modernised' in places by Davies in order to increase its appeal to contemporary audiences. Rigaud's comment on 'zis poxy weazzer', in response to the incessant rain making his journey on foot very uncomfortable, is a case in point. Similarly, Fanny Dorrit's rather pretentious but somewhat vulgar speech often employs turns of phrase more suited to contemporary soap operas.

REPRESENTATION

Once again, the huge gallery of characters appearing in this adaptation makes it necessary to select a small sample for discussion:

Amy Dorrit – Amy is a young woman, some twenty years old. She is small and slight of stature, and modestly pretty. In keeping with her change of fortune, she has two, somewhat different, representations. Before her family inherit their wealth, she displays a completely unadorned face and hair to match the plainness of her simple dress. Outdoors she tends to wear a bonnet and cloak. Her demeanour is quiet, respectful and anxious to please, particularly her father, whom she adores and looks after as a dutiful daughter. Her sensitive nature leads her to indulge her father in his attempts to maintain the pretence of status within the prison. She has the overall appearance of a servant girl.

William Dorrit – Amy's father, the self-styled 'Father of the Marshalsea' on account of the length of his stay in the prison (twenty-five years), is some sixty plus years old. He wears the smartest clothes he can manage, but his unkempt hair and sideburns, together with a general air of shabbiness betray his poverty. He behaves with kindness towards his family, especially Amy, but can often display considerable selfishness and a self-centred concern for his own position, treating Amy as a servant. He ingratiates himself with visitors, exploiting an over-zealous politeness towards them in order to secure gifts of money from them when they depart. He presents an air of refinement, believing that he is working hard to keep up a position within the prison for all of his family, but the effect is one of self-delusion, which the sensitive Amy pretends not to notice.

Analyse the representation of Amy and William Dorrit after they have inherited their fortune and have left the Marshalsea Prison. Consider their clothes, hairstyles, manner of speaking, attitudes towards others, especially with regard to matters of class and status.

Arthur Clennam – A youthful-looking man in his late thirties, with a kind and gentle expression, sober of dress representing a businessman of comfortable means. He can appear bemused at times, particularly when confronted with people or situations which he does not altogether understand – his mother's rejection of him, Pancks' puzzling conundrums concerning the Dorrits, Rigaud's cavalier behaviour towards Mrs Clennam, Flora's mildly flirtatious behaviour, for example. His love for Minnie Meagles is shown by his attentive behaviour towards her. His general manner is one of thoughtful and genuine benevolence.

Mrs Clennam – An elderly woman apparently confined to a wheelchair. She wears plain, dark clothing, and her expression is serious and, for the most part, lacking in emotion. Her mode of speaking is sharp, often betraying a deep-seated anger. She seems unable to show any love towards her son, Arthur, and is often antagonistic towards him, her partner and servant, Flintwinch, and her housekeeper, Affery. She does show some slight kindness towards Amy Dorrit. Her tight-lipped disapproval of almost everything, together with her conviction of her own innocence and the failings of others, all contribute to our understanding of her as the 'hammer-headed woman' that Flintwinch accuses her of being during one of their many arguments.

Fanny Dorrit – Amy's sister, Fanny, is represented in this adaptation as a flighty, selfish, vulgar airhead. She is always seen with an excess of cheap, tarty make-up, and flashy clothes, as befits her role as a dancer at the music hall. She could actually be pretty, but the extravagant nature of her overall appearance tends to create an impression of hardness. Her manner towards others tends to be bossy and dismissive, especially towards her eventual husband, Edmund Sparkler. His naïve view of her as a 'damn fine girl, with no begod nonsense about her' is ironically so far from the truth.

IDEOLOGY AND PERIOD DRAMA

Since many period dramas are adaptations of novels or plays produced at specific dates in the past, they are very likely, and in some cases deliberately designed, to reflect the ideological concerns of their authors. We have already seen how Dickens intentionally used some of his novels to expose what he regarded as the social and political ills of his day. In *Bleak House*, the labyrinthine structures of the legal system and its impact on all classes of people came under close scrutiny, and in for firm criticism. In *Little Dorrit* we meet the twin evils of imprisonment for debt and the red-taped bureaucracy of totally inefficient government departments, both of which lead to the ruin of good, innocent people. Such novels, then, can be seen as social critiques, and their television adaptations might well be opportunely used to throw light on current problems, as well as help us to understand the issues of previous generations.

Dickens also seems to have explored other themes and ideas prevalent in his day. In both *Little Dorrit* and *Bleak House* there is an ongoing emphasis on the integrated nature of society, where every cog, every wheel, every part of the social machine works together to create a social whole. It is not surprising that such imagery should emerge and be popular at a time when the economic stability of the times depended on the machinery of the industrial revolution and the technological developments of the day.

Period dramas, however, may also be said to exhibit their own intrinsic ideologies. For example, they appear to promote notions of the past as a site for historical reassurance – things were simpler, safer, more understandable, less threatening then, and, because such narratives are usually resolved with 'happy endings', they offer a kind of closure which real life so often fails to provide. For example, Dickens' highly contrived, intricately woven plots eventually connect all the narrative strands and loose ends to create a satisfyingly integrated conclusion.

Such adaptations also seem to project notions that the people of the past were, in most major ways, not so very different from 'us', and such notions seek to promote an historical continuum, which might serve to reassure us of our own place in the greater scheme of things.

What period dramas, arguably, do not do, is challenge any of the apparent established conventions of the periods they are representing. For example, class and gender divisions are still one of the major ideological structures of period drama, and, where they are not challenged by the original work, no critique is usually offered by the adaptation. The lower classes usually defer to the upper classes; females usually defer to males; the young usually defer to their elders.

A good example of this in *Little Dorrit* is the fluctuating relationship between Amy and Arthur:

- At first Arthur is financially comfortable and belongs to the business class; Amy is the daughter of a pauper and has to work as a lowly paid seamstress.

- Relationship possibility = zero.

- Arthur loses his company's money and ends up as a destitute inmate of the debtor's prison; Amy is now the daughter of a rich man, whose inheritance can easily support his entire family.

- Relationship possibility = zero.

- Arthur discovers he is the orphan of a long-dead, unmarried dancer and his now dead father, but his fortunes are restored by the success of his friend and partner, Doyce; Amy is now an orphan, having lost her mother soon after she was born, and her father more recently, and is also a pauper, having lost all her money in Merdle's collapse.

- Relationship possibility = zero.

- Amy then discovers she is entitled to the legacy left to her by Arthur's grandfather, and can, therefore, claim her inheritance; Arthur is now a wealthy businessman again.

- Relationship possibility = 100%!

Despite the apparent equality of their respective statuses, however, Amy is still happy to have her task of looking after Arthur. Some might argue that the disparity in their ages means that Amy has merely swapped her duty of care to one older man, her father, for a duty of care to another older man, Arthur. All of her previous expressions of such duty suggest that she is at her best and happiest when caring for someone else. This story is as much about emotional and psychological imprisonment, as it is about physical imprisonment.

There is no doubt that Davies intended his version of *Bleak House* to resonate with current issues. The problem of straitened economic circumstances is certainly one. Possibly the cult of celebrity is another. Merdle is courted by all levels of society for his business acumen, and feted by the wealthy as one of their own, only to be quickly condemned after his death and his empire has collapsed. Similarly, Fanny and Amy are tutored in the airs and graces of upper-class society, much as WAGS now have to make the transition from ordinary women to international celebrities. It is telling that Amy can see through the whole charade, whereas Fanny laps it all up, thinking that Merdle's step-son is her ticket to fame and fortune.

Political corruption and indolence, characterised by the Circumlocution Office, have probably never been off the agenda of writers campaigning for social and political change, but, as many politicians at the time of writing (June 2009) have been facing investigation for inappropriate financial practices with regard to their expense claims, it seems likely that Davies' focus is equally sharp in this area as well.

- It was one of the BBC's aims with *Bleak House* and *Little Dorrit* to make the adaptations accessible to a wider audience familiar with soap opera. Analyse some sequences from both adaptations in order to identify any similarities with soap opera conventions and generic characteristics.

- Explore the use of camera and lighting styles in the two adaptations in order to understand how these technical codes make meaning for the audience.

CHAPTER EIGHT — *LIFE ON MARS & ASHES TO ASHES*

'Take a look at the lawman...' – Hunt, Tyler and Cartright (l-r: Philip Glennister, John Simm and Liz White) in Life on Mars

LIFE ON MARS

In January 2006, one of the most innovative and intriguing pieces of TV drama for some time arrived on our screens. Ostensibly a police drama, *Life on Mars* uses all the familiar generic conventions of a contemporary cop show and then adds to them all the conventions of police series from the 1970s, some features we might expect to find in a sci-fi strand about time-travelling, and makes the total confection look and sound like a complex post-modern psychological thriller.

Life on Mars is the creation of Matthew Graham and Ashley Pharaoh who met while working as writers for *EastEnders*. Their intention was to produce an up-beat but serious police thriller, and to use the time-travelling device as a way of exploring how much has changed in British society over the last thirty-odd years by the familiar dislocation technique of placing a contemporary central character (Sam Tyler) in the unfamiliar environment of the 1970s policing scene in Manchester. Graham is on record as stating that the 'coma' motif came later, when it became clear that another dramatic dimension could be developed from Sam's disorientation, and his conviction that he was from 'somewhere else', i.e. his own mind.

GENERIC FEATURES

For students of television drama *Life on Mars* is a gift. It features an affectionate and, at times, humorous pastiche of 1970s TV cop series such as *The Sweeney*, with spectacular car chases, action-adventure sequences, and a central, tight-knit buddy-pairing – for Regan & Carter, read Hunt & Tyler; it also makes more than passing references to contemporary police and hospital dramas, such as *The Bill* and *Holby City*; it is also a taut psychological mystery thriller; it is a love story of sorts about Sam's relationship with WPC Annie Cartright, as well as with his present-day girlfriend, Maya; it taps into the time-travelling theme from *Doctor Who*, *Back to the Future* (1985), *Crime Traveller*; and it's a 'dislocation' drama, where the central character is placed deliberately in unfamiliar environments; it could also be seen as a social satire on prevailing attitudes to political correctness, multi-ethnic communities and the clash of cultures, then and now. On top of all this, it also finds every opportunity to showcase classic tracks from the 1970s.

After a familiar beginning involving some contemporary police work at a crime scene and back at the station, the leading DCI, Sam Tyler, distraught by the apparent kidnap of his girlfriend (fellow police officer, Maya) is suddenly and shockingly knocked down by a passing car and wakes up in 1973. As he puts it in the introduction to each subsequent episode: 'Am I mad, in a coma, or back in time?'

Apart from one confused copper on the beat who first discovers him and can make no sense of Sam's references to his 'Jeep' ('a military vehicle?'), his 'mobile' ('mobile what?'), his arrival in 1973 seems to have been expected by his new colleagues – he is, it appears, on transfer from Hyde (a suburb of Manchester) as a detective inspector, and has been allocated to DCI Hunt's section.

From then on both Series 1 and 2 focus on two quite distinct but overlapping storylines: Sam's attempts to integrate with his new colleagues and their involvement with 1970s policing in Manchester; and his attempts to understand what has happened to him and how he might achieve his goal of returning to his own time.

In the first of the twin themes Sam joins Gene Hunt and the other detectives in a series of crime-solving storylines, and is frequently appalled by the violent, sexist, racist way that Hunt deals with criminals and suspects, not to mention half of his own force. Sam and Hunt clearly have a love-hate relationship, and, despite his seniority, Sam's attitude, judgment and skills are frequently called into question by his junior colleagues. This disjuncture between life as it is in 1973, and Sam's attempts to understand how it is, form an edgy and mercurial backdrop to the criminal activities he finds himself involved with.

In the second theme, Sam is repeatedly surrounded by all manner of references to his situation and how he might seek to escape from it. The television in Sam's flat, for example, is definitely in on the act. The old 1970s test card with the little girl, the clown and the balloon sometimes talks to him. The scary little girl also appears to him in his room, carrying her clown and balloon. Other TV programmes make direct reference to him; presenters speak directly to him from the screen, such as the maths lecturer, with his 1970s haircut and clothes, in an Open University production.

Sam also hears unusual broadcasts on the police radio system referring to him as being in what seems to be described as a coma. In fact, the 'coma' explanation of Sam's state apparently holds sway for much of the first series, and his actual situation is not resolved, leaving the story open for the second and last series.

These two parallel themes occasionally intersect, and when they do, the dramatic force and tension increase considerably. One particular example of this intersection occurs in the last episode of Series 1, when Sam forms part of a team assigned to track down an elusive and rather shady young man mixed up in a murder, only to confront his own father, who walked out on the family when Sam was very young, the reason for which Sam can now understand.

A further occasion occurs in Series 2. The team are investigating what appears to be a drug-related killing, but Sam is convinced that the murder is racially motivated. The victim is a Ugandan Asian who runs a record shop. His white girl-friend, a bank clerk, had been helping with the accounts. Sam befriends her and discovers two facts about her which send him reeling – she is pregnant, and she is about to be the mother of Maya, Sam's girlfriend in 2005. These small coincidences, together with others (Sam also encounters his Auntie Heather in a murder enquiry, and his mother while investigating a corrupt night-club owner) help to build a personal context for him in 1973, and also serve to heighten the dramatic tension as Sam is brought face to face with his own life thirty years before.

REPRESENTATION

It could be argued that sexism hadn't been 'invented' in 1973, and that our response to the behaviour and attitudes of the 1970s cops, filtered through Sam's contemporary observations, is inevitably coloured by what we now know about sexism in particular, and political correctness in general. Hunt and co. are merely behaving as many men did in 1973, and Sam's reactions are obviously seen as strange and incomprehensible to them.

All the characters, their settings and locations are deliberately designed to reflect the fashions and environments of 1970s Manchester. Longer hairstyles, flares, wide lapel jackets and fashionable ties for the men all help to create an accurate sense of period. Choice of dialogue, with generous helpings of the slang of the time, firmly roots the action in a time when casual conversation and contemporary buzzwords were different from those in use today. Every object, from clunky dial phones to the new-fangled cassette recorders, looks as though it has come from the relevant 'heritage' museum to dress the set with 1970s period atmosphere.

Female fashion similarly reflects the extravagant designs and flamboyant colours of the day, although the female characters' more marginal roles within the drama tend to mirror their marginality within society at the time. Germaine Greer's feminist work *The Female Eunuch* may have been published three years before Sam turns up in Gene Hunt's macho world, and Hunt himself may use the title merely as a further way to insult and belittle Annie Cartright, but male attitudes towards women at this time had changed little as a result of such publications.

Being set in Manchester allows the writers to have a field day with police attitudes to ethnic minorities. 'Pakis' are viewed as a troublesome group of immigrants, always ready to screw the system, the Irish workforce are all regarded as undercover members of the IRA, while 'blacks' are represented as comic figures right out of the 'Uncle Tom' portrayals in American movies. In order to avoid being the butt of racist jokes from his colleagues, a new black officer, obviously lacking in confidence, introduces himself by cracking all the 'nigger' jokes first. In this particular instance we find out from Sam's knowledge of the 'future' that this officer will, in fact, go on to become one of the most respected senior officers in the Manchester force, and Sam's future mentor. Sam is understandably horrified by the way this future leader of police attempts to ingratiate his junior self with his overtly racist 'colleagues'. It is noticeable in this scene that Annie, no doubt taking her lead from Sam, whom she respects and tries desperately to understand, does not take part in this behaviour.

NARRATIVE

The narrative is littered with clues about its meaning, some deliberate red herrings, others hitting the nail on the head. DCI Gene Hunt's very name suggests some sort of a game for Sam to search for a possible parentage, but this proves not to be the case. Sam has been transferred from Hyde, suggesting a link with the horror/thriller *Dr Jekyll and Mr Hyde*, the nineteenth-century story of a man with a split-personality which is out of control. A mysterious senior officer, who seems to be helping Sam to 'get home', i.e. back to the future, is called Frank Morgan, the name of the American film actor who played The Wizard in the classic musical, *The Wizard of Oz*. In the film it is The Wizard who helps Dorothy return home to her beloved Kansas. One of Gene Hunt's favourite insults for Sam is to call him Dorothy.

The drama also contains a wide array of narrative enigmas, of which the opening question posed by Sam is the most pervasive. Although the crime-story segment of the narrative tends to get resolved at the end of each separate episode, the resolution of the overall enigma of Sam's presence in 1973 is not that clear-cut. Audiences are left to draw their own conclusions about the ending. And that ending was final – no 'Christmas Specials', no third series.

Except that it wasn't, quite; instead, *Life on Mars* borrows a neat idea from the old BBC police series from the 1960s and 1970s, *Z-Cars*, which spawned a spin-off in the shape of *Softly, Softly*, featuring some of the senior characters from the original series. In *Ashes to Ashes* (see below), it is goodbye to Sam Tyler, but it's hello to a new sidekick for Gene Hunt, now transferred to London in the 1980s. And this sidekick, too, finds herself (that's right, her-self) transported back in time from her contemporary role as a police officer in today's Met. She's DI Alex Drake, a psychological profiler, who is kidnapped along with her daughter and suffers a dreadful accident, leaving her trapped in 1981. Once again, a clash of policing styles and strong personalities will generate the necessary conflict to fuel the dramatic momentum.

So what makes *Life on Mars* such an outstanding piece of TV drama? These are arguably some of the contributory features; you may well think of others:

- Strong characters, full of idiosyncrasies which prevent them becoming stereotypes, played by an excellent cast of actors.

- Convincing production design which gets its 'period feel' right.

- A good balance between action sequences and psychological drama.

- Powerful storylines for each episode.

- A nice contrast between classic 'cop TV' and contemporary police drama.

- An enigmatic and intriguing theme running through both series.

- A successful combination of the serious and the comic, just like real life.

- First-class writing in every episode.

ANALYSING THE SCRIPT

One way of looking at how a TV drama sequence works is to analyse the script. The following sequence covers Sam's arrival in 1973, courtesy of the car accident. He has just discovered that the suspect he's been tailing seems to have kidnapped his girlfriend, Maya. Sam is understandably upset.

NOTE: This script is taken from an amended shooting version, but is not necessarily an accurate version of the final broadcast programme. For example, scene 19, overleaf, actually takes place in daylight in the broadcast version.

17 I/E. SAM'S JEEP – DAY 1/1 14:00

SAM at the wheel – distressed, but keeping a lid on it. 'Life on Mars' plays softly over his iPod. He brakes hard. The music floats around him as he tries to marshal his thoughts and feelings. He steps out of the car. Leans against it to pull in some clearing air. He is close to tears. He steps back to compose himself. A car smacks into him at speed and in half a second SAM is thrown down the street like a scarecrow full of straw. It's shockingly sudden.

[Sam's distress is clearly reflected in his body language. The abduction of his girlfriend by this villain has hit him hard – which is precisely how the car hits him, taking him into another time. The diegetic music playing on the iPod provides another dimension to his stress, but the juxtaposition of 1970s music playing on a piece of contemporary technology also serves to emphasise the clash of times and cultures inherent in the drama itself. Sam's vehicle is a 4x4, a big car for a big city. The surrounding concrete and tarmac environment also reinforces the urban location. Sam's emotional state, the hard-edged surroundings and the brutality of the hit-and-run all lead the audience to expect a hard-hitting piece of gritty realism.]

18 EXT. MANCUNIAN ROAD – DAY 1/1 CONTINUOUS

SAM is thrown in a tangle across the tarmac. 'Life on Mars' builds on the soundtrack. A short series of cuts brings us closer to SAM, as he lapses into unconsciousness.

19 EXT. WOODS – NIGHT – FLASHBACK

FLASH SHOTS – Woods at night. POV of a young boy – looking down at his own page-boy shoes pushing through the grass – brass buckles catching the moonlight. Looking up through the dancing branches at the stars. Magical. Serene. The boy's hands reach up for the stars in the sky.

TOTAL BLACKNESS. TOTAL SILENCE.

[This enigmatic sequence, visited at times throughout the episodes, is a reference to Sam's boyhood experience of the day when he last saw his father. It will become clear in a later episode that Sam is taking part in a wedding, and it is from the reception that his father absents himself. Its unexpected appearance here seems to comment on the time when Sam was left abandoned, as he is now.]

20 EXT. ROAD – DAY 1/2 14:20

SAM unconscious on dusty ground. He is wearing a dated brown leather jacket and bell-bottom cords. 'Life on Mars' can still be heard playing. SAM lifts his head. The music is coming from the 8-track playing in the Ford Granada that he is lying beside. The door is open. SAM heads towards the car. A COPPER arrives. There is something about his uniform that isn't quite right. He also has a large radio transmitter around his neck. COPPER helps SAM to his feet.

[We now have to make some sense, without explanation, of the fact that Sam is wearing 70s clothes, the music continues to play, but the technology playing it (8-track cassette player) is thirty years out of date, as is the car. As Sam begins to look around this unfamiliar place, the camera circles him slowly at a low angle, emphasising his isolation and detachment from the location, and allowing the audience to register his appearance. Even the supposedly reassuring arrival of a policeman is anything but, since his uniform is 'wrong', he fails to understand Sam's utterances, and his communications technology is a little behind the times.]

COPPER   What happened? Did you not see the signs?

SAM realises that he is standing in roadworks. A development plot for the very same road he was driving on moments ago. A road which now seems to be in the process of being built.

COPPER   Do you remember what happened sir? [Beat] Sir, can you tell me what happened?

SAM gawps at the Granada.

SAM   This ... This isn't my car. I was driving ... I was driving a jeep.

COPPER   You were driving a military vehicle?

[Sam's reference to his 4x4 confuses the beat bobby, who is represented as a matter-of-fact, unimaginative jobsworth, and is the first of many instances where he talks about things, events, places that have not yet come into being. The audience is receiving the first glimmer of what might be going on here.]

He removes paperwork from the car.

SAM   Just hang ... what's going on?

COPPER   Can I ask if you've been drinking?

SAM   I'm not drunk.

COPPER   Says here you're on transfer from C Division in Hyde. Detective Inspector.

[This common script device allows some of Sam's details to be conveyed to the audience, and to Sam himself.]

SAM   What? I'm a DCI. What the hell are you ..? I need my mobile.

COPPER   Your mobile what?

SAM   My phone.

COPPER   You brought your own telephone from Hyde?

[This short exchange introduces another riddle for the copper, as modern terminology gets in the way of understanding. It also introduces the notion of 'Hyde', both as Sam's place of origin, but also as a reference to the 'Jekyll & Hyde' idea of a split personality. This is one of the many 'clues' to Sam's identity and purpose scattered all over every episode of both series of the drama.]

The COPPER unstraps the bulky Pye Pocket Phone from his shirt.

COPPER   Eight- Six-Zero to Alpha One. Hello?

SAM has had enough. He strides away from the scene.

COPPER   No, hang on sir! Come back .. sir!

SAM breaks into a trot. He crosses the street. Above him looms a giant billboard with an artist's impression of the Mancunian Way and the words 'Opening Soon'.

COPPER   Come back here!

SAM breaks into a run.

[The old-style technology may work, but all Sam has to do to escape is run away, and the beat copper is useless. The billboard illustration is another short-hand device to reinforce the date and location of this scene. This is a good example of how different audiences will respond differently to a media text. For non-Mancunians, this location will simply mean somewhere, some time in the past; for locals it will root the scene precisely in time and place, and will remind older viewers of the trials and frustrations of trying to drive around Manchester before the road was built.]

21 EXT. SAM'S RUN – DAY 1/2 CONTINUOUS

SAM pelting through streets of old terraces. Collapses against a lamp post. Becomes aware of the cars parked nearby – Hillmans, Vauxhalls, Austins. He catches a glimpse of himself in the wing mirror of one of the cars. He crouches down to study his reflection and notices the change in his image for the first time. He rifles through his pockets and pulls out a police 'badge' – a leather wallet containing a card with the name SAM TYLER.

[The makes of the parked cars, the appearance of the shops and the streets, and Sam's very 70s clothing are further clues to the period. The production design laid great emphasis on the accuracy of its recreation of 1973.]

22 SCENE 22 OMITTED

23 EXT. POLICE STATION – DAY 1/2 14:50

SAM stands sweaty and panting staring in astonishment at numerous black bicycles that are lined up outside. A Panda car pulls out.

[Further examples of the period set dressing.]

He marches on. Pushes through dirty swing doors –

26 INT. POLICE STATION – CID – DAY 1/2 CONTINUOUS 26

A DOZEN CID stop and stare. Most are smoking. The air is opaque with it. Page 3 girls jostle for space with crime scene photos. Desks over-flow with ash-trays, coffee cups and paperwork. Most officers are dressed in cheap suits flecked with dandruff flurrys. The younger ones sport tight-fitting leather jackets. They look pallid and cynical. They are all and I mean ALL chewing gum. Every fibre of SAM'S being tries to assimilate this. A gangly, affable DC (CHRIS SKELTON) approaches.

CHRIS DC Chris Skelton. Plod's bringing in your stuff. One of the girls'll sort out your RTA. Don't sweat it if you've had a couple of stiff ones. Blimey, you look like you gone ten rounds with Big Henry.

SAM pushes by.

CHRIS   Someone needs to take a look at you, Boss. You're as white as a ginger bird's arse.

DS RAY CARLING   There's that nice little plonk on the next floor. Cartright?

CHRIS   She could kiss it better.

SAM (loud)   Shut up!

> [Sam's confusion has been largely caused up to this point by what he has seen and heard. For the first time he is now addressed by his new colleagues. They are clearly expecting him, and the details of his arrival – RTA, etc. – seem to be generally known. The sexist banter between Chris and Ray is offensive to twenty-first-century Sam, as he at least remembers his diversity training. However, he also seems to find the general untidiness irritating. The smoking, the pin-ups, the chaotic mounds of paper and coffee cups all point the audience towards an understanding of this place as one of disorganisation and inefficiency. We are meant to question with Sam how any good policing could ever get done in this rat's maze.]

Their good humour fades. SAM is standing with his back to an office which has the blinds down.

SAM   I don't know who the hell you lot think you are but this is my office. Right here (points into thin air). There's a door .. here. My desk. Here.

He looks down to see on the desk a calendar girl photo – all tits and arse.

SAM   Where's my desk? Where's my desk? Chair. PC terminal ...

RAY   Who? You want a constable up here?

SAM   What the hell is going on? This is my department! What have you done with it. ...?!!

CHRIS   Ssshhh! Keep it down, Boss.

RAY   Too late.

> [Sam expresses his frustration through his constant questioning, revealing again the disjuncture between his unexpected arrival in 1973 and his colleagues' matter-of-fact response to this bizarre situation.]

Movement from within the office. SAM steps back. DCI GENE HUNT emerges like a bear from a cave. He shoves an Embassy No6 into his mouth.

SAM (calming himself)   All right. Okay .. surprise me, what year is this supposed to be?

GENE grabs SAM'S arm, steers him into the office.

GENE   Word in your shell-like pal.

27 INT. POLICE STATION – GENE'S OFFICE – DAY 1/2 CONTINUOUS

SAM   wrestles free and rounds on GENE.

SAM   Big mistake!

GENE   Yeah? What about this?

He pushes SAM violently against the pre-fab wall which trembles. Clock, shelf, dartboard, darts trophies and notice-board all fall off the wall. GENE leers into SAM'S face. SAM grips GENE'S collars.

SAM   Get off me …

GENE   They reckon you got concussion. Well I don't give a tart's furry cup if half your brains are falling out. You don't ever waltz into my kingdom acting the king of the jungle.

SAM   Who do you think you are?

GENE   Gene Hunt. Your DCI. And it's 1973. Almost dinner time. I'm having hoops.

GENE'S face is inches from him. Quiet, gravelly menace.

The final two scenes of this sequence are a good example of how such dramas set character by the use of terse, punchy, elliptical dialogue. Gene's very first line contains no article or verb, or even an explanation of what 'shell-like' is, signing off with an ironic 'pal'. This man has no time to waste, enjoys a bit of wordplay, sarcasm and irony, and likes to use a seemingly polite overture before going for the throat. But then, 'Excuse me, but could I have a word with you, young man' doesn't have the same dramatic effect.

His physical response to Sam's behaviour is equally punchy – you do not mess with this man. His third speech is a brilliantly economic way of communicating his whole approach to life:

- He can acknowledge the facts of a situation.

- He can express his opinion about it in very basic, often vulgar language.

- He can issue his instructions in a very clear and unambiguous way.

- He can make it crystal clear that he is in charge, and that his rule is unashamedly despotic.

Even before we know who he is, his character has been accurately delineated for us.

His fourth speech spells out the detail, moving from the vital (name, rank), to the inconsequential (time, lunch menu), but surrounding the absolutely crucial piece of information for Sam ('and it's 1973'). In fact, the last three statements move, almost at the speed of light, from the earth-shattering (1973) to the banal (I'm having hoops). This last reference, to Heinz Spaghetti Hoops, is also revealing. These were meant to be for children, as a way of getting them to eat pasta. Such a meal was also meant to be quick, convenient, for people without much time to spare. Gene's choice, therefore, might suggest something of the over-grown child, who doesn't put eating very high on his list of priorities. There was also something of the 'junk-food' label about them, rooting them in a working-class diet.

- Choose a sequence from the script of a current police/crime drama and explore the way it uses the dialogue to convey situation and character.

ASHES TO ASHES

'I'm stuck with a valuable friend...'
– Philip Glennister reprising Hunt, with Keeley Hawes as Alex Drake

Following the success of *Life on Mars*, Graham and Pharaoh were prevailed upon to create a sequel. Having returned Sam Tyler to his 1973 existence, it was necessary to invent a new period and a new foil for Hunt. The 1980s seemed obvious – still far enough away to be thought of as another country, but quite distinct from the early 1970s. Gene Hunt, Ray Carling and Chris Skelton have been transferred to the Met, so we now have different locations to enjoy, and a new policewoman, Shaz Granger, has been introduced to provide a love-interest for Chris. Into their busy, metropolitan world comes DI Alex Drake. She has been shot in a dramatic stand-off, and has been taken back in time to 1981.

Like Sam, she is now in a coma in the present-day world. In 1981 she wakes up in the middle of an illegal sex and drugs party on a Thames cruiser, dressed as a high-class prostitute. She stumbles off the boat and comes face to face with the three detectives summoned to deal with the party. The fact that they are Hunt, Carling and Skelton, Sam Tyler's old colleagues, is enough to make her faint. She spends much of the rest of the first episode attempting to work out what has happened to her. Her university education and psychological training cause her to talk in academic language, which mystifies Hunt and the others. Because she has spent so much time studying Tyler's case, she starts to believe that her new colleagues and the environment they inhabit are a psychological construct of her unconscious mind. Needless to say, Hunt can make nothing sensible out of the thoughts she involuntarily puts into words.

At the time of writing, *Ashes to Ashes* has just completed a second series, and a third is planned. The second series ended with Drake being shot and sent into a coma in 1982, while her 2009 self wakes up from the coma she succumbed to at the beginning of Series 1, only to discover that every screen in the hospital has an image of Gene Hunt calling out her name.

Just like Sam, Alex experiences personal messages from her TV set. Characters from popular shows of the day, such as Zippy and George from the children's programme, *Rainbow*, speak to her directly. Even Hunt himself appears as a presenter on the story-time show, *Jackanory*, although he retains his bad-tempered and aggressive persona, threatening to stamp on the children's toys, if they don't listen. This last comment is a direct reference to *Life on Mars*, where he forces kids to watch his parked car for him, threatening to stamp on their toys if they fail.

Just like Sam, Alex is obsessed with finding out how she got to the 1980s, and with finding a way to get back. She is particularly distressed by the thought of her daughter, Molly, being left alone. She is convinced that she has returned to 1981 for a specific purpose. In fact, she learns in the final episode of Series 1 how and why her parents died, witnessing their deaths both as her present-day self and as the young girl she was at the time.

Just like Sam, Alex applies her twenty-first-century skills, knowledge and experience to the policing expected of her in the early 1980s; this, of course, leads to inevitable confusion and mistrust on the part of her colleagues. Nevertheless, Hunt seems to derive some kind of benefit from his sidekick's eccentricities.

NARRATIVE

The storylines of *Ashes to Ashes*, like its predecessor's, continue to concentrate on urban crime and police corruption, culminating at the end of Series 2 with alleged police involvement in the real Brink's Mat gold bullion robbery in 1983.

The narrative structure follows the usual pattern for linear narratives, with the main story told in chronological order. However, the present-time narrative flow is interrupted at intervals by flashbacks to Alex Drake's own narrative concerning her injury and comatose state. There are also occasions when these two narratives coincide, when the present meets the future — Alex witnessing her own parents' death as an adult and as a child, for example, at the end of Series 1.

The narrative pace is usually fast-moving, sometimes elliptical, and always moving forward relentlessly. There are slower moments for reflection and consolidation, but these serve to provide variations, and are often connected with Alex Drake's personal story.

In Series 2, Episode 8, a 'countdown' device is employed to remind Alex and the audience that time is running out. It is provided by on-screen reminders of the level of infection control being deployed to bring Alex out of her present-day coma. It is expressed in millilitres, but actually fits the passing of real-time minutes in the episode. For example, when 10ml appears on Alex's TV screen, it is approximately ten minutes into the episode; when 50ml appears, the action of the sixty-minute episode is approaching its climax.

In this way the progress of the narrative line can be followed quite literally on the screen as the action rushes to its conclusion

CAMERA, EDITING & *MISE-EN-SCENE*

The design, shooting and editing styles of these two shows re-work a number of filmic and televisual strands. They borrow lighting styles from the conventions of 1940s/1950s *film noir*; action sequences from action-adventure films of all periods; imagery from TV cop series of the 1970s; editing pace from more contemporary crime series.

ANALYSIS OF A KEY SCENE SERIES 2, EPISODE 8

Gene Hunt and his team are embroiled in an attempt to discover the precise nature of an imminent crime. While Alex Drake is questioning a suspect, Gene Hunt takes a break in his office.

The sequence opens with a CU of two whisky tumblers on Hunt's desk. One has a shot already in it, the other contains dregs. The camera tilts up to an MCU of Hunt pouring the dregs into the second glass.

[This is a slower-paced series of shots, helping us to understand Hunt as he tries to figure out what form the imminent crime could possibly take, with the aid of alcohol. He is shown here as someone who can be thoughtful, but his recourse to whisky as an aid suggests an isolated man, who needs support, but finds it hard to trust people. All the camera shots in this sequence are hand-held, but camera movement is minimal, although somewhat edgy at times, as if it doesn't quite know where to look.]

As he picks up the glass, we see a CU of it and a tape cassette on the desk, which he also picks up. His expression suggests that he has not seen it before. We cut to a low-angle CU of Hunt looking at the tape. We cut to a CU of him grabbing a cassette player from the shelf behind him, which he puts on his desk, inserts the tape and presses the 'play' button.

[We understand Hunt has only just seen the tape and does not know what it represents. With the exceptions noted below, Hunt is always shot from a low-angle camera position during this sequence, as if to suggest his dominating influence, and also, possibly, to place the audience in a subservient position to him. The cassette-player, now old-fashioned to a modern audience, is an intertextual reference which will remind those familiar with *Life on Mars* how difficult it was for Sam Tyler to convince Hunt how important tape recordings will become for modern policing. Eight years later, he seems to be using them without question.]

We cut to another low-angle CU of Hunt, whisky glass in hand, listening to the contents of the tape. It is the voice of Alex Drake, recording her innermost thoughts on Hunt, her situation both here and in the future. She comments on his centrality to her position, but how difficult it is to communicate with him, since he seems to pose a threat to her, which she doesn't specify.

[The use of voice-over is often a non-diegetic device, enabling the audience to hear important thoughts which others cannot. Here, the voice-over is diegetic and enables both Hunt and the audience to hear what Alex really thinks about her situation and the person she is working with.]

We see a CU of the player as Hunt presses the stop button. We cut to a low-angle CU of Hunt looking even more thoughtful. The camera tilts up to reveal a CU of Hunt listening even more intently to the recording. Her account is somewhat disjointed, failing to complete sentences and nail important detail. There are further cuts back and forth between Hunt and the player.

[The CUs of both Hunt and the player suggest that this listening sequence is a kind of very intimate exchange between Drake and himself. It is the closest he has come to hearing something of the truth from his enigmatic colleague.]

We cut to a shot of the inside of the office door, with Drake in the distance walking towards it; further cuts between the door and Hunt, still listening. Cut to Drake opening the door and facing Hunt, shot from low-angle. Cut to a CU of Hunt looking up at her, no emotion on his face. Cut to low-angle CU of Drake explaining the nature of the imminent crime, warning him that officers at the highest level are involved and that he should trust no one.

[The shots of Drake approaching the door from outside suggest that she is about to interrupt something private, which is, indeed, the case. However, she cannot know that she will actually interrupt a very private exchange between her recorded self and Hunt. The low-angle shots of Drake provide us with a Hunts-eye view of her, which reinforce for us how he is to react to her, given what he has heard.]

CU of Hunt as he responds to Drake's mention of trust by repeating the word. Cut to a low-angle mid-shot as he removes the tape from the player, stands up and walks round the desk to confront Drake face to face. When he stands to face her, he asks why she thinks he is a threat – a direct reference to what he has heard on the tape, which catches her by surprise. Hunt forces Drake to tell him the truth, which she begins to do in a sequence of shot-reverse-shot cuts.

[The CU of Hunt as he repeats the word 'trust' allows us to see the deliberate and controlled expression on his face – no sense of anger or confrontation as yet. The shot-reverse-shot sequence follows the conventional conversational exchange, used to present all kinds of different atmospheres, from close intimacy to hostile confrontation. We are still not sure what sort of exchange is taking place here.]

Suddenly we cut to a two-shot as Alex makes the bald statement 'I'm from the future'. We cut back to the shot-reverse-shot sequence as she tells Hunt how the bullet put her in a coma and she awoke to find herself in his world. Hunt listens and then tells her that she is 'pissing in his face', insulting his intelligence with her fantasies. She pleads with him to understand. We hear a romantic theme in the background. We cut to a CU of the tape, which he hands back to her, dismissing her from his office. She leaves; CU on Hunt as he continues to reflect on this 'confession of truth' from Drake.

[After the close-up intimacy of their exchanges, the sudden cut to a medium two-shot comes as something of a surprise, and fits Drake's statement of truth 'I'm from the future'. Finally the truth is out and they face one another in the light of it. As Alex pleads with Hunt, it is as though they are lovers, with Hunt accusing her of an infidelity, and Drake claiming that she is telling him the absolute truth. A last CU of the tape as Hunt hands it to Drake is almost where we came in, although at the beginning of the sequence it was an enigma, an unknown. Now it seems to carry a deep and significant meaning for both of them.]

- Select and analyse another confrontation sequence. Explain how camerawork, soundtrack and editing help to create and develop a confrontational setting.

IDEOLOGY

There have been some serious ideological shifts in the production of police/crime dramas over the decades. As we noted in the Introduction, the first significant police drama on British television, *Dixon of Dock Green*, promoted the notion that the police were a force for good. If there was a rotten apple in the shape of a bent copper, then it was just one in a barrel-full of otherwise wholesome, honest granny smiths. Furthermore, the programme supported the idea that the police were, for the most part always in the right, the bastion of a generally law-abiding, upright British populace.

Dixon of Dock Green was actually a TV spin-off from a British film, *The Blue Lamp* (1950). The film was a somewhat outspoken statement about the rise of violent crime and the lack of policing on the streets shortly after the Second World War. Interestingly, this was the first film to receive the full support of the Metropolitan Police, no doubt concerned about the state of policing in a city still suffering from the ravages of war. One issue was the effectiveness of an unarmed police force against criminals with weapons. During the course of the narrative, an authoritative voice-over comments that many of the perpetrators were young tearaways, who did not abide by the law-breakers' unwritten code, and were a liability to themselves and to the professional criminal class, who would have nothing to do with them. From this we may infer that, while the professional law-enforcers were going about their daily duties, and the professional law-breakers were sticking to the rules, then all was right with the world.

Knowing where you were, *vis-à-vis* age, class, gender, ethnicity and legal status was an important sociological idea in the 1950s and early 1960s. Dixon provided the answers. If you wanted to know the time, and just about anything else to do with life and how to live it in the mid-twentieth century, ask a policeman.

When *Z-Cars* aired in 1962, public perceptions of the role and status of the police force began to change. The police, it seemed, were not always right. Police behaviour towards suspects, towards the public, towards themselves could often be unacceptable. Intimidation, physical violence, corrupt practices, racism, sexism were all suddenly on the agenda. Later police series, such as *The Sweeney*, continued the trend, giving rise to the kind of storylines to be found in *Life on Mars* and *Ashes to Ashes*.

With *Life on Mars* and *Ashes to Ashes*, we are very much rooted in the ideological discourse of the 1970s and 1980s. Women and ethnic minorities come in for much verbal abuse. Women police officers are 'plonks', while most other women are 'tarts' or 'birds'. Even DI Alex Drake is affectionately called 'Bolly' or 'Bolly Knickers' by Gene Hunt. This particular appellation manages to combine Hunt's sneering disregard for posh, educated women (Bolly is short for Bollinger, the type of champagne he imagines posh women always drink), and 'knickers', arguably, evokes the unspoken sexual attraction he feels, but will not express, for his DI. However, he frequently shortens this nickname further to 'Bols', which really does sound like a genuine term of endearment. It also mirrors Alex's nickname for her daughter, Molly, whom she calls Mols. By contrast, Hunt is given to expressing his displeasure with her by using her second name, Drake.

The emphasis on realism found an echo in the real world, as enquiry after enquiry found corruption, institutional racism, sexism and many other malign influences in the real police forces in the UK. This blurring of the boundaries between law-enforcer and law-breaker continues to inform current crime series, such as the US show, *The Wire*.

Early police dramas tried to deal in certainties and reassurances, much as parents had told their children to respect the police and turn to them if they were in trouble. Later dramas posed questions rather than answers, expecting the audience to think about the moral dilemmas and make up their own minds about the issues raised. No longer would there be the comforting presence of PC George Dixon to take you by the hand and restore you to the safety of your place within the world.

- Compare an episode of *Life on Mars* with one from its more recent spin-off, *Ashes to Ashes*. Consider similarities and differences of character, plot and situation.

- Both series sent their protagonists, Sam Tyler and Alex Drake, back to the past. Develop some ideas for a possible series which sends Gene Hunt forward to the future. Write a short scene to explore Hunt's mystification when confronted with more modern policing methods – use episodes from *The Bill*, *Silent Witness*, *CSI*, *Prime Suspect*, *Touch of Frost*, and others to inform your ideas.

CHAPTER NINE – *HOUSE MD*

Hugh Laurie (centre) as the eponymous House

One of the more recent entries in the US tradition of medical dramas is the idiosyncratic series known as *House MD*, or more simply, '*House*' (2004 –). Its creator, David Shore, says that his original conception was to produce a 'CSI-type drama with germs and disease as the villains', but other aspects of the brand have largely overtaken this premise.

Shore admits that its inspiration is the Sherlock Holmes canon of detective fiction, by Sir Arthur Conan Doyle, published between 1892 and 1917. Holmes uses his encyclopaedic knowledge, much of it scientific, and wide powers of deduction to solve cases that have baffled the regular detective force. He is an enigmatic man, given to fits of depression and melancholy, an intermittent dependency on opium, and a detached, dispassionate and, at times, cynical regard for his fellow human beings. He has one long-standing, close friendship with Dr John Watson, an ex-army medical man, who is a willing and able assistant, even if he lacks Holmes' razor-sharp intellect and deductive genius. Watson suffers from a war wound which sometimes inhibits walking.

Conan Doyle claimed that the inspiration for Holmes was his old university medical lecturer, Dr Joseph Bell, who based his diagnoses on detailed observation and logical deduction. It therefore seems to make sense that Shore should return Holmes to the fount of his creator's inspiration by making House a medical genius.

Further reinforcement of this idea comes from one of the stories 'The Problem of Thor Bridge'. At the beginning Holmes angers a prospective client, a rich and powerful American, by suggesting that he is lying, because he is not willing to provide the truth about his relationship with the governess he employs for his two daughters. The American cannot see why such information might be relevant to the case. Holmes begs to differ, and the American then makes the comment that Holmes is like a surgeon who wishes to make a diagnosis but can only do so when he has been presented with all the symptoms.

The parallels are very close:

HOLMES	HOUSE
Unmarried, lives for his work.	Unmarried, lives for his work.
Solves crimes by reasoned deduction.	Solves medical problems by reasoned deduction.
Addicted to opium.	Addicted to pain-killers (Vicodin) for his leg condition.
Cold, detached attitude towards clients, whom he often suspects are not always revealing the whole truth.	Cold, detached attitude towards patients, whom he believes always lie.
Has one supportive friend, Watson.	Has one supportive friend, Wilson.
Plays violin as source of solace and escapism.	Plays piano and guitar as source of solace and escapism.
Avoids relationships with women.	Enjoys outspoken and often outrageous 'flirting' with women, but is not seriously involved with anyone.
Smokes a pipe as focus for thinking out problems.	Plays computer games and watches TV medical soaps as a focus for thinking out problems.
Is assisted in some of his cases by a small gang of street urchins, called the 'Baker Street Irregulars'.	Is assisted in all of his cases by a small gang of specialist doctors, whom some have dubbed 'The Ducklings' or 'The Maisonettes'.
Undertakes a variety of 'illegal' activities to obtain information and solve a case.	Undertakes a variety of unethical, sometimes illegal activities to arrive at a correct diagnosis.
Watson has a leg injury.	House has a leg injury.
Only enjoys cases he finds 'interesting'.	Only enjoys cases he finds 'interesting'.
Lives at 221B Baker Street.	Flat number is 221B.

Frequently makes astonishing deductions about a person's occupation, motivations, behaviour and habits, merely from a moment's observation.	Frequently makes astonishing deductions about a person's occupation, motivations, behaviour, habits and illness, merely from a moment's observation.
Holmes' arch-rival and enemy is Professor Moriarty.	House is attacked by a gunman called Moriarty.
Holmes' one slight instance of female susceptibility involves Irene Adler, in the case 'A Scandal in Bohemia'.	House's patient in the pilot episode is a female teacher called Rebecca Adler, although there is no romantic link.
Holmes' name.	House (home, homes).

GENRE

The medical drama genre has been discussed in Chapter 5, but *House* exhibits characteristics peculiar to itself, since it also borrows heavily from certain kinds of detective drama. The main generic features are:

- Set in a hospital, medical centre or similar.

- Regular staff consists of doctors, nurses, support staff, management.

- Patients tend to change from episode to episode ('guest' stories).

- Focus on interpersonal relationships among staff, often romantic.

- Moral dilemmas raised by treatment of patients.

- High degree of medical practice, terminology and technology.

Most medical dramas tend to focus on a combination of interpersonal relationships, often romantic, between the permanent medical staff, and the intense drama of saving a patient's life, medically or surgically, against all the odds. House is somewhat different. Interpersonal relationships are certainly a focus, but they are usually professional rather than personal/romantic, and the life-and-death struggle is usually concerned with finding a diagnosis for a patient's condition, rather than concentrating on treatment and cure. The medical input in *House* is very high, with much of the dialogue couched in medical jargon and obscure technical terminology.

A typical episode begins with a situation concerning the future patient experiencing a trauma (accident or injury), or suffering suddenly with apparently inexplicable symptoms. This results in their being referred to the diagnostic department, ruled over by House and his team of three medical assistants. After discussing and analysing a variety of diagnostic proposals, the team propose a possible condition and a likely treatment regime. The treatment invariably makes matters worse; further ideas are considered and rejected; until a final diagnosis, usually correct and treatable, is arrived at. The conditions are deliberately obscure or very rare, but medically accurate, making their identification near-impossible. The process of reaching a diagnosis tends to follow a similar pattern in every episode:

- Patient presents with symptoms.

- House considers whether the condition is 'interesting' enough for his involvement.

- Symptoms are noted on the 'whiteboard' and members of the team make diagnostic suggestions, often challenged by other members. This is known as 'differential diagnoses'.

- House invariably challenges all the suggestions with the manner of a sarcastic and self-opinionated referee.

- House, having recourse to one of his central ideas, that everyone lies, especially patients, proposes that one or two of the team explore at first-hand the domestic or work environment for contextual clues to possible allergens or other triggering factors. This unethical and probably illegal invasion of personal space is a recurring feature of House's method – he will insult, provoke, deceive and patronise patients and their relatives in order to reach the truth from which a correct diagnosis may finally be made.

- Armed with as much information as they are ever going to get, the team propose further, often changed treatment, until even this informed process results in near disaster for the patient, who is often brought to the brink of death.

- A final revelation, sometimes caused by a small medical detail or casual remark made quite out of context, and often totally unconnected with the central story, provides House with the last piece of the jigsaw, from which he is able to reach the right diagnosis and save the patient, just at the point where all hope appears to have evaporated. It is sometimes a significant part of the denouement that, despite House's insistence that they don't, the symptoms and conditions themselves might also lie, mimicking other conditions or concealing vital details necessary for their correct identification until the very last moment, when their 'deception' is unmasked by the infallible House.

Audiences should also be aware of a number of on-going narrative strands which both inform and develop from the main episode storyline. House abuses his prescription pain-killers in an attempt to reduce the pain of his injured leg, but also, perhaps, to satisfy the needs of his complex, sado-masochistic personality. He appears to enjoy inflicting pain and distress on others, both patients and colleagues, but is aware that this also causes a degree of stress for himself.

He has developed a friendly relationship with an oncology consultant, Dr James Wilson, who provides emotional support and a professional soundboard for House as he struggles to reach the correct diagnosis for a patient. Wilson is fiercely loyal to the seemingly misanthropic House, sometimes tendering advice, which appears to be openly rejected but secretly considered and, occasionally, acted upon.

House also has to interact with Lisa Cuddy, the Dean of Medicine at the Princeton-Plainsboro Teaching Hospital where he practises. Cuddy and House enjoy a finely-tuned love-hate relationship. He treats her with a subtle combination of intense admiration and withering contempt, while she matches her deep loathing of his public persona with a deep caring for, and emotional attachment to the person she believes he could be. Overarching all of this is her unshakeable belief in his genius as a diagnostician and his hopeless failure as a human being. One of Cuddy's less attractive features is a level of control-freakery which leads her to pin House down to a programme of general clinical duty, where he has to deal with ordinary patients and their seemingly trivial symptoms.

Much humour is derived from his brusque, eccentric and often brutally honest manner with what to him seem like time-wasters. His ability to deduce, like his detective almost-namesake, Sherlock Holmes, all manner of small details about their lifestyles from a cursory glance never fails to astound them. His resulting dismissal of their complaints, often with biting sarcasm and outspoken rudeness, never fails to horrify and mystify them in roughly equal proportions. On one notable occasion his direct insolence towards a patient who is a police detective leads to a catalogue of recriminations that result in House facing a long prison sentence for possessing and dealing in narcotics (his Vicodin habit). Wilson also faces jail for aiding and abetting (lying about a forged prescription), while his team have their bank accounts frozen and are interrogated about House and his addiction. His ultimate acquittal at the final moment is achieved by Cuddy convincingly perjuring herself to save the man who 'saves lives'. In this way House's brush with the law is analogous to his medical investigations which are frequently resolved as the patient is about to die.

It is a feature of this medical drama that, as a result of exploring symptoms and administering treatments, the three members of the supporting team, Eric Foreman, Allison Cameron and Robert Chase, are all forced to confront personal demons from their past personal history, and find ways to move forward to a better understanding of themselves and others. House, too, is living through his own demons and seems to be enjoying the experience, but situations and the people within them occasionally make him stop and take stock of his life and its repercussions. It is, however, an important part of the overall dramatic structure of all four series of episodes that he does not significantly shift his position, morally or medically.

NARRATIVE

The narrative structure of a typical episode is linear and very straightforward. The narrative disruption occurs at the very beginning, namely the sudden onset of symptoms which will result in the patient being investigated, treated and, in most cases, cured. The patient will be subjected to batteries of tests and tentative treatments, while the diagnostic team, under House's acerbic tutelage, will strive to identify the mysterious and usually very rare condition afflicting the patient. The narrative is resolved by the establishment of a cure.

A range of ongoing sub-narratives co-exists with the central narrative strand. These include: House's long-standing feud with Cuddy and hospital protocol and management generally; Foreman's endurance of House's constant attempts to belittle and undermine his practice; Cameron's almost unshakeable loyalty to House's ability to arrive at the correct diagnosis; Chase's occasional scepticism when faced with House's greater excesses; House's reliance on Wilson's support as both colleague and friend; Cuddy's insistence that House fulfil a regular tour of duty in the out-patients' clinic, where an apparently inconsequential remark or small medical detail sometimes leads House to a reappraisal of the central case. None of these narratives is ever resolved but each one provides a background canvas for the central narrative.

Together with the Todorovian traditional structure of narrative disruption and resolution, we might also notice some Proppian characteristics. The narrative is a quest for a diagnosis and cure, with House cast as the hero, assisted by his team and Wilson as helpers. There are many blockers or false helpers: the patient's refusal to be honest; the patient's relatives who also conceal the truth, don't know it or refuse to face it; Cuddy and the hospital management who often seek to derail House's attempts to resolve the case; occasionally one of House's team members who persists in following false leads. Despite all the red herrings and dead ends, the correct diagnosis is always reached by the end of the episode, often with lessons or morals to be learned, or at least considered by one or more of the permanent team. This soul-searching often takes place during a narrative coda, and the episode may end with some unfinished business for one or more of the regulars.

REPRESENTATION – THE ORIGINAL TEAM (SERIES 1–3)

Gregory House, MD – He visually reflects his chaotic, troubled persona. He is frequently unshaven, his hair is unruly, his clothes and footwear casual and untidy. He refuses to wear a doctor's white coat, even though his assistants do. Because of the muscle-damaged condition of his leg, he walks with a limp and the help of a cane. He has a sharp, sarcastic tongue, and speaks with a tone of voice which is frequently dismissive, patronising and insolent. He 'speaks his mind' and seems not to care if he upsets patients or their relatives in his obsessive and unorthodox quest for the truth of his patient's condition. He is seen taking pain-killers to ease the agony of his leg, but is clearly addicted, often employing a variety of subterfuges, including self-prescribing, in order to obtain his medication. He is often shown in 'thoughtful' mode, playing with a variety of toys and gadgets, such as a yo-yo, a play-station, a portable TV and a stress ball. He is also a talented pianist and guitarist, often using music as an escape from reality. Above all, he is a loner. He admits to having been in a long-term relationship some time ago, and does his best to avoid any similar occurrence disrupting his single status. He is forced to confront his feelings about this when his ex-partner, a lawyer, brings her sick husband to be diagnosed by him, and later joins the hospital staff as an attorney in Series 1. This situation leaves House feeling very ambivalent towards her, and they do come together for a very brief period. For all his cynical misanthropy, he can occasionally evince signs of sensitivity, and can sometimes seem genuinely sorry for the plight of those who come into his care. He prefers, however, that such feelings remain unobserved by others. Because of his position, that 'everybody lies', it is infuriatingly difficult, if not impossible, for his colleagues to determine what his true feelings really are. After his original team decide to leave at the end of Series 3, he holds auditions among a large group of willing aspirants, until he settles on a final group of three. Foreman returns in a senior advisory role to the new team.

Lisa Cuddy, MD – Dean of Medicine, she is an attractive woman in her forties, who exudes confidence and efficiency in her management role. She wears smart, businesswoman clothing, and tries to take a no-nonsense approach to House and his bizarre behaviour. Her dominant manner is sometimes betrayed by the genuine concern she feels, both for the patients and also for House. She rarely rises to his bait, however, and they seem to be about even in the mutual trumping stakes that take place between them. In later episodes she is seen trying to get pregnant, a sub-plot which intrigues House and is the cause of much banter between them.

James Wilson, MD – House's only friend. He is portrayed as a friendly, calm and supportive person, often given to dispensing good advice for House largely to ignore. As a cancer specialist, he is often useful to House's diagnostic team. The fact that he rarely becomes emotionally involved in the lives of the rest of the team makes him something of a moral compass for House. On his own admission, his marriage is going nowhere, and he shows sporadic interest in the opposite sex. His relationship with House often has the air of 'college buddies' about it – they talk sport, hang out together – and seems to provide the only socialising that House is willing to get involved with. As the series progress, Wilson is drawn more into the lives of House and his colleagues, especially as a major part of the police investigation into House' drug use.

Eric Foreman, MD – A black-American neurology specialist who frequently feels that he is the target for much of House's abuse and criticism. He is a tall and somewhat imposing figure and always maintains a very friendly and professional manner with his patients. He had some brushes with the law in his youth, which gives House some ammunition, and his manner tends to be one of exasperation with the others when he feels he is right and they can't see it. He is seen having a difficult relationship with his parents, especially his mother who is suffering from Alzheimer's and clearly does not recognise him. In later episodes he is motivated to resign from the team because he fears that he is gradually becoming too much like House himself. Although his resignation is accepted in Series 3, he returns in Series 4 as a kind of senior partner in the department, when House, having lost Cameron and Chase, is forced to create a new team.

Allison Cameron, MD — An immunologist, she is one of the two younger members of the team. She is represented as a beautiful young woman, but tends to dress and wear make-up conservatively. In the earlier episodes she has a quiet, almost shy demeanour. Her long hair is often pinned up and drawn back, giving her a rather reserved appearance. She wears it down in more relaxed situations. Her glasses and serious manner project an image of a knowledgeable and committed doctor, but in the earlier episodes her exchanges with House often make her look and behave like an enthusiastic student very much in awe of her older and wiser mentor. She is dedicated to her work and exhibits a very caring manner towards her patients. This transfers to her feelings for House. She is able to recognise his vulnerability, even when he states bluntly that he does not like her. As the first season progresses she quite clearly falls in love with her damaged superior, but this is managed in a very low-key, understated way, and, beyond one awkward dinner-only date, does not reach any kind of mutual fulfilment. In later episodes she begins to be represented as a more complex character, whose motivations are sometimes difficult to assess. In the poignant scene, for example, when Cameron (together with the rest of the team) believes House is dying of cancer, she caresses and kisses him in what looks like a passionate fulfilment of the hitherto unspoken feelings between them, which House appears to reciprocate until he discovers by a movement of her hand that this open display of affection is merely a subterfuge for her to use a syringe to get a sample of his blood for testing. House's analysis of her during their only dinner-date leaves her in silent thought. He describes her as someone who is damaged herself, looking for a damaged person to care for, just as she cared for her terminally ill husband — House is not willing to be that person.

Robert Chase, MD — A young, good-looking Australian doctor. He is presented as a son in the shadow of his father, a renowned medic in Australia with a world-wide reputation. Nevertheless, he makes his mark in House's department, always ready to pursue all lines of enquiry suggested by House, although not reluctant to argue against his boss if he believes him to be wrong. His flowing, blonde hair and boyish good looks make him an occasional target for romantically inclined patients ('the cute one'). This side to his persona places him at considerable professional risk when a rather precocious nine-year-old female cancer patient, who is likely to die, begs him to kiss her, so that she has at least one chance to 'feel what it's like'. He is attracted to Cameron and, after one fling, reminds her of this on a weekly basis (Tuesdays), although initially she does not succumb. Later in the series they do develop a matter-of-fact physical relationship.

ANALYSIS OF A SEQUENCE – FROM THE PILOT EPISODE

The pilot episode, which cleverly puts in place all the fundamental features of *House MD*, begins with a pre-title sequence introducing the principal character for that episode and some of the symptoms she suddenly begins to experience.

She is Rebecca Adler, a twenty-nine-year-old kindergarten teacher. Rebecca is arriving unusually late for school. She meets up with a colleague, Melanie, who is puzzled by Rebecca's uncharacteristic lack of punctuality. She accuses her of sleeping over at her boyfriend's house.

In the dialogue that follows, two details are revealed which have ironic overtones for the episode as a whole:

Rebecca: I didn't sleep with him.

Melanie: Girl, there's...[Interrupted]

Rebecca: I missed the bus!

Melanie: There's something either very wrong with you, or there's something very wrong with him.

Rebecca: There's nothing wrong with him.

We shall quickly discover, though, that there's something very wrong with her. As she enters her classroom and greets her pupils, Melanie fires a parting shot:

Melanie: You're lying aren't you?

Rebecca: I wouldn't lie to you.

It quickly becomes apparent in the early part of this episode that House believes everybody lies. He sees it as part of his professional diagnostic process to break through the lies until all that remains is the truth.

Rebecca begins talking to her class about her weekend. After a few sentences, she degenerates into meaningless gibberish, manages to scrawl a message on the board, and collapses to the floor.

Rebecca: Absolutely! You should never keep anything from your parents. And I told them [gibberish]

Class: [giggles]

Rebecca: Wh..

Class: [more giggles]

Rebecca: [gibberish]

Class: [Laughs and giggles]

[Rebecca goes to the board and starts writing]

Class: C, A, L, L, T, H, E….

Sidney: 'The.'

Boy: We know that word, 'the'.

[Rebecca collapses, on the board the words 'call the nurse' are written. It might be worth noting in passing that one of House's diagnostic 'tools' is a whiteboard on which he writes a patient's symptoms and any diagnostic suggestions made by the team – it's like a working diagram of the diagnostic process.]

Following the title sequence, we cut to the hallway of a large hospital. A close-up lower-half shot of two men walking reveals that one is wearing a doctor's white coat, the other has a cane, is limping and dressed casually. Their first exchange puts in place several important features of this couple, their relationship and their attitude to medicine. Wilson, the white-coated MD, is succinctly summing up the symptoms of the young woman we saw in the opening sequence:

Wilson: [matter of fact] 29-year-old female, first seizure one month ago, lost the ability to speak. Babbled like a baby. Present deterioration of mental status.

House, the limping man, seems more interested in the reactions of others to his apparent disability:

House: [apparently changing subject] See that? They all assume I'm a patient because of this cane.

Wilson immediately engages House in an exchange of friendly banter which is going to characterise their relationship in all future episodes. Although it begins in a light-hearted way, House quickly darkens the mood by introducing some of his key attitudes to his work and to women:

Wilson: So put on a white coat like the rest of us.

House: I don't want them to think I'm a doctor.

Wilson: You see where the administration might have a problem with that attitude.

House: People don't want a sick doctor.

Wilson: Fair enough. I don't like healthy patients. [tiring of badinage and returning to the point] The 29-year-old female…

House: The one who can't talk, I liked that part.

Wilson: [stopping to face House with a more serious, personal point] She's my cousin.

House: [maintaining his air of detachment] And your cousin doesn't like the diagnosis. I wouldn't either. Brain tumor, she's gonna die, boring.

In this brief dialogue we learn that House has scant regard for hospital management, a sexist attitude towards women, and that last sentence sums up what he thinks about his role as a diagnostician – the woman's prognosis is straightforward and therefore holds no interest for him. We also learn, as an audience, to expect blunt, outspoken dialogue which pulls no punches.

Wilson is not prepared to let House off that lightly. In his attempts to provoke a response, Wilson very neatly lets us know about House's set-up at the hospital. He heads a department of diagnostic medicine and he has assistants.

Wilson: [lightening the mood, but still trying to be persuasive] Come on! Why leave all the fun for the coroner? What's the point of putting together a team if you're not going to use them? You've got three overqualified doctors working for you. Getting bored.

At which point we encounter one of the show's recurring motifs: CGI sequences of the inside of a human body, representing the condition or the results of treatment of the patient in question. In this case we enter Rebecca's bloodstream via her nose, as she undergoes an MRI scan, the results of which are then viewed by House and his team.

Foreman: It's a lesion.

House: [with his usual level of sarcasm] And the big green thing in the middle of the bigger blue thing on a map is an island. I was hoping for something a bit more creative.

Foreman: [concerned about the correct protocol] Shouldn't we be speaking to the patient before we start diagnosing?

House: Is she a doctor?

Foreman: No, but…

House: [stating his profound belief] Everybody lies.

House is sarcastic, patronising and cynical. It is left to another of his assistants, Cameron, to define House's working principle:

Cameron: [an explanatory remark whispered to Foreman] Dr House doesn't like dealing with patients.

Notice her use of the phrase 'Dr House', which manages to be both deferential and ironic without revealing which. House continues to offer some more choice tenets from his philosophy:

Foreman: [almost as a reply to Cameron but picked up by House] Isn't treating patients why we became doctors?

House: No, treating illnesses is why we became doctors; treating patients is what makes most doctors miserable.

Foreman: [making a bid for human beings] So, you're trying to eliminate the humanity from the practice of medicine.

House: [the last word] If you don't talk to them they can't lie to us, and we can't lie to them. Humanity is overrated. I don't think it's a tumor.

Another feature of this show is the quick-fire dialogue, which shifts gear in an instant from general speculation to a bald statement of opinion without missing a beat. He then leads his team into the area he knows best – differential diagnostics. Everyone is invited to join in with suggestions until, gradually, each one is ruled out, leaving, hopefully, the right one.

House: [getting down to business] Differential diagnosis, people: if it's not a tumor what are the suspects? Why couldn't she talk?

Chase: Aneurism, stroke, or some other ischemic syndrome.

House: Get her a contrast MRI.

Cameron: Creutzfeld-Jakob disease.

Chase: Mad cow?

House: [referring to an earlier comment from Foreman, not quoted] Mad zebra.

Foreman: Wernickie's encephalopathy?

Note House's use of the word 'suspects', as though this is a criminal investigation. And so it goes on. House orders tests which the others carry out, systematically eliminating all the possibilities until the real culprit is exposed.

It should not escape our attention that this process – eliminating all possibilities until whatever remains, however improbable, must be the truth – is very closely modelled on the methods of House's literary forebear, Sherlock Holmes.

After House has ordered an MRI, we cut to his first encounter with Dr Lisa Cuddy, Dean of Medicine, and House's immediate boss. He's waiting for the lift, which he impatiently tries to summon more quickly to avoid her. The exchange is, as we might expect, sharp and sparky. House is acerbic, detached and insulting, but Cuddy gives as good as she gets.

Cuddy: I was expecting you in my office twenty minutes ago.

House: [dismissive tone] Really? Well, that's odd, because I had no intention of being in your office twenty minutes ago.

Cuddy: [accusatory] You think we have nothing to talk about?

House: No, just that I can't think of anything that I'd be interested in.

Cuddy: I sign your paychecks.

House: [tit for tat] I have tenure. Are you going to grab my cane now, stop me from leaving?

Cuddy: That would be juvenile.

In a few short words we begin to understand the rocky relationship that exists between these two. As a manager she is duty bound to take him to task for his lack of organisation.

Cuddy: I can still fire you if you're not doing your job.

House: I'm here from 9 to 5.

Cuddy: Your billings are practically nonexistent.

House: Rough year.

Cuddy: You ignore requests for consults.

House: I call back. Sometimes I misdial.

Cuddy: You're six years behind on your obligation to this clinic.

House: [there's no answer to that] See, I was right, this doesn't interest me.

Cuddy: Six years, times three weeks; you owe me better than four months.

House: [looking for the escape route] It's 5:00 I'm going home.

Cuddy: [the ultimate put down] To what?

House: [wincing as the knife goes in] Nice.

In keeping with his medical role, House has a snappy answer for virtually anything thrown at him. Obscure illnesses are very tricky for him to pin down; Cuddy ought to be more of a pushover. What Cuddy does have to acknowledge is that House is, quite simply, a brilliant diagnostician and doctor, and the hospital would be the poorer for losing him.

Cuddy: [beseechingly] Look, Dr House, the only reason that I don't fire you is because your reputation is still worth something to this hospital.

House: Excellent, we have a point of agreement. You aren't going to fire me.

Cuddy: [with an air of pleading against which he cannot argue] Your reputation won't last up if you don't do your job. The clinic is part of your job. I want you to do your job.

House: [the last word] Well, like the philosopher Jagger once said, 'You can't always get what you want.'

So there it is in a nutshell:

- A dramatic introduction to the patient's condition.

- A brief and witty exchange between House and his only genuine friend, Wilson.

- The differential diagnosis procedure with the team: Foreman, Cameron and Chase.

- House's attitude towards his boss, Cuddy, and her attitude towards him.

- House's attitude towards hospital officialdom.

- CGI to illustrate the effects of the condition and/or treatment.

- Popular culture reference ('Jagger' is Mick Jagger, singer/composer with the Rolling Stones; this is a quote from one of their songs).

MISE-EN-SCÈNE

This episode: Public transport images – bus, railway track, footbridge, pavements; typical kindergarten environment – corridors, classroom, desks, teacher's table, bright, lively; modern hospital environment – busy, bustling, corridors, treatment rooms, consulting rooms, medical technology, offices with staff names + MD, staff clothing (white coats, uniforms).

More generally: Lighting and general production design attempts to reflect the normal environments of patients and staff. Night sequences sometimes allow more low-key, melodramatic lighting. One significant feature of the design is the regular use of CGI graphics to illustrate the interior of the human body, usually accompanied by appropriate sound effects/music. Most of the audio is diegetic sounds and dialogue, but some episodes, especially the later ones, feature a popular song played over the montage of concluding scenes (dubbed a songtage by some critics), whose lyrics help to enhance the meaning of those scenes. The words may echo unconscious thoughts on the part of patients, friends, relatives, medical staff or others drawn into the drama, sometimes drawing parallels between their respective experiences.

GENRE

This episode: Serious medical-mystery drama, based on the idea behind the stories of Sherlock Holmes – diagnosis is the logical deduction of a condition by scrupulous examination of the 'evidence' (symptoms).

More generally: This generic mixture can subvert audience expectation, although, once the formula is learned, there is no difficulty in following the episodes. There are several ways in which standard expectations are undermined:

- Most medical dramas emphasise the permanent staff and their relationships – the patients are secondary and transient; House foregrounds the illness, although the characters and their complex and often contradictory personal lives are gradually fleshed out as the series progress.

- Most mysteries involve criminals, wrongdoing, justice; House treats the diseases as villains, the patients usually recover, the means to recovery are sometimes unorthodox and even criminal.

REPRESENTATION

This episode: White, middle-class, young female teacher; white, middle-class kindergarten children; the choice of the name 'Adler' foregrounds the 'Holmes' connection.

More generally: See earlier section for representations of main characters. Apart from these, other medical staff are usually silent and anonymous. Members of the public tend to represent a cross-section of the US population; occasionally patients are of other nationalities. There seems to be a conscious effort to avoid overt stereotyping, although some 'types' do feature in the 'clinic' sequences – inadequate males with sexually-related conditions or young, attractive females, provocatively dressed, for House to ogle.

AUDIENCE

Adult, with an informed interest in medical dramas; some inheritance from previous knowledge of Hugh Laurie (*Jeeves & Wooster, Blackadder*); African/American interest via Foreman, male interest via Cameron, Jewish/female interest via Wilson/Cuddy, Australian/female interest via Chase. Some inheritance also from the long line of US medical dramas (see Introduction).

IDEOLOGY

The mission of doctors is to care, diagnose and treat – represented as an honourable and ethical vocation by all the doctors except House, who regards his practice as a single-minded, obsessive pursuit of truth = the right diagnosis and the right treatment, even if this involves lying, cheating, unethical and personally intrusive practices; the philosophy of the end justifying the means. As a result many episodes raise, but do not resolve, ethical problems and serious conflicts of interest, leaving the audience to continue the debate at the end of the episode.

House's misanthropy and cynical world-view appear to be presented as an extreme position at odds with the dominant ethos of the hospital staff. However, each of the main characters chooses or is forced to adopt similar, if less extreme, positions as the stories and the series progress: Foreman puts on a certain false persona in the company of his parents; Cameron attempts to deceive House over the embrace/blood sample incident; Cuddy goes so far as to perjure herself when House faces criminal charges, imprisonment and the end of his career as a result of persecution by one police officer who did not take kindly to House's insolent treatment methods in the clinic.

Although the ethical stance of the self-less doctor saving patients' lives may appear to be the driving force of the drama, it is clear that the human condition as presented in *House MD* is much more morally complex and by no means as ethically clear-cut as the simple narrative style might suggest.

INSTITUTION

Companies involved in production have credit spots after the programme credits; the Fox/NBC and Universal connections locate the show with companies who have interests in both TV and film; Heel & Toe Films and Bad Hat Harry Productions are the two producers; the casting of British and Australian actors ensures international marketing potential. Many internet sites host blogs and a wealth of background information and trivia about the show. The show, its creators, and some of its individual actors have been nominated for and/or won a huge variety of entertainment and TV awards. Hugh Laurie himself was also awarded an OBE in 2007 for services to television drama.

- Choose similar diagnostic sequences from *House* and other UK and/or US medical dramas. Discuss their similarities and differences in terms of narrative, representation and filmic styles.

- Select a sequence from *House* and discuss the use of camera, lighting and sound to create meaning.

- Compare *House* with the recent US medical drama *Nurse Jackie* (2009), especially in terms of narrative structure and representation.

CHAPTER TEN — *LOST IN AUSTEN*

Amanda (Jemima Rooper, left) finds herself Lost in Austen

One of the biggest challenges for writers and producers of TV drama is to find something innovative which will still ring familiar bells with the audience, but surprise them with a different slant on traditional genres and narratives.

This book has already highlighted some of these successful innovations (*Life on Mars/ Ashes to Ashes* – novel twist on crime/police dramas + time-travel; *Doctor Who* – complete re-branding of established and familiar show; *Bleak House/Little Dorrit* – different approach to serialisation and presentation of period drama).

A relatively recent (autumn 2008) entrant in the innovation stakes is *Lost in Austen* (ITV), universally acknowledged as 'Life-on-Mars-meets-Pride-and-Prejudice'. The premise of this four-part whimsical drama is simple: twenty-first-century office-girl, Amanda Price, obsessed with Jane Austen's *Pride and Prejudice*, and dissatisfied with her slobbish boyfriend and his laddish maners, swaps places with the heroine, Elizabeth Bennet, by means of a time portal in her Hammersmith bathroom, which leads into Longbourn, the Bennets' family home, leaving Elizabeth stranded in contemporary London. The confusions that arise lead directly to some serious re-workings of the novel's original plot, as Amanda's interventions play havoc with the relationships which are supposed to develop throughout the story.

Cue for culture clashes, lashings of intertextuality and large helpings of period drama iconography – brooding, booted heroes; high-bosomed, simpering heroines; large stately homes; even larger annual incomes; courtly, Regency manners; love interests; marriage.

NARRATIVE

The narrative of this quirky take on period drama follows the linear pattern of the original novel as far as some of the events are concerned, although Amanda's unwitting interventions cause some serious disruptions to the established order of Austen's original story. The first major disruption for the Bennets is the absence of Elizabeth, although Amanda's explanation involving Hammersmith seem to be accepted without too much pertinent enquiry.

The first clever device of this drama is to make the initial narrative disruption in the real world (Elizabeth's arrival in Hammersmith and Amanda's departure for Longbourn) become a serious disruption in the novel (Elizabeth's absence and Amanda's arrival), because the 'proper' narrative disruption in the novel is supposed to be the arrival of Mr Bingley and Mr Darcy at Netherfield. They do arrive, of course, and the Bennet girls are immediately thrown into their expected state of romantic confusion and intrigue, but it is the presence of Amanda that disrupts Bingley's and Darcy's expectations. In this version Bingley shows all likelihood of falling for Amanda, while Darcy, although keeping his distance, is also intrigued by the feisty and puzzling persona of this new arrival.

The narrative progresses in this way, with the 'wrong' women falling for, or marrying the 'wrong' men, until the need to pursue matters back in Hammersmith brings both Amanda and Darcy back to the twenty-first century, where they encounter a very modernised Elizabeth (cropped hair, make-up, contemporary clothes). They all return to Longbourn to attend an injured Mr Bennet, but Darcy shows no signs of falling in love with Elizabeth. Amanda forces herself to return to the modern day, but confronting her original circumstances sends her back to Darcy and 'Austen-Land' where she appears destined to remain forever locked in his romantic embrace.

GENRE

Lost in Austen is primarily a light comedy drama. However, it borrows heavily from period drama adaptations in its production style, much of its dialogue, its narrative structure and its representational features. It also employs the characteristics of more recent time-travelling dramas such as *Life on Mars* and *Doctor Who*, with its emphasis on not altering the course of what has already happened, for example. In addition, there are elements of 'dislocation' drama, where the main character finds him/herself in unfamiliar environments. In this case, for example, Amanda is unfamiliar with Georgian domestic routines, even if her reading of Austen does provide her with some idea of Georgian etiquette.

REPRESENTATION

Amanda is an attractive, contemporary young woman with a typical hairstyle and wardrobe to match. She lives in a small, two-bed flat, has a nine-to-five bank clerk job and a stereotypical laddish, chauvinistic boyfriend. She shares the flat with another young woman, Pirhana, whose more extravagant hairstyle, make-up, dress sense and even her name project an air of someone who enjoys a good time by going out, having fun and living a bit dangerously.

Amanda has a standard London accent, enjoys reading classic fiction, especially Austen, and is shown to possess a bright personality and a great deal of quick-wittedness. She is more critical of herself, especially when she asks Darcy which Amanda he prefers: his first impression of her as 'spiky and vulgar and argumentative', or her later attempts to be 'simpering and fanning and trying hard to fit in'. Darcy replies, in keeping with the Firth interpretation, that he found both versions 'equally disagreeable'.

Her love of Regency manners and language enables Amanda to fit into Longbourn life fairly well. Because of her obsession with the novel, she is shown as someone who has a warm, friendly and caring regard for the characters who people it.

The representation of the characters from the novel is rather more complex. In appearance, behaviour and language, they all conform to the images projected by the classic BBC adaptation of *Pride and Prejudice*, first transmitted in 1995, starring Colin Firth and Jennifer Ehle. They are all played by different actors, but every effort has been made to replicate the overall effect conveyed by the 1995 cast.

The women are dressed in appropriate Regency costume, with an emphasis on elaborate hairstyles, jewellery and other finery. The men are also extravagantly dressed in long coats, breeches, boots, flamboyant shirts and waistcoats. Servants and other 'ordinary' people are more modestly dressed, generally in dull colours.

The appearance of Amanda among them begins to have a material effect on their behaviour, attitudes and language. In particular, Mrs Bennet eventually becomes much more outspoken and confident, especially towards the arrogant Lady Catherine de Bourgh, and her daughter, Jane, who has 'accidentally' become married to Mr Collins instead of Mr Bingley, is very critical of the stupid behaviour of her idiotic husband. Meanwhile Elizabeth's experiences in modern-day Hammersmith have changed her appearance and her whole personality, making it more difficult for her to fit into her old way of life.

Mr Darcy remains true to his 1995-Colin Firth representation, but Mr Bingley seems much taken by some of the more 'modern' manners introduced by Amanda, particularly her propensity for a quick snog and a secret smoke. In the novel, Mr Wickham is certainly depicted as a villain, but for Amanda, he seems to represent an ordinary bloke who actually assists her to put right some of the mix-ups she has caused.

AUDIENCE AND INSTITUTIONAL ISSUES

This clever take on the classic literary adaptation was well-received by critics and audiences alike. It was regarded as a 'witty and high-concept tale', and *Daily Telegraph* reviewer, James Walton, wrote 'This is not a sentence that you often hear – but it's been a good week for drama on ITV1'. The reason for Walton's slightly cynical comment is the plight of ITV1 at the time, beset on all sides by phone-in scandals, programmes of all kind that failed to capture the audience's imagination or their viewing time and a heavy reliance on reality shows.

The problem for ITV1 is the nature of its funding, based on the revenue from advertising, in turn based on audience numbers. Andrew Stephens, quoted in Stephen Armstrong's *Guardian* article of 6 October 2008, explains:

> *Lost in Austen* attracted huge numbers of ABC1 viewers, as much as 22% up on that slot's usual performance. The problem is, it averaged 3.5 million viewers over the series, where the slot (9.00 pm) usually gets 4.2 million.'

Fewer viewers for a slot, no matter who they are, will mean a lower income for ITV1, because of the rules governing the sale of airtime. As Stephens puts it:

> 'I loved the show. I thought it was clever, funny and exactly the kind of show you need to get a new audience. The CRR [the rules governing airtime trading], however, means it may be bad news for the channel.'

Armstrong finishes his article by commenting:

> 'Ofcom is reviewing the CRR – but in the meantime, the only way ITV can earn more money from its airtime is to schedule wall-to-wall *Coronation Street* and *X-Factor*, in order to increase its viewing figures – which is surely to nobody's benefit, least of all viewers. The health of the British creative industry depends on exactly the opposite.'

- Select three current TV dramas, two 'popular' and one more 'specialist', and research their audience figures (including social-class breakdowns), and any reviews they may have received.
- Discuss audience issues that arise from your research.

TECHNICAL ANALYSIS

CAMERA

Period dramas are not usually noted for their fast and flashy camerawork, although this is sometimes a feature of *Bleak House* (see Chapter 7). The camerawork in *Lost in Austen* tends to conform to the normal conventions of much TV drama: establishing shots of the settings and locations, two/three-shots to introduce characters and dialogue, shot-reverse-shot to emphasise conversational dialogue and close-ups to highlight individual emotional responses. Camera angles are mostly eye-level and camera movements tend to be controlled and stately to reflect the nature of the images, although there is some hand-held camerawork, which is no doubt designed to reflect the contemporary nature of the production.

- Choose a sequence and try to identify any unconventional use of camerawork.

- For your chosen sequence prepare your own camera script in order to give it a more contemporary feel.

SOUND

The audio characteristics of the dialogue and ambient sound tend to reflect the shooting environments, where real locations rather than studio sets are used for the action: some natural room reverb for interiors and a sense of the precise placing of sounds help the process of realism to a very great degree.

At appropriate points in the narrative, non-diegetic orchestral music is used to create and reflect a romantic atmosphere, in keeping with the period drama feel of the production.

Some advantage is taken of the contrast between the chaotic noise of present-day London and the tranquillity of the Regency countryside. In particular, the ambient sounds that make up the canvas of a twenty-first-century location – traffic noise, music, the sounds of contemporary technology, the barrage of people going about their business – are replaced by birdsong, light chatter, the occasional carriage, the odd sheep or cow.

- Choose a sequence, switch off the vision and try to identify all the sounds which can be heard.

- For your chosen sequence consider other sounds which might add to or change the meaning.

EDITING

Most of the editing in *Lost in Austen* is conventional continuity editing, suitable for a straightforward linear narrative. Some of the sequences are edited elliptically, with no obvious establishing shots, audiences having to work out changes of time or location. Generally, however, sequences are introduced by establishing shots which enable audiences to understand the progression of scenes from one place and time to another.

Shot lengths tend to reflect the more measured pace of a period drama, but Amanda's modernity and sharper dialogue often make for a faster-paced editing style at appropriate moments.

> - Measure the average length of shots over a selection of sequences, and compare the result with similar sequences from the 1995 TV adaptation.
>
> - Select a sequence and suggest ways in which it could be re-edited to create different effects, or to emphasise different features.

MISE-EN-SCÈNE

Every attempt has been made in this production to emulate the settings, locations, shooting and editing style of the original BBC adaptation. Even the title music (and Amanda's ring-tone!) uses the original BBC theme. Some of the title imagery reflects the 1995 adaptation, but the photographic reproduction of the main characters, with its emphasis on a photo-art style, lends a contemporary feel to the sequence.

The lush English countryside, large country houses, grand interiors, balls, music, horse-riding, plush carriages, and all the other iconography of period drama are present in abundance in this version. The comic and dramatic interest arises largely from the disjuncture between this world and the contemporary imagery and behaviour of twenty-first-century London. One of the big contrasts is between the unceasing noise and bustle of the Hammersmith streets, and the peaceful, sedate environments of Georgian England. This is partly reflected in the initially outlandish and clumsy interventions of Amanda in the quiet, unhurried life of Longbourn, where the loudest noise tends to be the giggling of the younger Miss Bennets and the occasional scrunch of carriage wheels on the gravel drive.

Despite the references to modern London and contemporary lifestyles, the major part of this drama is unashamedly presented as a reflection of the 1995 TV adaptation of the romantic fiction on which it is based. Environments, wardrobe, décor, manners and behaviour, lighting styles, camera movements, soundtrack, non-diegetic music all take their cue from the 1995 production.

> - Compare the *mise-en-scène* of the 1995 adaptation and Lost in Austen, noting significant similarities and differences. Try to explain what effects these might have on the meaning for audiences.
>
> - When Amanda asks 'Darcy' to take a dip in an ornamental pond in order to replicate a famous scene from the 1995 adaptation, she comments to herself 'I'm having a bit of a strange post-modern moment here.' Explore what she means by this statement and look for other examples of such moments.

TEXTUAL ANALYSIS – THE OPENING OF THE DRAMA

Our heroine, a self-confessed Jane Austen fanatic, Amanda Price, (already an Austen reference: Fanny Price is the heroine of Austen's *Mansfield Park*) has to face a daily barrage of the insolence and bad behaviour of ordinary people in her job, only to return home to find her flatmate is tarting herself up for an evening on the pull. Amanda has opted for an evening in with *Pride and Prejudice*.

A big close-up of a glass of red wine being poured, signifying the prospect of a relaxed evening, dissolves into a shot of Amanda, curling up with a good book and the wine glass. Some romantic classical music is playing on the soundtrack as she begins to read to herself, heard in voice-over, the sequence in the novel where Elizabeth Bennet expresses her disapproval of Mr Darcy and his proposal of marriage. This is accompanied by a superimposed image of a Darcy-like figure standing in a forlorn pose by a large ornamental pond, clearly meant to suggest to the audience the object of Amanda's imagination at this point in her reading. The image fades as she comes to the 'had you behaved in a more gentleman-like manner' put-down.

Immediately her reading is interrupted by a furious buzzing from the door. We cut to a shot of her boyfriend, Michael, falling flat out onto the sofa with a bottle of beer glued to his lips. We are meant to understand that he has ignored Amanda's request not to come after a drunken night out with his mates. We are also meant to register his 'un-gentleman-like manner' – he's drunk, semi-comatose – very much the stereotyped 'lad'. Nevertheless, he seems determined to propose. He uses a ring-pull as an engagement ring, a nasty line in belching to replace any romantic requests he has in mind, and promptly falls asleep on the sofa, snoring loudly. This behaviour further reinforces his representation as a beer-swilling, chauvinistic, 'out-with-the-lads' bloke. Amanda expresses her disgust at the lack of romance shown by her boyfriend, and makes herself some toast.

The sequences so far have been shot in relatively low-light to indicate the comfortable atmosphere of a small flat and the camera is at a low-angle, as though we might be sitting in an armchair.

Distracted by an unexpected noise from the bathroom while Michael snores on the sofa Amanda goes to investigate. The bathroom light is off, but we can just make out a figure stumbling about in the dark. Amanda pulls the light-switch to reveal a young woman in Georgian period cap and nightdress examining Amanda's drying underwear. This apparition addresses Amanda as 'Miss Spencer' (cf. the 'Calvin Klein' underwear mistake in *Back to the Future*), while announcing herself as 'Miss Elizabeth…', which Amanda

completes with '…Bennet', knowing uncannily that she is encountering her favourite fictional heroine. The lighting scheme is now bright, as though things might be a little clearer for Amanda, and the camera angles are now at eye-level, suggesting that we are now standing with them as the unseen observer.

After her initial surprise, Amanda is told by Elizabeth of a mysterious door in the Bennets' house which apparently led nowhere, until now. Elizabeth's dialogue is deliberately couched in the Austen style, whereas Amanda still speaks in a contemporary mode. This first meeting is interrupted by Amanda's boyfriend calling from the living room. Her attention is diverted towards him, but when she turns back, she finds that Elizabeth has gone. Treating this as an hallucination, she reflects on talks she has had with her divorced and disillusioned mother, who tries to persuade her that marriage, even to her loser boyfriend is better than a lonely old age. Amanda does her best to explain to her mother why she likes the Austen lifestyle so much, with no success. Cigarettes and alcohol are used by her mother as a cushioning against the loneliness of her life, but they also support the representation of her as a lonely older woman with no prospects.

Back on the couch, Amanda's reading of her favourite novel is disturbed again by persistent clicking from the bathroom. She enters to find a now dressed Elizabeth playing with the light-switch. Elizabeth's fascination with this piece of simple technology reinforces our understanding of the disjuncture between the two worlds.

In the ensuing conversation Amanda tries to secure some evidence that Elizabeth is real, by asking for some point of detail which she could not possibly know. When Elizabeth announces that Netherfield Hall is let, Amanda immediately responds that she knows (from her reading of the novel). This surprises Elizabeth who, it appears, has only just learnt this, enabling Amanda to realise that she has stumbled upon Elizabeth at the point in time when the novel begins. A geographical point about Alaska, which Amanda does not know, is enough to convince her that Elizabeth is real, and she demands to be shown the door through which Elizabeth has entered her world. This whole exchange highlights the whole premise on which this drama is based – do characters in a novel have an existence beyond that which is described in the novel? Can they know and experience things which have not been overtly presented in the novel? The fact that Amanda is about to enter the world of the novel raises this very question, because she was not in the original story.

Elizabeth shows her the door at the rear of the bathroom. When Amanda pushes on it, it swings open and Amanda steps through into what appears to be an attic corridor. Before

she has a chance to step back, the door swings shut, resisting all of Amanda's attempts to open it, and a servant appears. Not too taken aback, the servant asks Amanda whether she will be dining, since Mr Bennet likes to know how many to expect at table. Amanda, attempting a clumsy curtsey, says that she will be dining and that the servant should say she is a friend of 'Miss Elizabeth'. The servant departs and Amanda makes her way down the servants' staircase to the main landing of the house.

This transitional moment, as Amanda enters the world of the novel, is actually presented as a moment of normality. The servant accepts her presence without expressing surprise or alarm as though her arrival has been expected (this event mirrors Sam Tyler's expected arrival, in Gene Hunt's 1973 police station, in *Life on Mars*).

She hears female voices chattering and a piano playing, but before she can make it all the way down, Mr Bennet suddenly appears at the foot of the stairs. He is a little startled to see Amanda, but her curtsey and polite, short greeting quickly impress him as the husband and father of a family of females 'promiscuous of speech'. She tells him her name and they descend to his study, where the storyline of the original novel now begins to develop apace, except that Amanda is now there in Elizabeth's stead to witness the events she has read about so often. The author's purpose, of taking a reader into a book, has never been more literally achieved than here.

RESOLVING THE NARRATIVE

Towards the end of the series of four episodes Amanda is intent on returning Elizabeth and Darcy to their world and regaining her own place in twenty-first-century Hammersmith. She has already engineered an annulment for Jane so that she can marry Mr Bingley, and it begins to look as though the plotlines of the original novel are starting to get back on track. Elizabeth, however, seems reluctant to play ball, presumably having found her 'holiday' in the modern world more conducive to her happiness than the prospect of marriage to Mr Darcy. Amanda does her best to convince her otherwise, urging her to 'keep talking to him'. As she puts it, 'from the talking comes the love'.

This may have been true for the characters in Austen's novel, but, let loose in London, Elizabeth seems to have other ideas. Amanda does succeed in resolving this problem in a surprising, yet ultimately logical way.

We talk of being 'lost' in a book while we're reading, allowing the words, ideas and descriptions to take us over. We also talk of identifying with the characters, enabling us, in our imaginations, to become the person we feel most affinity with.

Lost in Austen takes these two ideas to their logical conclusion. Amanda is, quite literally, lost in the novel, its ideas, its locations and its characters, unable to return to her own world. She also identifies strongly with Elizabeth, as Austen, no doubt, intended her female readership to do. Logically, therefore, to resolve the narrative, Amanda must stay 'lost' in the world of the novel, fall in love with Darcy as he does with her, and marry him. After all, every female reader does as much in her fantasies of the novel; Amanda merely does it 'for real'.

Given that there are points of comparison between *Lost in Austen* and *Life on Mars*, we should note that at the end of Series 2, Sam Tyler, faced with a modern lifestyle and the constraints of modern policing, 'returns' to the 1973 world of Manchester law enforcement, and to Annie, the girl he left behind: the world he had spent all of his time trying to escape from in the other episodes. Amanda simply does the same.

FURTHER WORK

- Read and analyse the following reviews. Discuss how far you either agree or disagree with them.

'It's a bit silly but quite fun, in a jolly, frothy kind of way. *Life on Mars* basically, but going back a bit further – so lacy frocks and bulging breeches instead of flares and brown leather jackets, tinkling pianos instead of Bowie, and the crunch of carriage wheel on gravel instead of the screech of a cornering Mark I Cortina. *Life on Mars* for girls, in other words, because it is a truth universally acknowledged that women like Jane Austen better than what fellas do.' (Sam Wollaston, *The Guardian*)

'Of course, as many people have already spotted from its shameless blending of *Pride and Prejudice* with *Life on Mars*, the series does come with a distinct whiff of commercial calculation. Yet, so far at least, this only goes to show that commercial calculation can sometimes work rather well. The result can't be called profound. Nonetheless, it does triumphantly achieve its main aim of being enormously good-natured fun.' (James Walton, *Daily Telegraph*)

The Times's Tim Teeman was moved to give the drama four stars and labelled it a 'funny, clever breeze'.

'Not quite enough happens in the way of culture clash. There are little dabs of historical instruction, as when Amanda asked to clean her teeth and was shown a bundle of birch twigs and a block of chalk. And there is some fun to be had with the mismatch between modern clothes and idiom and local manners. But oddly (given that the plot involves a kind of temporal exchange programme) we learn nothing of how Lizzie is getting on in West London, and the drama lacks the edge of terrified uncertainty that gave *Life on Mars* its extra emotional depth. At worst, Amanda simply seems exasperated that she can no longer get a mobile-phone signal, which may not be quite enough to persuade us that she really thinks this is happening at all.'

Carry out some research into other texts (films and TV dramas) which use the device of including someone from the 'readership' or audience in the action.

- Choose a favourite novel, film or TV drama, and devise some scenes, including yourself (or a volunteer) as a character in the narrative, for which you can then create some scripts. Consider how you will deal with issues of genre, representation, narrative, *mise-en-scene* and technical features.

CHAPTER ELEVEN – APPROACHES TO STUDYING TV DRAMA

Current exam specifications require you to understand and explain the technical codes of television drama production:

- The use of the camera.

- The production and purpose of diegetic and non-diegetic soundtracks.

- The techniques of editing.

- The creation of *mise-en-scène*.

They also require you to understand and explain how these technical codes make meaning for the audience in the areas of:

- Genre.

- Audience response.

- Narrative structure.

- Representation.

- Ideology.

- Institutions.

The requirements are detailed in the specifications published by the exam boards, and they are available to download from their websites. Make a point of becoming very familiar with the exact requirements published by them for the year of your exam.

Although the technical and analytical categories are listed as separate codes and areas, they should not be thought of as discrete: each code or area works with all the others to create an integrated meaning.

For example, in *Life on Mars*:

A low-angle medium close-up shot (camera – suggests power) of Gene Hunt interrogating a suspect (generic features of a cop drama accompanied by sound – diegetic dialogue) is inter-cut (editing – to suggest the cut-and-thrust of such a session) with a high-angle medium close-up shot (camera – suggests suspect is powerless) of the suspect. This interrogation takes place in a dark and shadowy basement room (*mise-en-scène* as revealed by the camera to intimidate the suspect). Hunt is wearing his trademark coat, loosened tie, unbuttoned shirt, untidy hair. He shouts brusquely in a northern accent – Manchester – at the suspect, making disrespectful and abusive comments, and then grabs him by the lapels in order to intimidate him (development of narrative, representation – maverick eccentric, diegetic dialogue – northern accent accepted as a guarantee of gritty realism, ideological issues – police brutality versus crime, audience response – Hunt appeals to our emotive sense of 'justice', or appals us by his violent behaviour).

This sequence takes place in a police drama (genre – detective, suspect, interrogation room), on a mainstream terrestrial channel – BBC1 – after the 9.00 watershed (institutional scheduling, audience targeting – adults, mostly male?).

What do we understand from this sequence?

- This is a no-punches-pulled cop drama dealing in the hard realities of policing crime on the streets of Manchester.

- The camera angles position Hunt as a powerful and threatening figure, while the suspect is powerless, both as an intimidated suspect and as a human being who might wish to seek redress for the violence he is suffering.

- Hunt's appearance and manner suggest he is a maverick cop, with no respect for the 'rules', but with an obsessive mission to clean up crime on the city streets. For this stance, we are expected to admire his motives if not his methods.

- The scheduling suggests we are watching an 'adult' drama, where we might expect to see violence, swearing, sexual behaviour and other adult themes.

- The production company – BBC – suggests that we may be watching a 'quality' drama – the BBC has a reputation for producing quality drama.

- Hunt's behaviour and mode of speaking to suspects mark him out as a colourful eccentric, who always works on the edge in his pursuit of criminals – the drama presents Hunt as a 'character', whose efforts we should cheer.

AND SO ON...

The key factor is that every point of description that you make (the camera is doing 'this'…) must be accompanied by an analytical point which explains how the audience can make meaning from it (…because it reveals Hunt as….). If you merely describe what you see and hear in a sequence, you cannot hope to convince the examiners that you really understand how the media text you are studying creates meaning for the audience.

There are also other issues to explore. TV dramas are marketed as commodities, products to be bought and sold, both by the TV companies who transmit them, and by the audiences who view them in a variety of contexts – on terrestrial channels, freeview and satellite channels, Internet sites, as pre-recorded boxed sets purchased in retail chain stores or through Internet sites. They spark Internet forums and blogs, and are, of course, studied as academic artefacts. Just like other marketable products, they have brands, trademarks, USPs, niche markets, loyal consumers and a 'support network' to provide a kind of 'after-sales service'. A fruitful area for research would be to investigate how TV dramas are marketed and with what success.

SELECT BIBLIOGRAPHY

Books and Articles

Armstrong, S. 'Pride before advertising fall' in *The Guardian*, 6 October 2008

Carpenter, H. *Dennis Potter – the Authorised Biography*, Faber & Faber: London, 1998

Cook, J. R. *Dennis Potter – a Life on Screen*, Manchester University Press: Manchester, 1995

Cooke, L. *British Television Drama*, BFI Publishing: London, 2003

Ellis, J. *Visible Fictions*, Routledge: London, 1992

Creeber, G. *The Singing Detective*, BFI Publishing: London, 2007

Giddlings, R. & Sheen, E. (eds) *The Classic Novel – From Page to Screen*, Manchester University Press: Manchester, 2000

Hare, D. 'Theatre's great malcontent' in *The Guardian 'Review'*, 8 June 2002

Williams, R. *Television: Technology and Cultural Form*, Routledge: London, 1974

Wilson, L. (ed.) *House Unauthorised*, Benbella Books Inc.: Dallas, 2007

On the Web

The BBC website 'Writers Room' section has downloadable scripts for *Ashes to Ashes*, *Casualty*, *Doctor Who*, *EastEnders*, *Holby City*, and *Life on Mars*, amongst others:

http://www.bbc.co.uk/writersroom/insight/script_archive.shtml

The extract from the script to *Life on Mars* series 1, episode 1, has been extracted from the script available on the 'Writer's Room' web site. The copyright for the script lies with the BBC and Matthew Graham:

http://www.bbc.co.uk/writersroom/insight/downloads/scripts/life_on_mars_ep_1.pdf

The extract from the 'General Notes and Background' planning note about *Doctor Who* has been extracted from the BBC online archive of documents. The full version can be accessed at:

http://www.bbc.co.uk/archive/doctorwho/6403.shtml

The ITV website – www.itv.com – for pages relating to *Coronation Street*

INDEX

Note: In order to prevent multiple page references, the main case study dramas are not included here.

STILLS INFORMATION

The publisher has attempted to correctly identify the copyright holders of the images reproduced herein and belives the following copyright information to be correct at the time of going to print. We apologise for any omissions or errors and will be delighted to rectify any errors brought to our attention in future editions.

The Sweeney © ITV / Aquarius Collection; *Coronation Street* © Granada Television / Joel Finler Archive; *The Singing Detective* © BBC TV / Joel Finler Archive; *Clocking Off* © BBC TV / Red Productions; *State of Play* © BBC TV; *Casualty* and *Holby City* © BBC TV / image.net; *Doctor Who* © BBC TV / image.net; *Bleak House* and *Little Dorrit* © BBC TV; *Life on Mars* and *Ashes to Ashes* © BBC TV / Kudos / image.net; *House* © NBC Universal TV / image. net; *Lost in Austen* © ITV.